HUMAN BEHAVIOR OR TECHNOLOGY INFLUENCES ORGANIZATIONAL

PERFORMANCE IMPROVEMENT

JOHN LOK

Made with ♥ on the Notion Press Platform
www.notionpress.com

Contents

Preface

Introduction

Nowadays, we are experiencing new economic development period. Many countries societies will have significant unpredicted change, however, we will difficult to predict whether what our societies will change or how and why we future societies will have these possible changes. I write this book aims to explain whether what some social changes will be causes to influence our daily living in possible future development. Due to we are experiencing new economic development period, so we ought to attempt to predict whether what our societies will be influenced to change by new economic development.

How will (AI) influence human job change?Advances in artificial intelligence (AI) technology is for the progress in critical areas, such as health, education, energy, economy inclusion, social welfare and the environment.Thus, it brings this question: Which (AI) workers be instead of traditional human workers in these different new markets? In recent years, machines had been used to be human's tasks in the performance of certain tasks related to intelligence , such as aspects of image recognition. Experts also forecast that rapid progress in the field of specialized artificial intelligence will continue. Then, it also brings this question: Does (AI) exceed that of human performance on more and more tasks? If it is truth, will some of human jobs to be disappeared? (AI) will be instead of human some simple jobs, then unemployment rate to the low skillful and low educated workers will be increased. Whether (AI) will be raised either production or performance or unemployment to bring human job market more advantages or more disadvantages? Can robtics workers bring what positive or negative influences to office working environment ?Artificial intelligence had been developed to be applied to any service , working aspects, e.g. auto-driven cars. In the future, it may replace manual transport drivers in possible, e.g. non-manual driven tram, train, bus, taxi etc. public transport service. In factory warehouse environment, it can replace some workers to deliver any goods in warehouse. In shopping center service environment, it can replace security to do patrol jobs. In restaurant, it can replace waiter to deliver food to client's table. So, AI will assist or replace any service workers to do any kinds of simple jobs in any working environment in possible future.Final chapter, I shall explain why one organization has excellent facility management strategy, which can help it to prolong or expand long time to stay on mature life cycle stage in possible. In my this book, I shall let readers to make judgement whether technology or organizational employees behavior can improve performance for their whole organizations.

Prologue

Table of content

How to spply consumer choice theory to predict Consumer Behavior Marketing at Apple Computer

Microeconomics Models and Theories solve customer problems

Developed countries low skillful labour market wage grows up causing factors

labour market excess supply and shortage demand factor

- the division of labour concept
- Surplus value of labour theory

Refugee immigration factor

Technological development factor

Chapter 3

Explaining technology or employee behavior influences organizational performance

Engagement (Building good organizational culture) Strategy solves Hill Wood Medical Centre organization international different culture difficult cooperation problem

- How and why can engagement strategy solve medical organizational departments difficult culture cooperate problem ? p.56-80
- suggestion engagement strategy influences to medical centre departments' staffs build kindly culture efficient cooperative method

.What barriers did this medical centre face in implementing the strategies or achieving success?

.Did it overcome those obstacles and if so, how?

England NHS public hospital patient price structure of marketing strategy

1. What do you understand by the concept of a pricing model? Critically discuss their relevance to a public sector service ,such as the NHS.
2. What factors should influence the level of charges at an NHS car park?

What are the important factors that the leaders of Willard and Eastern must consider in order to be effective?
What could each have done to be more effective?

- Outsourcing service Strategy solves Unversity cost raising challenges
- Outsoucing service strategy can help this university to solve staff management challenge.

Building effective organizational international communication strategy solves broadcasting television department and file producing entrepreneur cooperation challenge

- upward communication strategy solves broadcasting television department communication challenge
- film producing entrepreneur downward communincation strategy solves team cooperation challenge

Fair compensation strategy solves factory workers and baseball players cooperation challenge

● Factors cause electronic assemblies factory workers team performance

● What factors seem to be influencing team performance?

● If I was Dave, shop supervisor, what team concepts should I apply? why?

● Fair compensation solve baseball organization players cooperation challenge

● Describe the types of conflict that seem to exist within the Bluebirds organization.

● Fair compensation strategy solves compensation director poor working performance challenge

Crisis management and time management strategy solves nuclear factory team cooperation challenge

● Nuclear factory team making the most right decision challenge

● What alternatives do you use for reducing the possibility of a similar problem in the future?

● Time management hotel staff workplace stress emotion challenge

Marketing mix strategy solves supermarket store organizational cooperation challenge

● Critically discuss the factors influencing Tesco's sourcing of fresh fruit and vegetables.

● Assess the level of power that Tesco exercises in the supply chain for fruit and vegetables.

A national chain of restaurant mobile advertising promotion strategy

● Discuss methods that could be used to assess the effectiveness of mobile advertising.

● Discuss the relationship between mobile advertising and other elements of the promotion in campaign planning.

Can AI facility management technology improve organizational performance

Facility management influences airport and logistic employee performance

● Facility management assists employees reduce

maintenance service expenditure p.91-119

- Facility management role in organization
- Can (FM) create value to organization?
- Facility management brings departmental benefits

CHAPTER ONE

How airport service technology or employee may improve performance

Our global tourism development had been developed from birth cycle stage to decline life cycle stage nowadays. From 1960 beginning, when airplanes were popular to be increased need to global travelers. Hence, from 1960 to 1970 is whole global tourism industry birth cycle stage. Till to 1971 beginning, many Asia, e.g. Singapore, Japan, China and Western, e.g. UK, UK etc. countries people, they have jobs to do ,and they have more extra money to prepare to choose any leisure activities. From 1971 to 1980, it is growth life cycle stage to global tourism industry. Many airplane manufacturers had been beginning to manufacturer many airplanes because they felt global traveler number would increase. In fact, in this ten years, global traveler number had been increasing every year. Then, from 1981 to 2019 this fourty years, it is global tourism industry nature life cycle stage. It means that every year travel number had been increasing more significantly to compare past. Also, many travelers feel need to travel every year. So, global travel tourism industry may reach the most top travel clients level in this fourty years. However, till to 2020 , due to COVD19 human mouth and disease occurrence, it influences global travelers feel fear to catch air planes to travel because this kind COVD 19 human mouth disease may cause lung disease from air. When many travelers are sitting in the close window air plane, if one person has ths kind COVD19 human mouth disease. The sick person may contact air to let the persons to breath to cause lung disease in possible in airplane. So, global travelers number is decreasing after 2019 . Also, it implies that tourism industry is facing decline life cysle stage.

It brings these questions: IS it right time to develop space tourism? Can space tourism help future tourism industry to re-grow its life cycle stage from nowadays decline life cycle stage? Can space tourism develop to nature stage from birth life cycle stage ? I shall attempt to give evidence to explain whether space tourism may be developed to let human has more one kind tourism . It may be future leisure new trend for travelers, instead of earth travel. Because one day earth tourism destination may not bring leisure interesting to global traveler, then space tourism may be attempted to replace this kind of travelling activity . So, space tourism is birth life cycle stage. However, our earth tourism may define moral tourism, nature tourism, green tourism, responsible tourism in future new travelling leisure trend.

It bring these questions: Can our future tourism industry meet the expectations with the terms " ecological tourist"? Which factors affect the product life cycle of eco tourism? Nature and green tourism may be our earth new kind of travel activities, when many young and old age travelers like to climb mountains, they feel life nature scene more than non-man made) nature scene in their journeys, they do not like to visit cities to travel. It is possible that they often work in offices, this office working factor may influence many travelers like green tourism in the future. So, green or nature tourism will be our future popular tourism leisure activities. It may influence nowadays our tourism decline life stage to re-grown to nature life cycle stage in possible in this COVD19 people mouth disease influential environment.

New economic development in Tourism and oil industries

- How to develop new economic tourism industry

How to develop tourism industry in new economic environment? Any examination of the new economic development of travel and tourism requires definitions of the subject and its components, which are suitable for economic analysis. However, in new economic development to tourism industry, it is also important to look at tourism conceptually, in order to set the scene for a deeper understanding of the future new tourism industry development.

Tourism is neither a phenomenon nor a simple set if industries, however, in new or old economic development environment. It is a human activity which encompasses human behavior, use of resources, and interaction with other people, economies and leisure enjoyment environment. It is also involved physical movement of tourists to locales other than their normal living places.

In future new economic environment, traditional travel needs to include these element in order to satisfy traveler enjoyment and leisure feeling: They may include: Tourist needs and motivations, tourism selection and behavior and constraints , travel away from home , market interactions between tourists and those supplying products to satisfy tourist needs and impacts on tourists , hosts, economies and environments.

In new economic environment, the tourism products may include: carriers, in any forms of transport for tourist travel accommodation, man-made attractions, which could also include the managed areas of natural attractions, private sector and public sector support services, middlemen, such as tour wholesalers and travel agents.

The tourism resources may also include: Natural resources, lands , minerals, water and biological; labor resources, human work, and enterprise; capital resources, manmade enhancement and other resources. The travel and tourism resources problems may include: As there is frequently a mismatch between producer and consumer perception of what constitutes the tourism product , there may be conflict in ideas of which resources are properly involved as well as many of the resources likely to be in demand for tourism are public goods , or even free resources.

In new economic development to tourism industry view, we need to consider that tourism and travel has the reputation of being a relatively clean and pleasant industry in which to work or invest in order to attract a greater number of resource suppliers than as less well-perceived industry, which therefore keeps rewards prices down by competition, how to attract those retiring from or travel business for example, if their finances are already sound, income from travel is not expected to be optimal , travel and tourism is frequently highly seasonal , offering rewards that are competitive with other industries only some of the time, destination products are often in locations which are of little use to other industries, so that competition for resource use if minimal and hence rewards are low.

In general, tourist purpose may include: recreational purpose : holiday, health and sport and religion as well as business purpose: company business , e.g. conventions and sales trips. So, in new economic tourism development aim, tourism industry need consider hoe to achieve incentive trips to let these both tourists to feel. For example, the overall type of tourism required, destination arrangement, travel mode, accommodation and attraction visiting and purchasing method or distribution channel. The purchasing method choices may include: whether to buy an inclusive package or separate service, whether to buy direct from suppliers, such as airlines or hotels or use an agent , which tour wholesaler or operate or agent to use.

I predict the tourism development in new economic view, it may have these characteristics: Few enterprises in travel and tourism are large, highly cashed-up and have a large asset base, enterprises within travel and tourism that are not in a financial position to diversify, and those do well success to the above –average growth obtainable in travel and tourism compared with many other industries, they would therefore tend to expand within the sector. The result of individual enterprise growth and integration within travel and tourism is an increase in the concentration of that industry. The degree to which output is produced of fewer and fewer enterprises. This can be only be accounted for realistically with the context of an individual economy, Levels of concentration in any part of travel and tourism in the future are likely to depend on two opposing factors: The constant demand by many tourist market segments for new experiences and products, which encourages the development and survival of more and diverse enterprises, and therefore leads to the reduction of concentration as well as technology, which in travel and tourism frequently calls for large capital outlays and requires mass markets for efficient use, promotes integrations and large scale enterprise, especially in air travel and non-personal services (marketing and information communication, travel insurance , tourism payment methods). IN these areas, concentration will undoubtedly increase in future new economic development environment.

HOW TO PROLONG TOURISM LEISURE MATURE LIFE CYCLE STAGE AS WELL AS AVOID DECLINE AND DEATH LIFE CYCLE STAGE OCCURENCE FROM COVID 19 HUMAN DISEASE

Any businesses expect to reach the mature life service cycle stage and they also hope to prolong to stay in this stage and avoid to have chance experience decline life service cycle stage, even death stage in future whole business life cycle stages. However, in fact, there are many businesses need to spend long time to have effort to reach mature life cycle stage from birth and growth both stages, even when they have effort to experience this the topest level stage, many can not stay to prolong time in this stage, then they will reach next stage, such as decline life cycle stage, even final death life cycle stage possibly. Hence , research whether how can reach the mature life cycle stage in short time and prolong to say in this stage. It is one common researching value question to any businesses. Such as COVID 19 human disease had been occurrence in 2019 end , it bring global tourism industry traveller number began to reduce. I shall attempt to explain how airline organizations implement strategies to avoid to enter decline service life cycle stage as below:

- How to avoid to reach the decline service life stage rapidly to global airlines tourism service industry due to COVID 19 human disease occurred

Strategies for growing and maturity a product or raise service performance, and increasing profit margins and prolonging to stay on the mature service life stage. I believe that it is any service businesses final aim. However, in any service life cycle stages, when the service , e.g. airline tourism leisure service industry will experience the decline service life stage , due to the COVID19 human disease influences to global travelers began to feel fear to catch airplanes to avoid air contact to give this kind of disease from 2020. So, nowadays, airlines ought have the suitable or right strategies to help them to solve travelers reducing number to influence their profit growth to encounter decline life service cycle stage later.

Life cycle strategy is based on product or service life cycle thinking from marketing, the factors may influence when the business can reach the mature life cycle stage, but some unpredicted factors may influence their clients number reduce, such as this airlines organizations traveler number reduces is due to COVID 19 human disease influences they feel fear to catch airplanes to travel case, their strategies may include: market growth rate, market growth potential, breach of service lines, number of competitor, distribution of market, share among competitors, customer loyalty , barriers to entry and technology improvement etc. factors to influence the global airlines tourism service industry can continue develop or expand to future overseas tourism market, when COVID 19 human disease may be killed by new medicine later.

Such as this COVID 19 human disease influences travelers feel fear to catch airplanes to avoid get this kind of disease and it influences global travelers number is decreasing in 2020 case, when the airline organization reaches the growth life service cycle stage from the birth stage, if it expects to spend short time to reach the mature life service cycle stage. Before COVID 19 human disease had not been killed by new medicine, if they hope to attract many travelers to choose to catch their airplanes to fly , the extension strategies that any airline organization can attempt to achieve, they may include, rebranding, establishing airline service in order to differentiate the other airline competitors tourism service , ticket price discounting and seeking new marketers, rebranding is the creation od a new look and feel for an established airline tourism service from the airline's competitors.

The airline service life cycle extension strategies also may include these methods to help the airline organization to grow or grow up or develop its airline tourism market rapidly, e.g. repackaging and new sizes, the appearance of airline tourism service can be crucial gaining a passenger's attention and developing tourism interest , new formulas or additional airline tourism features to the tourism country, lower ticket prices to maintain interest or liquidate surplus stock new airline tourism service advertising campaign, altering the new airline channel of destination, such as online ticket purchase.

Hence, after COVID 19 human disease had been skilled by new medicine , any airline organizations need to consider how to choose the most suitable strategy from different kinds of key strategies to expand their airline new tourism channels throughout the different airline tourism service life stages, in these four distinct stages: introduction, growth, maturity and decline or possible death stage, when this COVID 19 human disease had occurred from 2019 end, it may influence global travelers number had significant been reducing to bring any airline organizations may enter the decline life service cycle stage rapidly, even death life service cycle stage comes consequently.

Any airline organizations can use various marketing strategies in each stage to try to prolong the life cycle or attempt to reach the mature life cycle stage in short time. Avoiding to experience decline life service cycle stage, such as the COVID 19 human disease occurrence causes global travelers number began to reduce. It is ensure that any airline organizations do not expect to experience or reach the decline service life stage due to this COVID 19 human disease influences. The question is that how the airline organizations can maintain a strategy in the decline stage , such as COVID19 human disease influences global travelers number reduced and it brings many airlines income began to reduce, for example, reducing the airline promotional expenditure in this COVID 19 human disease occurrence period, reducing the number of airline distribution outlets , e.g. Hong Kong to New York airline flight channel reduces implementing ticket price cuts to get passengers to but the maintaining the airline tourism service and waiting for airline competitors to withdraw from the global airline tourism market.

Thus, following the initial growth, in this COVID human disease occurrence period, when the new airline organization enterprise enters the expansion stage during which the routing operation succeeds. The new airline organization can either reach the mature life service cycle stage either it can prolong to stay in this stage or it can not prolong to stay and enters to decline service life cycle stage , even death service life cycle stage. So , how to avoid the decline service life cycle stage comes to the new airline organization in this COVID 19 human disease occurrence period. It is any airline organizations concerning question when they are experiencing in the mature life cycle stage, but when COVID 19 human disease occurs to influence global travelers number began to reduce. May the airline organization experience the decline service life cycle stage rapidly when the COVID 19 human disease occurs ? It depends on whether it's strategies implementation are effective , its' strategies are effective, it may avoid to reach the decline life service cycle stage in short time easily due to COVID 19 human disease influences.

For this COVID 19 human mouth disease case , since 2019 had occurred, it brought serious tourism industry economic loss to any countries, many people loss jobs, many people feel fear to enter any shops when they are in crowd shop environment, e.g. restaurants can not permit to allow many people to sit closely, because when one person has COVID 19 human mouth disease, he can bring this disease to another person from air. So, many restaurants lose many clients in morning, lunch and night busy eating time, even ships also can not permit many people to enter their ships, because they avoid many people may contact, if one or some people has/have COVID 19 mouth disease, when he/she talks to the salespeople in the shop. It has high chance to cause many people get COVID human disease by mouth. So, any shops can not allow crowd in themselves shops to avoid any people have COVID 19 human disease occurrence. So, this COVID 19 human mouth disease may influence many businesses are experiencing decline life cycle stage, because clients number is continue decreasing, unless drug invention succeeds to fill this kind human mouth disease. Otherwise, on the consequence, many businesses will face death life cycle stage in short time possible. So, it is good example to explain unpredicted external environmental factor to bring global businesses will face decline life cycle in 2020 or next year, even after two years latter. So, COVID -19 human mouth disease may also influence any businesses had been experiencing long time in the mature life cycle to change to decline life cycle stage in possible.

Instead of the businesses are experiencing in either birth or growth life cycle stage. for example, UK Cathay airline had been experiencing long time in the mature life cycle stage from 2000, when its clients number had been increasing, but when the end of 2019, COVID-19 human mouth and air contact disease had occurred in global to influence any people feel fear to catch airplanes to travel or business travel frequently, due to airplanes have none windows, its none window environment will bring COVID-19 disease to any passengers when the airplane has many passengers are sitting together closely, if anyone has COVID-19 disease, he will cause any one airplane service waiter, passenger , even pilot to have COVID-19 disease easily.

So, global airline industry is experiencing decline life cycle stage. even Cathay airline is one big UK developed airline , it's passengers number is large in the past, but when COVID-19 disease occurs to cause travelers number had been decreasing. Hence, Cathay airline is experiencing decline life cycle stage from mature life cycle stage. It needs to implement dismissing staffs to keep salaries expenditure reducing strategy in global, e.g. HK will have 4,000 front line airline service staffs or airport check in service staffs , they will be dismisses in HK Cathay airline market. Although, HK government had given money to support it to continue to alive in order to avoid dismissing employees decision . But, Cathay airline had made decision that it will dismiss many airline service staffs in different countries.

In fact, if Cathay airline expects it would not reach to the decline life cycle stage later, this dismissing employees strategy aims to avoid spending much salaries expenditure , it may be one good method to avoid decline , even death life cycle stage occurs in this year or latter.

On conclusion, it is difficult to predict what factors may cause the business itself will face decline life cycle stage occurrence in any time. Hence, any businesses ought to spend time to research whether which methods or strategies can help them to continue to expand their market or fight any kinds of threats in those four identified business life cycle stages. To avoid business can not continue develop or die, when the business is experiencing in the decline life cycle stage, the strategy is that , the organization needs to spend time to observe or learn how and why its market environment is changing in order to make the most accurate or effective strategies decisions to solve any challenges in any one of these four life cycle stages successfully.

- How new economic development in oil industry

The future global economic growth, it will influence personal incomes and GDP rise. They would carry different weight in different countries at different times. Starting from low levels of incomer and economic development. Household consumption will change from being dominated by basic heat to rapidly rising energy use for higher levels of comfort in space heating and cooling (and large dwellings), and greater use of electrical appliances, finally to a degree of saturation influenced by the income distribution patterns of the country concerned. Income distribution typically changes very slowly, so that the technical market for heart will never be saturated because there will always be a proportion of poor people living in small spaces less comfortably than the average. Industrial energy consumption will be influenced by technical efficiency within each sector, and by changes in the structures of the economy, e.g. changing proportions of agriculture, heavy and light industry, and services. One may eventually see evidence of diminishing marginal returns to additional energy inputs compared to other inputs. Energy consumption in the energy transformation sector may be influenced by income, which drives the demand for electricity to influenced by income, which drives the demand for electricity to grow faster than the demand for heat, but is also subject to the chosen technology of transformation, which is influenced by the cost and availability of primary energy inputs (fuels) in new economic development environment.

IN new economic development environment, it will influences that fuels do not compete in all sectors; for example, the transport sector is dominated by oil. Nuclear and hydroelectric power (and most renewables) reach the user through electricity; electricity itself competes with the direct burning of fossil fuels. Electricity provides the means by which other fuels can compete with oil and gas in sectors, such as space heating and process heat. It also is the only means of powering applications such as motors, computers and lighting: these subsectors are difficult to analyze. However, there is strong evidence that higher incomes do not weaken the demand for electricity so much as the demand for energy in total (in contrast to the effect on the demand for non-electric energy forms).

Econometricians look at the historical record of change in fuel prices and quantities to distinguish several factors between the new economic development and old economic development to oil industry in the future. An income effect. Increasing (reducing) fuel prices reduces (increases) the purchasing power of consumers' income: higher incomes caused by lower prices will increase energy consumption; the consumers' allocation of the increased income to energy purchases may reduce as income rises. Thus income may be heading in a different direction from fuel prices that the effect of fuel price changes when incomes are rising means simply that rising incomes have increased demand. Reducing the cost of using energy through win-win efficiency measures causes a similar problem . On the consequence, in future new economic development environment, it may influence in both cases demand will be less than if the future oil price or efficiency has not changed. The other effect is that an efficiency or substitution effect. An increase in fuel prices may cause consumers to spend more on new equipment, building materials and management operations, which will reduce the amount of fuel required to give the same energy result to the user. The extent of the efficiency effect depends on what happens to the price of the new equipment or building: if those price s rise in line with the fuel price, changes in the balances between fuel and capital or management will not occur. A new user technology , such as the development of the combined cycle gas turbine generator may increase efficiency and thus greatly reduce the quantity of primary fuel needed to produce the required output in this case electricity. If electricity prices had remained sticky, and the electricity and gas markets were not competitive, some of this advantages could have accrued to the gas suppliers in the form of an increase in price, because th4 unit of gas produces more output of electricity, it would have a higher value. In reality, the development of new economic competitive environment in both gas and electricity has tended to ensure that the benefits of such technical advanced accrue to the consumer through lower final prices. The same many apply in the case of improved efficiency in future non-manual driving auto vehicle development: the consumer's cost of motoring is reduced in new economic non-manual driven auto vehicle (Artificial intelligent vehicle) can replace manual driven vehicle , even electricity battery can replace oil energy to be used in vehicles. So, oil price may be influenced to reduce in future new economic development environment.

New and old economic theories explain oil is not main factor to influence tourism income

- Can economic theory explain old price change to influence tourism income?

I shall attempt to apply old and new economic theory to explain whether oil changing price has direct relationship to influence global tourism indusry development or tourism income as below:

Is oil changing price the main to influence tourism income or tourism development or economic growth ? If oil price rises ar falls, it will or won't cause tourism income decreases or increases? If they have cause and effect relationship, what are the main factors to influence tourism income changes by oil price rises or falls ?

I aim to investigate how any why among oil price shocks will influence tourism income variables. We may distinguish between these oil price shocks: Supply-side , aggregate demand and oil specific demand shocks. I assume that oil specific demand shocks affect inflation and the tourism sector equity index. By constrast, I also believe that aggregate demand oil price shock exercisr an effect, either directly and indirectly tourism generated income and economic growth. So, in old economic theory, supply-side , aggregate demand view to oil specific demand shocks will influence tourism income varies. So, governments ought implement strategies against future oil price movements or plan for economic policy development.

In fact, instead of oil price changes will influence tourism income, it could also harm economic growth and tourism activities, due to the effect they expert on transporation, production cost, economic uncertainty.Because tourism activities is one important sector to influence any country's leisure consumption GDP income source. So, sudden fluctations in oil prices may also influence economic growth. It is based a hyphthesis known as the tourism led economic growth. So, it seems that they have direct or indirect relationship to case effect between oil price and tourism activities and development. So, increase on tourism income, the called " economic-driven tourism growth". In addition, high oil prices are affecting certain tourism industry segments , e.g. airlines, cruises lines, hotel, rent travelling car services etc. for oil, importing countries example, with reference to macro economic effects, higher oil prices generally lead to higher inflation, when they negatively influence to country's income.

Hence, from a micro-economic perspective, positive oil price shocks lead to a decline in disposable income. for low income people, it will bring an immediate and negative impact on tourism, mainly due to they feel tourism leisure is regarded as a luxury good, when oil price shocks to rise suddenly . It influences any airline or cruise entertainment service providers' costs are influenced to raise. Then, they need to increase air ticket or cruise ticket price. It will bring on negative tourism leisure demands-side the oil price increases low income group, potential tourism leisure consumers. Hence, it seems that oil price may have indirect relationship to influence tourism leisure consumers' needs.

- How the price of oil changes influences global tourism industry growth or recession?

In macro-economic view, sudden mid and long term oil price shock can influence global torusim industry growth or recession. For example, a oil price of US$180 per barrel was considered only a few years ago, now this has a realistic scenario to which all plaers in the T&T sector have to adapt. At such a high level, the price of oil will become even more critical to almost every part of the tourism value chain. Although, weak global demand, caused by global economic recesson, resulted in a steep oil price decline to US$45 per barrel by the fourth quarter of 2008 in the past low oil price occurrence history, this won't change the mid to long -term oil forecast.

In fact, the past oil price occurrence history of the dramatic structural had changed a high price imposed on airlines, travelers, and destination countries, all of which will have to navigate through times of shifting or even declining travel demand. I assume that a high oil price scenario is assumed in the long term in order to highlight the changes , such a senario would mean for consumer behavior and the competitiveness of several destinations.

Low oil price in the 1970 and early 1980 did not bring significant growth of international air travel, but its growth has been strongest between 1980 and 2004, a period with stable and relatively moderate oil prices. Also, the rapid development of the low-cost carrier business model in the 1990s further fueled air travel growth by capturing tourism leisure demand , such as weekend leisure travel to cities using mostly secondary airports in any big area countries, such as UK, US . However, the tourism growth is whole influenced by high oil prices, due to oil price had been continue rising in possible.

Basis of oil is shortage supply product, oil is assumed to be the main energy source for the aviation sector for the nest 30 years. Although, second-generation biofuels seem to be on the horizon, the economics as well as the production scalability and aviation biofuel shortage will be a main challenge to airline industry. So, I assume that oil price will continue rise up, if there have none any aviation biofuel can be reflected to oil to use for air plane energy.

Until 2004, the only factors to have affected air travel growth, negatively were in external shocks , such as 9/11, causes catching air plane crisis or US regional geopolitical conflicts. It brings some travelers feel fear to go to US travel, as well as until recently 2019, human mouth disease can influence air to have disease to anyone from mouth. So, global travelers number had been continue decreasing, because they are fear to get disease by air when many themselves every stranger travelers are sitting on the without windows air planes. Although, mouth human and air disease and US 9/11 air attack both matters may influence oil price falls effect, because air planes flying times will reduce. They won't need frequent to fly, to cause aviation oil energy need reduce. Consequently, oil price will decrease, due to travelers number reduces and air planes flying times are also influenced to reduce. (oil demand decreases cause oil price decrease). Although, air lines ' cost will also be influenced reduce, but oil price decrease can not bring travelers number increase , when air ticket price reduce because global many leisure and business trip travelers feel fear to catch air planes frequently when human mouth air disease occured in 2019. So, oil price decreases can not grow up tourism industry growth or rise tourism income.

However, the obvious impact of a high oil price is an increase in the operating costs of airline. Moreover, fuel cost as a percentage of airline operating costs vary significantly based on the length of the flight. The longer the flight, the higher the fuel costs as a percentage of the airline operating cost. So, from an online's perspective, long -hauel flights represent the most criticial challenge to profitable operation because the share of fuel on these flights, compared with other cost items, is largest, because of the unfacorable fuel economics, due to fuel costs even at high-load factors. For example, Thai airways dropped its non-stop Bongkok to US flights in the summer of 2008 for commercial reasons, because fuel reached operating cost levels of 55 percent on this route, a cost burden that could not be passed on to their customers. So, the estimated price elacticity of passengers demand at this Bongkok to US flights route is high, if Thai Airways rises less air ticket price, it will influence many travelers to choose other airlines to catch air plan to fly. Hence, due to Thai Airways can not make decision to rise air ticket price, because it believes that it will lose many travelers, so it only chooses to drop this non-stop Bongkok to US flights to avoid fuel cost rising economic loss.

However, although micro and macro economic theories may also that oil price variable or change, it may influence global tourism income. But, recently, on 2019, human mouth and air diseases, it can influence global individual leisure and business trip travelers feel fear to catch air plans to avoid their bodies get this kind of death sickness when they sit in the no fresh air supplying air planes. They feel that they reduce leisure travelling flying times or business trip flying times with strange travelers to sit in crowd air planes together. Then, they must many avoid human moth and air disease to avoid death crisis. Hence, in this global human mouth and air diseases threat environment occurrence, even oil price sudden reduces to low price, it brings airline's cost reduces and air ticke price reduces. However, when air ticket price reduce to be very cheaper, it can not still attract global many leisure or business trip travelers to buy air tickets to fly frequently. Why does air ticket reduction, it can not attract many leisure or businee trip travelers to buy air ticket to fly ? The main reason is because human mouth and air disease influences global many travelers feel fear to catch air planes frequently. In psychological view, this kind of human mouth and air sickness will bring long time negative influence to global traveles do not want to catch air planes for business trips or travelling leisure frequently. So, it implies that oil price changing to influence air ticket price reduction factor ought not main factor to influence tourism income. It may include traveler individual negative emotion psychological factor, such as human mouth and air disease or 2019 9/11 attack both cases, they can influence global travelers feel fear to catch air planes to fly to avoid death threat. So, oil changing price ought not be only one absolute main factor to influence global tourism income significantly.

On conclusion, in economic view, it seems that oil chang price may have indirect or direct relationship to influence tourism income, instead of some unpredicted external environment factors influence, such as US 9/11 attack crisis and human mouth and air disease factors, they may be main factors to influence travellers number to reduce in non-economic external unpredicted environment view.

How can artificial intelligent tools predict travelling consumer behavior in airline and air agent travelling market

I believe that applying (AI) big data tool to predict vehicle buyer consumption choice behavior, it is similar to predict traveler consumption choice behavior. In this chapter, I shall indicate how to apply (AI) big data gathering tool to predict vehicle buyer consumption choice behavior. Then, I shall its what its similar points to be applied to predict traveler consumption choice behavior.

Nowadays, many vehicle manufacturers hope their vehicles can attract to vehicle buyers to choose to buy their vehicles. However, there are many different brands of vehicles to provide to them to choose, so the vehicle market competition is very serious.

How to judge their different kinds of vehicle price which is reasonable acceptance to attract vehicle buyers to choose to buy the brand of vehicle manufacturers‘ any kinds of vehicles, e.g. fast speed sport style vehicles, comfortable and slow speed common cars, for four passengers common small size or more than four passengers common large car size?

How to evaluate the vehicle prices issue is important factor to influence vehicle buyers’ choices. Either if the brand of vehicle price is too high to compare other brands of similar vehicle price, it will influence many vehicle buyers choose to buy other brands‘ vehicles or if the brand of vehicle price is too low, it will influence vehicle buyers feel this brand’s vehicle machine quality or safe driving level or manufacturing steel material or speed or not comfortable sitting etc. different factors is worse to compare to other vehicle brands’ similar vehicle products.

Thus, if the brand of vehicle manufacturers can predict how to design vehicles which can attract many vehicle buyers to choose to buy whose any vehicle products. What are future vehicle buyers‘ favorable vehicle styles? Then, the vehicle manufacturer can concentrate on manufacturing the kind style of vehicle products to sell already. It will reduce its vehicle manufacturing investment risk.

How to apply (AI) tools to predict vehicle buyers’ behavioral consumption model? Whether artificial intelligent tools can predict automotive buyers‘ behavioral consumption model and predict future vehicle design trend. In fact, automotive brands and dealerships are facing an increasingly competition when attempting to manually gathering the vast quantities of data required to create customer focused programs that increase retention, ultimately new sales and service automotive business.

Building a based on that client’s intrinsic needs and interests to any kinds of automotive vehicles at any given time. This is especially true in the automotive industry where the time span between purchases is measured in years. Because vehicle buyers would not like often to change their old vehicle to another new one. So, their decisions to buying another new vehicle, the time is usually after one year, even longer time. Hence, it seems any vehicles won’t be frequent consumption products to the owned at least one vehicle family consumers (vehicle buyers). It implies that why vehicle manufacturers ought need to spend time to predict future vehicle buyer design choice for whole year vehicle buyer number growth because they won’t often change preferable vehicle design to change another new vehicle more easily.

Hence, how to predict vehicle consumers’ taste or preferable which styles of vehicle choices issues is very important.

If the vehicle manufacturers can not manufacture any attractive vehicles to sell easily in this year. Then, it will lose time, money in this year because it won't know when the owned least one vehicle users or non-owned any vehicle users who will decide to buy one new vehicle or change another new vehicle ensure. The different brand vehicle dealers will possible wait more than one year to attract them to buy their vehicles if their styles are not attractive to compare other brands of vehicle competitors.

However, artificial intelligence and machine learning can help any vehicle manufacturers to find solution to solve patterns in highly to solve patterns in highly complex data-sets that are beyond the capability of a human brain, and then building and automatically acting on the customer insights it generates.

Given the automotive customer need for individualized communications, this technology is positioned to become a critical component of any successful vehicle retailer's domestic or/and overseas vehicle markets. How can vehicle manufacturers and retailers use (AI) to enhance their vehicle marketing campaigns? How will (AI) affect their vehicle sale marketing strategy? What criteria would they use when selecting on (AI) solution?

Vehicle consumers today are able to quickly access different brands of vehicle information, research vehicle products and reviews, negotiate prices and compare one vehicle brand or retailer to another resulting of the brands of vehicle customers. At the same time, the rise of " big -data mining", wearable devices that track user's every move and preference and greater contextualization in advertising and social media has resulted in consumer expectations of individualized. Thus, it seems that (AI) tools can be used to gather " big-data" and then they can make human's mind to analyze how to design kinds of vehicles to satisfy vehicle buyers' needs.

As automotive vehicle marketers can apply (AI) tools to achieve messaging strategies to meet the needs of this new generation of informed vehicle consumers, using data from a variety of sources to move from a variety of sources to move from mass- messaging to more personalized messages aimed at particular vehicle buyer segments, e.g. fast speed sport vehicle buyer segment, slow speed comfortable small size or large size of buyer segment. However, when 90% of vehicle marketers believe having a single vehicle buyer view is important, only 6% have achieved it.

However, one of the main issues vehicle marketers are facing the lack of capacity to efficiently sift through and analyze the massive vehicle buyer amounts of data required to create vehicle buyer individualized vehicle customer experiences easily. This is especially difficult for automotive dealers, the long periods between purchase cycles, and the highly considered nature of the vehicle purchase means that each vehicle dealer needs to not only track a large number of potential vehicle customers for an extremely long period of time, but each of those vehicle customers will generate a huge amount of different kinds of vehicle behavioral consumption data as they research their next vehicle purchase. However, by choosing the right (AI) technological tools and programs , vehicle dealers can solve this big data gathering challenge into a major advantage.

For Forrester vehicle brand example, vehicle consumers have more power over the Forrester vehicle brand's reputation than ever before. Mayne, L. (2014) indicated that Forrester calls this new (AI) tools is the " age of the vehicle customer", a 20 year business cycle in which the most successful vehicle enterprises will reinvent themselves to systematically understand and serve increasingly powerful vehicle consumers. To win in this new age, Forrester declares companies must become vehicle customer obsessed and the only sustainable competitive advantage is knowledge and engagement with customers, such as (AI) gathering data knowledge.

Thus, the biggest challenge vehicle businesses currently face is not the collection of a large quantity of vehicle consumer data, but what to do with that data once they have it. Even at a large vehicle data research firm, the data sets are often too big for a single analyze, or even a team of analysts to sort through and draw conclusion from. However, enter artificial intelligence and machine learning , an efficient technology solution that can continuously find patterns in highly complex data sets that are way beyond the capacity of a human brain and then automatic drive action based on the customer insights is generated.

What is (AI) machine learning tool? Machine learning is a type of (AI) that learns from data and is not explicitly program. Think Amazon, face book. Machine learning serves up relevant content based on an individual vehicle purchase behavior and experiences. More simply, machine learning is a computer program that can learn relationships between data, subject those learnings to errors functions, and then learn from its errors. The program in effect, trains itself.

Lee, T. (2016) explained that "Thus, (AI) tools can learn deep a more advanced branch of machine learning inspired by how our brain's nervous function, has also been found to be especial effective in identifying patterns from data." When this way sound is complicated from a vehicle dealer perspective, the implementation of a marketing program driven by artificial intelligence can take care of these tasks in an automatic vehicle fashion with little to no manual intervention required from the staff at time vehicle stores.

In practice at a vehicle dealership, the program will continue track vehicle customer behavior online, merging that data with any offline source (like CRM or DMS data) and then analyze this aggregated vehicle buyer data set to predict what vehicle customer may be shopping for and what information they might like to relevance from different kinds style of vehicle design photos.

Why does travelling market seem to similar to vehicle market which can apply (AI) learning tool to predict travellingconsumer behaviors?

Artificial intelligence refers to complex in vehicle market and travelling entertainment market which is very seem to be applied to predict consumer behaviors.

(AI) machine learning that posses the same characteristics of human intelligence and that have all our sense, all our reason and think just like human vehicle buyer who prefer vehicle purchase choice or travelling consumer who prefer travelling package or travelling destination and airline choice. Besides, machine learning is the practice of using algorithms to collect and examine data, learn from it, and then make a determination or prediction about something in the world.

So, it can be attempted to gather data concerns that travelling consumer past travelling destination choice and air ticket price choice and different travelling package, e.g. high, middle, or low class hotel and foods supply and entertainment places choice in their past travelling journeys.

The machine is " trained" using large amounts of data and algorithms that give it the ability to learn how to automatically perform a task with increasing accuracy. Otherwise, deep learning is primarily based on artificial neural networks inspired by our understanding of the biology of human's brains.

Thus, (AI) big data can gather all these past traveler consumption behavioral choice data to make reference to analyze whether how many travelers will choose to go to the specific travelling destination in any time by the past traveler number record to different travelling destinations, then it can gather the past air ticket sale price to different destinations and past travelling package design to different destinations in order to analyze whether it is the cheap airline ticket price factor or attractive travelling package factor or attractive travelling entertainment etc. in order to predict which factor is the most potential influential factor to they choose to go to the destination to travel in different time within one year. Then, traveler agent or airline can collect these big data to judge how to design their package to attract travelers to go to anywhere to travel or what the main factor influence most of them to choose to visit the destination to travel.

For example, travel agents or airlines can apply "Deep learning" breaks down tasks in ways that enables machines to assist them to predict when travelling consumer choice will be changed and why their travelling choice will change and how their travelling choice will change with increasingly complex tasks.

So, such as why (AI) technology can be applied to predict how travelling consumer behavior changes to bring to judge whether anywhere will be many travelling consumers who will prefer to choose travelling hot destinations next year or next month.

Then, travel agents and airlines can gather overall past travelling consumer data to analyze and conclude the more accurate prediction of different travelling destinations to the number of traveler. Then, they can choose how much air ticket price is more reasonable to charge to the travelling destination or how to design the travelling package which can bring more attractive to the prediction number of different travelling destination travelers in order to achieve to raise the different travelling destination number next year.

Thus, (AI) big data machine learning can help airlines or travel agents to solve how to design any attractive travelling package challenge. A travelling package is both one of the most important and carefully considered travelling entertainment consumption the majority of travelling people will ever make in their lifetime at least one travelling time.

It is also a prediction how travelling package will be designed that tends to be fundamentally tied to a travelling person's travelling destination choice identify and travelling package view of themselves. As the same time, travelling consumers' travelling choice changing lifestyles result in changing travelling destination needs, e.g. the country's young travelers can choose to change non-extreme exciting travelling entertainment package from past extreme exciting travelling entertainment package. Due to personal feeling factor in general. However, I believe that (AI) big data can also be attempted to predict when the country's young travelers will choose to change non-extreme exciting travelling behavior.

It is similar to automotive dealers need to remember that vehicle customers and prospects are individual human beings with risk, complex and ever-changing lives factors, these factors will influence every vehicle consumer why who feels has vehicle purchase need, and how who choose to buy the first vehicle if who decided to buy the first vehicle.

It seems that travelling agents or airlines need to remember that travelling consumers and different features or designs are very traveler beings with risk, complex and ever-travelling package attitude personal changing factors in different travel season, these factor will influence every individual traveler why who feels has travel entertainment need, and how who choose to buy different feature or design travelling package if who decide to travel.

The (AI) big data technological travelling customer behavioral prediction tool seems to be the best travelling behavioral prediction tool in the world are those that know every one of different country's traveler need. Their likes and dislikes which style of travelling package, preferences and travel destination changing tastes to travelling destination choices.

The capacity of the human brain, however, limits us from achieving these different type of travel package sales. In this competitive travelling destination choice entertainment environment, (AI) big data machine learning enables platforms to assist the air ticket and travel package sales team by tracking the travelling consumer behaviors of each travelling customer, learning and memorizing their preferences and predicting their future travelling destination choice and travelling package design needs.

Finally, I recommend that for a travel agent or airline travelling marketing platform to make their travelling customer engagement efficient and fully-functional, I should be able to: applying (AI) tools to track every travelling customer behavior across the web, connecting to a society of data sources, CRM, DMS, third-party, web travelling brands, social traveler email, click etc., aggregating and accurately cross-reference data from a variety of sources, leveraging this data to drive insights on a mass scale, as well as on an individualized basis, driving actions and automatically direct travelling customer engagement via multiple channels based on where each customer is in their travelling individual lifecycle.

Why is (AI) big data gathering tool better than psychological and survey methods to predict traveler individual travel choice behavior?

Prediction travel behavioral consumption from psychology and survey methods.

How to predict travel consumption? It is one question to any travel agents concern to use what methods which can predict how many numbers of travelers where who will choose to go to travel more accurately. I think that who can consider how to predict travel behavioral consumption from psychology and survey travel choice prediction method, but it is better to apply (AI) big data gathering method to predict travel consumer's destination choice more accurate. The reason is as below:

The first reason is that traveller individual travel psychological desire is difficult to predict accurate more than (AI) big data gathering method, it is due that the data is past traveler's destination choice and travel package and ticket price actual data from (AI) big data gathering method. Otherwise, survey investigation is only traveler psychological thinking method. It lacks enough past actual traveler data gathering.

The second reason is that on the weakness of traveler individual psychological thinking view of survey investigation. It has evidence to support the relationship between self-identify threat and resistance to change travel behavior to any travelers, controlling for whose past travelling behavior, resistance to change if a psychological phenomenon of long standing interest in many applied branches of psychology.

Past travelling behavior has been acknowledged as a predictor of future action. Such as travelling behavior that is experienced as successful is likely to be repeated and may lead to habitual patterns. Some psychologists differentiate habit between two concepts, such as goal oriented and automatic oriented both. Although repeated past travelling behavior is addition goal oriented and automatic oriented. Further non-deliberative nature of habit may make appeals to judge and to predict future individual traveler's behavior accurately.

However, repeated one traveler will choose the destination to repeat to travel without a necessary constraint of goal orientation and automatic oriented both. So, it seems that psychological factor can influence any individual traveler why and how who choose to decide to repeat to choose the destination to travel.

So, survey investigation is only the traveler's thinking to answer the travel firm. It is not sure that the traveler's past travel experience is real answer. Otherwise, (AI) big data gathering method is computer gathering method which gather past traveler consumption actual data to analyze and conclude future traveler possible repeated travel destination choice and travel package choice more accurate.

The third reason is that on the strength of (AI) big data gathering method computer statistic view to predict future traveller consumer's destination and travel package choice. It is structural equation modeling is an extremely flexible linear-in-parameters multivariate statistical modeling technique. It has been used in modeling travel behavior and values since about 1980 year. It is a software method to handle a large number of variables, as well as unobserved variables specified as linear combinations (weighted averages) of the observed variable.

Can (AI) big data gather data to predict when climate will change to influence poor travelling behaviours?

(AI) big data tool can predict the flexibility of human travelling behavioral change is at least the result of one such mechanism, our ability to travel mentally in time and entertain potential future. Understanding of the impacts is holidays, particularly those involving travel.

Using focus groups research to explores tourists' awareness of the impacts of travel own climate change, examines the extent to which climate change features in holiday travel decisions and identifies some of the barriers to the adoption of less carbon intensive tourism practices.

The findings suggest many tourists don't consider climate change when planning their holidays. The failure of tourists to engage with the climate change to impact of holidays, combined with significant barriers to behavioral change, presents a considerable challenge in the tourism industry. In the future, computer (AI) big data tool can attempt to predict when the country's climate change to influence travelers to choose to go to the country to travel, e.g. next month or next half year or next year hot travelling destinations.

Tourism is a highly energy intensive industry and has only recently attracted attention as an important contributions to climate change through greenhouse gas emissions. It has been estimated that tourism contributes 5% of global carbon dioxide emissions. There have been a number of potential changes proposed for reducing the impact of air travel on climate change. These include technological changes, market based changes and behavioral changes.

However, the role that climate change plays in the holiday and travel decisions of global tourists. How the global tourists of the impacts travel has on climate change to establish the extent to which climate change, considerations features in holiday travel decision making processes and to investigate the major barriers to global tourists adopting less carbon intensive travel practices.

It will bring this question: Will tourists aware the impacts that their holidays and travel have on climate changes to influence their travelling decision?

When, it comes to understand individual traveler's behavioral change, wide range of conceptual theories have been developed, utilizing various social, psychological, subjective and objective variables in order to model travel consumption behavior. These theories of travel behavioral change operate at a number of different levels, including the individual level, the interpersonal level and community level. Whether pro-environmental behavior can be used to predict travel consumption behavior in a climate change. However, the question of what determines pro-environmental behavior in such a complex one that it can not be visualized through one single framework or diagram.

Despite the potentially high risk scenario for the tourism industry and the global environment, the tourism and climate change ought have close relationship.

However, (AI) big data tool can be applied to find what factors to influence the time of travelers' travelling choices. What are the important factors and variables which can limit tourism? e.g. money, time, family problem, extreme hot or cold weather change, air ticket price, journey attraction etc. variable factors.

Mention of holidays and travel were deliberately avoided in the recruitment process, so as not to create a connection factor to influence traveler's individual mind. However, the dismissal of alternative transportation modes can be conceived as either a structural barrier, in the sense that flying is perhaps the only realistic option to reach long-haul holiday destination, or a perceived behavioral control barriers in that an individual perceives flying as the only option open to whom.

The transportation tool factor will be depend to extent on the distance to the destination. This can also be interpreted in a social perspective as an intention with the resources available where much international tourism is structured around flying. To increase the availability of different transportation modes, tourists could choose holiday destination closer to home.

Finally, also how to predict future travel behavioral consumption. I feel that travel agents need to predict whether any country's random daily variation of weather factor is also important to influence travel behavior. e.g. in weather, temperature, rainfall and snowfall with traffic accidents factors will have relationship to cause travel demand.

Some scientists estimate suggest that when warmed temperatures and reduced snowfall are associated with a moderate decline in non-fatal accidents, they are also associated with a significant increase in fatal accidents. Thus increase in fatalities and temperature. Half of the estimated effect of temperature on fatalities is due to changes in the exposure to pedestrians, bicyclists and motorcyclists as temperature increase.

So, if any countries have rainfall, snowfall and low temperature to cause traffic accidents, whether this accident occurrence will influence the travelers who liking climb snow hills, riding bicycle, running sports who will avoid to travel to these countries' bad weather after occurs. So, why I feel that this natural climate factor will also be one serious factor to influence travel behavioral consumption. However, (AI) big data tool can predict more accurate than survey method when climate change to influence the country's climate to be poor, then it can predict when which countries are not popular acceptable to global country consumers' travel choice next month.

How can apply (AI) to provide travelling businesses with better-informed decisions ?

I shall explain how (AI) big data gathering technology can provide travelling businesses with better-informed decisions to drive top-line growth, deliver meaningful experience for travelling customers and smooth their path along the travelling consumer journey. The widely understood definition of (AI) involves the ability of machines or computers to learn human thinking, reasoning and decision-making abilities.

So, such as (AI) learning machine system can attempt to learn travelling consumer's travel destination or travel package thinking, judgement of their reasons why they choose to go to the destination to travel or why they choose to buy the travel package and learn how and why they make their past travelling decisions from their past travel big data gathering.

A Narrative science study in 2015 year identified that (AI) was being used primarily in voice recognition, machine learning virtual assistants and decision support. This study also highlighted the many branches of (AI) and that techniques and their definition are used interchangeably. It is possible that (AI) can be used to gather big data , then to analyze to help travel businesses to predict travelling consumer travel destination and travel package choice behaviors. For example, one of the most common techniques is traveler machine learning, where algorithms are used to perform tasks by learning from the airline or travel agent whose past all travelers' travelling destination choice and travel package choice historical data.

However, during 2017 year, search engines will begin to find what additional factors can influence past traveler personal travelling destination and travelling package travelling behavioral data into prediction of future travelling customer behavioral results, such as the online traveler (user's) history of travelling data searches, such as anywhere are the most popular travelling locations or travelling destinations and previously captures conservations.

Artificial intelligence will use this past travelling destinations and travelling package information to power predictive search results, e.g. predictive future travelling consumer's choice behavioral processing for where will be their preferable travelling destination choice and how to design travelling package to satisfy future travelling clients' needs. Predictive search will improve the quality of online travelling search results, and provide new insights into travelling consumers' travelling destination and package behavior and the moments which matter to them. Search will give recommendation into tailored how travelling consumer individual travelling destination choice in travelling decision making process. Several of the largest online platforms already use (AI) travelling machine learning to improve predictive travelling consumer behavioral search results.

For example, Google's rank brain technology adds research by understanding the context in which the travelling consumer has entered it. Over time, rank brain will learn further from user behaviors Amazon's DSSTNE (pronouned destiny) learns from shoppers' purchasing habits and consumption behavior to offer better product recommend actions, which Amazon can offer before a consumer has entered anything into the search bar.

Such as (AI) big data can gather past online travelers' e-ticket purchase transactions to conclude that online traveler's travelling choice habits and online traveler consumption behavior to offer better travelling destinations and travelling package opinions to travel agents or airlines. However, this technology is not independent of human input. For example, Google engineers will periodically retain the rank brain system to improve the models it uses.

For another example, in 2016 year , Apple computer revamped its travelling scene photos app to allow travelling consumers to search for specific travelling destinations in the travelling scene phots, they want to find anywhere travelling destination photos, not just dates and locations. Each travelling photo that an intelligent phone or intelligent pad user takes goes through 11 billion computations, so that travelling scene photos can understand exactly where is the travelling destination photography to let online travelling consumer to feel anywhere they plan to go to the location to travel. So, (AI) learning machine can make online travelling photos more attractive to influence potential travelers choose to the destination to travel after they see the travelling destination scene photos from internet.

It seems that in future, (AI) machine learning will allow online travelling search to evolve even further. Search engineers will deliver refined recommendations to airlines' online traveler e-ticket search users and use less human input to predict travelling consumers' needs from internet channel. For IBM computer example, it indicated 90% of the data that exists today has been created in the last two years.

This huge explosion of past traveler's e-ticket consumption data gives the opportunity to quickly spot and react to the latest trends, fashion and fads among its travelling clients and potential clients. This will allow airline or travel agent companies to better engage with younger travelling consumers, who gain influence access to the latest travelling destination and package trends.

They associate with to help define who they are as individuals. Thus, travelling company brands have to identify and make use of them before travelling consumers move on, but the vast quantity of past e-ticket purchase data available makes from internet channel. This a resource-intensive task. For next example, Lesara, a based online clothes store, uses this machine learning to inform its product decision often gathering information from internal and external sources.

When its trends -spotting shoes. Lesara has a range of over 20 styles and sells hundreds of pairs a day. It focus on giving consumers, the very latest trends allow Lesara to develop on average of 50,000 new items each year. It compared to 11,000 old items each year. Thus, travelling agents or airlines can attempt to apply (AI) big data gathering method to gather all past e-ticket purchase data, concerns where they prefer to choose to go to the destinations to travel and what travelling packages are the most attractive to the travelers to choose to buy. It aims to help them to predict where future travelers will prefer to choose to go to travel or what travelling package they will prefer to choose to buy next year.

For another (AI) big data prediction example, Lesara is one online clothes store, uses machine learning decisions after gathering information from internal and external sources. One of its most popular products, shoes with LED started life when its trend spotting software flagged up a blogger wearing similar shoes. Now Lesara has a range of over 20 styles and sells hundreds of pairs a day. Its focus on giving consumers the very latest trends allows Lesara to develop an average of 50,000 new items each year, compared to 11,000 for its competitor Lara.
It seems (AI) big data gathering machine learning can help Lesara business to predict what kinds of shoes design or style that shoe consumers will prefer choose to buy in future shoe market trend. Thus, Lesara can predict shoe consumers' taste successfully and it can manufacture many attractive style of shoes.
(AI) machine learning can gather global past shoe consumer's shoe shopping experiences, then analyzes to make conclusion to give lesara recommendation successfully. This will make the experience more enjoyable for shoe consumers and allow Lesara to advert whose different new style or design of shoes to deliver them move relevant messages by understanding the context of the experience.
So, online travel agents or online airline can also attempt to apply (AI) big data gathering method to predict where travelers will prefer to go to travel and how they ought design travelling packages to attract them to choose to buy next year. Hence, (AI) big data gathering technology can conclude how to design traveler agents' travelling package products to be the most attractive to excite many travelers choose to buy their travelling package, due to it has more accurate to predict travelling consumer destination and travelling package choice behaviors to compare human themselves prediction judgement effort, e.g. travelling survey or marketing research, or telephone enquire. It seems that (AI) machine judgement effort is more accurate to compare to human judgment effort in travelling industry.

Future travel consumption behavior

Can (AI) big data gathering tool predict traveler individual habitual behavior , e.g. renting travel transportation tools ?

Can (AI) big data gathering tool can predict past traveler destination and travelling package choice habit and it can be intended to predict of future traveler behavior to people are creatures of habits judgement of future anywhere travelling destination choice next year or next month or next half year destination prediction ?
Many of human's everyday goal-directed behaviors are performed in a habitual fashion, the transportation made and route one takes to work, one's choice of breakfast. Habits are formed when using the some behavior frequently and a similar consistency in a similar context for the some purpose whether the individual past travel consumption model will be caused a habit to whom. e.g. choosing whom travel agent to buy air ticket or traveling package; choosing the same or similar countries' destinations to go to travel ; choosing the business class or normal (general) class of quality airlines to catch planes.
Does habitual rent traveling car tools use not lead to more resistance to change of travel mode? It has been argued that past behavior is the best predictor of future behavior to travel consumption. If individual traveler's past consumption behavior was always reasoned, then frequency of prior travel consumption behavior should only have an indirect link to the individual traveler's behavior. It seems that renting travel car tools to use is a habit example. So, a strong rent traveling car tools useful habit makes traveling mode choice. People with a strong renting of traveling car tools of habit should have low motivation to attend to gather any information about public transportation in their choice of travelling country for individual or family or friends members during their traveling journeys.

Even when persuasive communication changes the traveler whose attitudes and intention, in the case of individual traveler or family travelers with a strong renting travel car tools habit. It is difficult to change whose travel behaviors to choose to catch public transportation in whose any trips in any countries. However, understanding of travel behavior and the reasons for choosing one mode of transportation over another. The arguments for rent traveling car tools to use, including convenience, speed, comfort and individual freedom and well known.
Increasingly, psychological factors include such as, perceptions, identity, social norms and habit are being used to understand travel mode choice. Whether how many travel consumers will choose to rent traveling car tools during their trips in any countries. It is difficult to estimate the numbers. As the average level of renting travel car tools of

dependence or attitudes to certain travel package policies from travel agents. Instead different people must be treated in different ways because who are motivated in different ways and who are motivated by different travel package policies ways from travel agents.

In conclusion, the factors influence whose traveler's individual traveler destination choice behavior The factors include either who chooses to rent traveling car tools or who chooses to catch public transportation when who individual goes to travel in alone trip or family trip. It include influence mode choice factors, such as social psychology factor and marketing on segmentation factor both to influence whose transportation choice of behavior in whose trip. So, (AI) big data can be attempted to gather past traveler transportation tool choice, rent travelling car tools choice or catching public transportation tools choice to predict where destination can provide what kind of transportation tool to attract many travelers to choose to go to the place to travel.

How (AI) big data determine future travel behavior from past travel experience and perceptions of risk and safety for the benefits to travel consumers?

How (AI) big data determine future travel behavior from past travel experience and perceptions of risk and safety for the benefits to travel consumers? Why does individual traveler avoid certain destination(s) is(are) as relevant to tourist decision making as why who chooses to travel to others?

Perceptions of risk and safety and travel experience are likely to influence travel decisions. If travel agents had efforts to predict future travel behavior to guess whether travelers will feel where is(are) risk and unsafe to cause who does not choose to go to the country to travel. Then, the travel agents will avoid to choose to spend much time to design the different traveling package to attract their potential travel consumers to choose to travel. The reason is because in the case of individual traveler's tourism experience, the traveler whose past disappointment travel experience (psychological risk) will be a serious threat to the traveler's health or life (health, physical or terrorism risk). The past safety or unhealthy risk to the country(countries) will influence the traveler decides to choose not to go to the countries(country) to travel again in the future.

What is push and pull factors to influence any traveler who chooses where is whose preferable travelling destination ?

How to apply (AI) big data to predict individual traveler's behavioral intention of choosing a travel destination?

Understanding why people travel and what factors influence their behavioral intention of choosing a travel destination is beneficial to tourism planning and marketing. In general, an individual's choice of a travel destination into two forces.

The first force is the push factor that pushes an individual away from home and attempt to develop a general desire to go somewhere, without specifying where that may be.

The other force is the pull factor that pull an individual toward in destination, due to a region-specific or perceived attractiveness of a destination. The respective push and pull factors illustrate that people travel because who are pushed by whose internal motives and pulled by external forced of a destination. However, the decision making process leading to the choice of a travel destination is a very complex process.

For example, a Taiwanese traveler who might either choose new travel destination of Hong Kong or another old travel Asia destinations again or who also might choose any one of Western country, as a new travel destination. The travel agents can predict where who will have intention to choose to travel from whose past behavior and attitude, subjective and perceived behavioral control model. When (AI) big data gather past every country traveler number who chose to go to which countries to travel in order to judge where destinations will be the country travelers' travelling choice destinations in the future.

The factors influence where is the traveler choice, include personal safety, scenic beauty, cultural interest, climate changing, transportation tools, friendliness of local people, price of trip, trip package service in hotels and restaurants, quality and variety of food and shopping facilities and services etc. needs. So, whose factors will influence where is the individual travel's choice. It seems every traveler whose choice of travel process, will include past behavior. e.g. travelling experience, travelling habit, then to choose the best seasoned travelling action to satisfy whose travel needs. This process is the individual traveler's psychological choice process, who must need

time to gather information to compare concerning of different travel packages, destination scene, climate change, transportation tools available to the destination, air ticket price etc. these factors, then to judge where is the best right destination to travel in the right time.
Hence, (AI) big data can gather past different countries' climate changing data, transportation tool changing data, destination scene environment changing etc. different data to give opinions to travelling businesses whether any country's these above factors will influence about how many traveler number will be increase or decrease in the future.

Why can expectation, motivation and attitude factor influence travelling behavior?

Social psychology is concerned with gaining insight into the psychological of socially relevant behaviors and the processes. For instance, on a global level bad influence to global warming, it influences some countries extreme cold or hot bad climate changing occurrence, then it ought influence some travelers' behavioral decision to change their mind to choose some countries to go to travel at the moment which do not occur extreme hot or cold climate (temperature). e.g. above than 40 degree in summer or below than 0 degree in winter. Due to the extreme climate changing environment in the countries, it will cause them to feel uncomfortable to play during their trips. So, the global warming causes to climate changing factor will influence the numbers of travel consumption to be reduced possibly. This is global climate changing environment factor influences to bad or uncomfortable social psychological feeling to global travelers' mind of traveling decision. What is individual traveler expectation, motivation and attitude? Tourism sector includes inbound (domestic) tourism and outbound (overseas) tourism both incomes to any countries. According to recent article, a tourist behavior model has been developed, called the expectation, motivation and attitude (EMA) model (Hsu et al., 2010).

This model focuses on the pre-visit stage of tourists by modeling the behavioral process by incorporating expectation, motivation and attitude. Travel motivation is considered as an essential component of the behavioral process, which has been increasing attention from the travel; industry. The economic approach defines "tourism" is an identifiable nationally important industry. It includes the component activities of transportation, accommodation, recreation, food and related service. So, tourism behavioral consumption is concerned the individual tourist's usual habituate of the industry which responds to whose needs, and of the impacts that both the tourist and the tourism industry have on the socio-cultural, economic and physical environment.

However, travel motivation means how to understand and predict factors that influence travel decision making. According to Backman and others (1995, p.15), motivation is conceptually viewed as " a state of need, a condition that services as a driving force to display different kind of behavior toward certain types of activities, developing preferences, arriving at some expected satisfactory outcome." So, motivation and expectancy which has close relationship to any tourist before who decided to do any tourism of behavior.
Some economists confirmed motivation and expectancy which has relations, such as expectation of visiting an outbound destination has a direct effect on motivation to visit the destination; motivation has a direct effect on attitude toward visiting the destination; expectation of visiting the outbound destination has a direct affection on attitude toward visiting the destination and motivation has a mediating effect on the relationship in between expectation and attitude.
Hence, (AI) big data can gather all the country's climate environment change, transportation tool change, entertainment scene change, hotel price and restaurant price change etc. data to give opinions whether the country will attract how many traveler to choose to go to travel in the year.

What is (AI) deep learning techniques to forecast travelling environment behavioral consumption

Prediction how many travelers will choose to go to the country to travel. It is similar to apply deep-learning technology to predict how to raise the agricultural farming productivity in the agricultural export country.
The (AI) deep-learning technology leads to performance enhancement and generalization of artificial intelligent technology. It influences the global leader in the field of information technology has declared its intention to utilize the deep-learning technology to solve environmental problems, such as climate change.
So, it will help agriculture farming businesses can raise any plant food: vegetable, fruit, rice which grow up very

easily if farmers can apply (AI) deep-learning technology to solve environment problems to influence their plant food grow. If the whole year seasonal change is very good and it is suitable for any plant food to grow in farming land easily, e.g. rain is enough and soil is enough for any plant food to grow in the farm lands. Then, fruit, rice, vegetable etc. agriculture businesses will have much beneficial attribution to global farmers.

The question is how to use deep-learning technologies in the environmental field to predict the status of pro-environmental consumption. We predicted the pro-environmental consumption index based on Google search query data, using a recurrent neural network (RNN model). To certify the accuracy of the index, we compared the prediction accuracy of the RNN model with that of the ordinary least square and artificial necessary network models.

For example, the RNN model predicts the pro-environmental consumption index better than any other model. we expect the RNN model to perform still better in a big data environment because the deep-learning technologies would be increasingly as the volume of data grows. So, deep-learning technologies could be useful in environmental forecasting to prevent damage caused by climate change to influence any rice, vegetable, tomato, potato, fruit etc. different plant food grow in any countries' farming land easily.

For South Korea example, over 800 government agencies spent 2.2 trillion Korea won on eco-products in 2014 year. However, green products are rarely purchased outside these agencies. This phenomenon occurs because there is a gap between consumer attitudes and behavior , that is environmental attitude is a major factor in decision making vis-a-vis the consumption of " green" food and services (Jorea Ministry of Environment, 2015).

Therefore, it is necessary to understand those consumer attitude, that will lead to sustainability-conductive behavior and consumption. (AI) Deep learning system can be applied to attempt understand those traveler attitude to environment protection to fly to which country. For example, (AI) deep learning system can attempt to gather data concerns how many Hong Kong people concern air pollution challenge to influence their health, then it can attempt to predict how many Hong Kong travelers do not choose to go China travel, due to the air pollution challenge to influence their health.

Environmental travel consumption prediction

Recently, many researchers have studied pro-environmental consumption and household indexes as well as suicide rate predictions using messages posted by internet users on Google trend, Tweets etc. channel.

Whether can environmental consumption be predicted by (AI) deep-learning technological internet channel to influence how many travelers choose to go to the country to travel?

How can impact the pro-environmental consumption attitudes of green policies to influence how many travelers choose to go to the country to travel?

For example, Korea scientists estimated pro-environmental attitudes using search query data provided by Google trend and confirmed through regression analysis, that pro-environmental attitude has a positive correlation with the pro-environmental attitude index. They also explained that environment-friendly attitude of residents plan an important role in policy making. In the past, most household consumption indexed were calculated through surveys, but (AI) deep-learning technological tool " big data" have recently gained research attention (Lee et al. 2016). So, (AI) deep learning technology can attempt to gather whether how many Korea residents who concern environment pollution to influence their eating green food attitude then to judge whether how many Korea residents hope to leave their country to travel anywhere either high risk environment pollution countries to travel or low risk environment pollution countries to travel in the future.

It seems that (AI) deep-learning technology can help agricultural export countries' farmers , e.g. US, UK, Canada, New Zealand, Australia, Japan, China, India etc. they can predict environmental behavioral consumption to any rice, tomato, potato , fruit, vegetable etc. plant food consumers. The beneficial advantages to them include as below:

(a) Assuming they know their countries' weather, when it has less rain to cause drought or when it has more rain in any seasonal time in the year. They can choose not to grow any kinds of above these plant food to avoid loss.

(b) They can make any kinds of above these plant food price raising after their prediction of these bad seasonal time to cause their plant food shortage supply challenge. Because these plant food consumers' demand number is more, but the supply of these above plant food supply number is less. However, due to they had predicted when the bad seasonal time can not allow them to grow these above plant food before. So, they have enough time to grow many these above plant food number in predictive good seasonal time to prepare to supply to their plant food import countries' plant food consumers to eat. Thus, these predictive environmental consumption plant food export countries can raise their plant food price to sell to them. When, the other non-pre-predictive environmental consumption plant food export countries can not supply any one of those plant food to them to eat, due to the bad climate to cause them can't grow any one of these plant food to export to sell.

Thus, (AI) deep-learning technology can be applied to predict how to raise the plant food supply number in order to raise price to the import plant food countries consumers to eat, due to they feel difficult to buy these plant food to eat in the bad climate seasonal time in whole year.

(c) (AI) deep-learning technology can help climate scientists to find what reasons cause their countries; rain sudden increases or cause their countries' rain sudden decreases. After its gathering data analysis, it can assist climate scientists to find solution methods to attempt to control the rain level can be right falling down level to let agricultural export farmers who can grow their plant food to sell to agricultural import countries in whole year.

(d) The agricultural export countries' farmers can apply (AI) deep-learning technology to help them to choose whether growing which kinds of plant food in that whether climate time to earn more plant food consumption number more easily.

Due to the agricultural countries climate will often change, for example, tomato, potato, rice, fruit etc. plant food can be adapt to grow in more rain time, but vegetable can not be adapt to grow in more rain time. If farmers can apply this technology to predict when it will have move rain or when it will have less rain to fall down in their countries. Then, they can choose to grow which kinds of plant food number more, in the suitable seasonal climate time in order to raise plant food growing number productivities to supply to sell to satisfy any agricultural food import countries' demand effectively.

(e) (AI) deep-learning technology can help agricultural import countries to solve agricultural food shortage challenge in long term. When this technology can be popular to base applied by the agricultural plant food export countries. It will solve global agricultural food shortage challenge. For example, when one agricultural export countries' farmers can popular accept to apply this technology to predict when to grow which kinds of plant food more to rise number productivities to sell. e.g. vegetable, fruit, rice Besides another agricultural export countries' farmers can also accept to apply this technology to predict when to grow plant food, e.g. potato, tomato to raise number productivities to sell. Then, they can concentrate on growing the specific kinds of plant food in order to raise the specific plant food number productivities in every seasonal change time every month. Then, global agricultural plant food supply must be raised, due to these predictive environmental change farmers can know who ought grow which kinds of plant food to sell to raise number productivities.

Consequently, (AI) deep learning can gather where countries will have high risk environment pollution to influence health food supply. Then, it can give opinions to travelling businesses when these high risk environment pollution countries will encounter the traveler number to be decreased, due to the environment pollution serious challenge will occur.

What methods can predict future travel behavioral consumption ?

How to use qualitative of travel behavioral method to predict future travel consumption from (AI) big data ?

I also suggest to use qualitative of travel behavioral method to predict future travel consumption. Methods such as focus groups interviews and participant observer techniques can be used with quantitative approaches on their own to fill the gaps left by quantitative techniques. These insights have contributed to the development of increasingly sophisticated models to forecast travel behavior and predict changes in behavior in response to change in the transportation system. I shall indicate the weaknesses of human travelling investigation methods as below:

First, survey methods restrict not only the question frame but the answer frame as well, anticipating the important issues and questions and the responses. However, these surveys methods are not well suited to exploratory areas of research where issues remain unidentified and the researched seek to answer the question "why?".

Second, data collection methods using traditional travel diaries or telephone recruitment can under represent certain segments of the population, particularly the older persons with little education, minorities and the poor. Before the survey, focus group for example can be used to identify what socio-demographic variables to include in the survey, how best to structure the diary, even what incentives will be most effective in increasing the response rate.

After the survey, focus, focus groups can be used to build explanations for the survey results to identify the "why" of the results as well as the implications. One Asia Pacific survey research result was made by tourism market investigation before. It indicated the travel in Asia Pacific market in the past, had often been undertaken in large groups through leisure package sold in bulk, or in large organized business groups, future travelers will be in smaller groups or alone, and for a much wider range of reasons.

Significant new traveler segments, such as female business traveler. The small business traveler and the senior traveler, all of which have different aspirations and requirements from the travel experience.

Moreover, Asia tourism market will start to exist behaviors in the adoption of newer technologies, a giving the traveler new ways to manage the travel experience, creating new behaviors. This with provide new opportunities for travel providers. The use of mobile devices, smartphones, tablets etc. and social media are the obvious findings to become an integral part of the travel experience. Thus, quality method can attempt to predict Asia Pacific tourism market development in the future. It is such as (AI) big data gathering tool can give traveler quality opinions to any travelling businesses to make the more accurate where will be the popular travel destination choice next month or next half year or next year.

However, improving the predictive power of travel behavior models and to increase understanding travel behavior which lies in the use of panel data(repeated measures from the same individuals). Whereas, cross-sectional data only reveal inter-individual differences at one moment in time, panel data can reveal intra-individual changes over time. In effect, panel data are generally better suited to understand and predict (changes in) travel behavior. However, a substantial proportion was also observed to transition between very different activity/travel patterns over time, indicating that from one year to the next, many people renegotiated their activity/travel patterns.

How to apply advanced traveler information systems (ATIS) to predict future travelling behavior?

Nowadays, information can impact on traveler behavior and network performance. For example, when steadily growing levels of vehicle ownership and vehicle miles traveled information has been identified as a potential strategy towards man aging travel demand, optimizing transportation networks and better utilizing available capacity. Toward, this goal to predict further tourist behavioral consumption. Many countries, government tourism development institutes has applied advanced traveler information systems (ATIS) which travel behavior models and high-fidelity network performance models made increasingly feasible through the rapid advances in computer power. Crucial components of this problem domain are the modeling of individual tourist drivers' response to travel information and the development accurate guidance of relevance to real would trip makers. So, this advanced traveler information systems (ATIS) can assist the tourist who like to rent travelling car tools to travel in any countries own free traveler information systems service conveniently. Also, this travel information system can be intended to assist travelers to make better travel choices. e.g. this system can improve the decision making of individual traveler rather than improvements of network performance overall. So, we need to understand how tourists make their travel plans. Also, understanding decision process that lead to booking of the trip is equally important, as it allows of a potential behavior.

How can online tourism sale channel influence traveling consumption of behavior?

Nowadays, internet is popular, it seems that booking air ticket behavior of using internet is predicted to influence overall tourism air tickets payment method. Tourism industry has grown in the previous several decades. Despite its global impact, questions related to better understanding of tourists and whose habits. Using online travel air ticket booking benefits include booking electronic air tickets can be made from entering any electronic travel agents websites in the short time and electronic travel ticket payers do not need leave home, who can pay visa card to pre booking any electronic travel ticket from online channel conveniently.

How can analyze activity based travel demand ?

Nowadays, human are concerning the traffic congestion and air quality deterioration, the supply oriented focus of transportation planning has expanded to include how to manage travel demand within the available transportation supply. Consequently, there has been an increasing interest in travel demand management strategies, such as congestion pricing that attempts to change aggregate travel demand. The prediction aggregate level, long term travel demand to understanding disaggregate level (i.e. individual levels) behavioral responses to short term demand policies, such as ride sharing incentives, congestion pricing and employer based demand management schemes, alternate work schedules, telecommuting limitation of travel agent traditionally work nature shall influence oriented trip based travel modelling passenger travel demand indirectly.

Finally, online travel purchase will be popular to influence the number of travel behavioral consumption nowadays. Any travel package products can be sold from websites to attract travelers to choose to pre-book air ticket for any trips conveniently. In the past ten years, the internet has become the predominant carrier of all types of information and transactions. Regarding travel decisions, internet has also become an important sales channels for the travel industry, because it is associated with comparably lower distribution and sales costs, but also because it adapts to high supply and demand dynamics in this industry. Consequently, the travel and tourism industry tries to increase the internet sale specific share of sales volumes. So, internet sale channel has changed travel consumption behavioral pattern and characteristics and travel experience. For example, Switzerland has one of the highest population-to-computer ratio in Europe. It is also one of the most highly internet penetrated countries in terms of use of the WWW on a day-to-day basis, with more than 75 percent of the population older than 14 years using the WWW daily (ICT, 2005).

The reason of booking online tourism may include: convenience, fast transaction, finding traveling package choice easily, more airline seats available. So, online booking tourism will influence the traditional tourism agents visiting of sales and air tickets and travelling package numbers to be decreased. Finally, the online booking tourism market shares will be expanded to more than traditional tourism agents visits sale market in the future one day. So, the travel agents who still use the traditional tourism visiting sale channel which ought raise whose features to compare to differ to online tourism sale channel if these traditional tourism agents want to keep competitive ability in tourism industry for long term.

What is actively based patterns of urban population of travel behavioral prediction method?

Actively based patterns of urban population. It is a method of motivational framework means in which societal constraints and inherent individual motivations interact to shape activity participation patterns. It can be used to predict one city or urban the numbers of travel demand in the year. It has two elements: First, capability constraints refer to constraints are imposed by biological needs, such as eating and sleeping and/or resources, such as income, availability of cars etc. to undertake the urban or city's family activities in the year. Second, coupling constraints define where, when and the duration of planning activities that are to be pursued with other individuals. So, this method needs to gather information (data) to get the relationship between activities, travel and spending work time and space time to evaluate whether there are how many families who have real needs to spend time to go to travel in the year.

What is trip based versus activity based approaches?

What is trip based versus activity based approaches? The fundamental difference between the trip-based and activity based approaches is that the former approach directly focuses on trips without explicit recognition of the motivation or reason for the trips and travel. The activity based approach , on the other hand, views travel as a demand derived from the need to pursue travel activities. So, it is better understand the individual or family behavior basis for individual or family travelling decision regarding participation in travelling activities in certain places or cities or countries at given times and hence the resulting travel needs. This behavioral basis includes all the factors that influence the why, how, when and where of performed activities and resulting individuals and household, the cultural/social norms of the community and the travel surrounding environment.

Another difference between the two approaches is in the way travel is represented. The trip based approach represents travel as a collection of trips. Each trip is considered as independent of other trips, without considering the inter-relationship in the choice attributes , such as time, destination and mode of different trips. As tours are chains of trips beginning and ending at a same location , say home or work. The tour based representation helps maintain the consistency across and capture the interdependency and consistency of the modeled choice attributed among the trips of the same tour.

In addition to the tour based representation of travel, the activity based approach focuses on sequences or patterns of activity participation and travel behavior, using the whole day or longer periods of time is the unit of analysis. Such as approach can address travel demand management issues through an examination of how people modify their activity participation, for example, will individuals substitute more out-of-home activities for in home activities in the evening of who arrived early form work due-to a work schedule change?

The major difference between trip based and the activity based approaches is in the way, the time dimension of activities and travel is considered. In the trip based approach, time is reduced to being simply a cost making a trip and a day's viewed as a combination, defined peak and off peak time periods. On the other hand, activity based approach views individuals' activity travel patterns are a result of their time use decisions with a continuous time domain. As individuals have 24 hours in a day or multiples of 24 hours for longer periods of time and decide how to use that travel among or allocate that time to activities and travel and with who, subject to their socio-demographic, transportation system and other and scheduling of trips. So, determining the impact of travel demand management policies on time use behavior is an important step to assessing the impact of such policies on individual travel behavior. The final major difference between this two approaches relates to the level of aggregation. In the trip based approach, most aspect of travel, e.g. number of trips etc. are analyzed at an aggregate level.

Consequently, trip based methods accommodate the effect of socio-demographic attributes of households and individuals in a very limited fashion, which limits the activity of the method to evaluate travel impacts of long term socio-demographic characteristics of the individuals who actually make the activity travel choices and the travel service characteristics of the surrounding environment. So, the activity based models are better equipped to forecast the longer term changes in travel demand in response composition and the travel environment of urban areas. Also, using activity based models, the impact of policies can be assessed by predicting individual level behavioral responses instead of employing trip based statistical averages that are aggregated over defined demographic segments.

Can apply (AI) big data gathering method predict senior age will be main travelling target?

In the past, Germany government had established tourism survey analysis to analyze survey data in order to arrive at reliable conclusions on future trends in travel behavior. To aim to find how demographic change will influence the tourism market and how the industry can adapt to those changes. The travel analysis provided data on tourism consumer behavior, including attitudes, motives and intentions. Since, 1970 year, it is based on a random sample, representative for the population in private households aged 14 years or older. Then, a continuous high scientific standard combined with a national and international users makes the travel analysis a useful tool and reliable source for tourism industry and policy decisions. It aimed to gather statistical data. e.g. on the age structure and on demographic trends, quantitative and qualitative analysis with time series data from the travel analysis. It shows e.g. not only the future volume , quite different from today's seniors, or how who will travel of family holidays will change, e.g. single parents of low, but grandparents of growing significance for tourism.

Demographic change is said to be one of the important drivers for new trends in consumer traveling change behavior in most European countries (e.g. Lind 2001). Because the growing number of senior citizens in the European Union and other industrialized countries, such as the USA and Japan, looks to become one of the major marketing challenges for the tourism industry. United Nations statistics predict that the share of people being 60 age or older will grow dramatically in the coming future, and is expected to rise from 10 percent of the world population in 2000 year to more than 20 percent in 2050 year (United Nations Population Division, 2001). From its statistic, some data showed that travel propensity increased throughout life until the age of about 50 years of age and was then kept stable until very late in life 75 age. The most important results is that the travel propensity when getting older is not going down between 65 and 75 age of course, the overall development of this variable is influenced by a lot of other factors which are responsible for quite a variation over time. It is now possible to suggest that the general pattern of travel propensity is one of the key indicators for holiday life cycle travel behavior, includes three stages. The growth stage tends to increase from early adult hood until 45 age old or when reaching some 80%. The next stage is stabilization from the ages of around 50 age, until 75 age old, starting with a lower increase. Finally, the decrease stage is a slight decrease occurs once people reach the more advanced age of 75 age to 85 age old (Lohmann & Danielsson 2001).

So, it seems Germany government tourism prediction to future travelers' behavior indicated these findings, such as on how future senior generations will travel, who had used survey data to examine the patterns of travel behavior of a generation getting older and applied the findings to draw conclusions on the future. Also, it predicted that on the future of family trips, family segmentation will be the travel behavior patterns in the future. These findings together with the statistical data on demographic change allowed for a better understanding of the coming tends in family holidays. It's aim developed in consumer behavior related to demographic change and predicted what will happen future of tourism one had to consider other influences and drivers as well, for example, trends on the supply side. e.g. low cost airlines or in travelling consumption behavior in general whether how the past may provide a key to predict travel patterns of senior citizens to the future.

Given the projected growth of the senior citizens market, designing specific marketing strategies to meet the prospective needs of elderly tourists will become increasingly important. It has been an implicit assumption that it will be a close relationship between the travel behavior of today's senior citizens and the those of future ones. The growing number of senior citizens in the world. e.g. China, Hong Kong, Japan, USA etc. countries. Global senior citizen tourism market will be based solely on demographic predictions about the future of the population's age structure. However, many of these seniors won't only live longer but will be fitter and more active until later in life. Many of the will also have plenty in life. Many of them will also have plenty of time and money to spend on travel. So, will these new seniors behave like today's senior citizens? Will they adopt the same travel behavior as the previous generation or become a new market of oldies for the leisure and tourism industry? However, to determine the actual number of senior citizens who will be travelling and to sought to evaluate and specify certain difficult to predict the actual numbers of senior citizen to any country. However, they can be based on the implicit assumption that there is a close relationship between the travel behavior of past, present and future seniors. But is this a valid assumption? As the revise- analysis travel analysis survey, which was conducted in Germany every year, offered some interesting data possibilities. It was designed to monitor the holiday travel behavior, opinions and attitudes of Germans and has been carried out since 1970 year, questions in the questionnaire. Data are based on face to face interviews, with a representative sample of more than 7,500 respondents, the interviews being carried out in January each year. All results refer to the average for the defined generated, which ranges generally over ten years. The group of people then at the age of 60 to 69 age is described. This corresponds to the same generation ten years ago, when they had an age of 50 to 59 age. When this methodological approach is not necessarily very sophisticated, it does have the important advantages of being cost effective.

IS (AI) big data gathering method a better psychological method to compare human marketing research method predict travel behavioral consumption?

On the psychological view point, I think individual traveler's character will have those kind of personal characteristics. First, simplicity searchers value above everything ease not transparency in their travel planning and holiday making, and are willing to avoid having to go through extensive research. Second, cultural purists use their travel as an opportunity to immerse themselves in an unfamiliar looking to break themselves entirely from their home lives and engage. Sincerely with a different way of living. Third, social capital seekers understand that to be well travelled is a personal quality, and their choices are shaped by their desire to take maximum of social reward from their travel. They will exploit the potential of digital media to enrich and inform their experiences, and structure their adventures always keeping in mind they are being watched by online audiences. Finally, reward hunters seek a return on the investment who make in their busy , high-achieving lives. Linked in part to the growing trend of wellness, including both physical and mental self-improvement who seek truly extraordinary and often indulgent or luxurious‘ must have experiences.

Why needs to know the personal character of individual traveler's characteristics? Because if travel agents could feel which kinds of individual traveler's character, then who can predict which kind of travel package to design to them more easily. For example, how to determine future travel behavior from past travel experience and perceptions of risk and safety? We need to concern that the influences of past international travel experience, types of risk associated with international travel and the overall degree of safety feeling during international travel on individual's travelling experiences likelihood of travelling to various geographic regions on their next international vacation trip or avoidance of those regions, due to perceived risk. Because individual traveler's experience of safety risk degree to the countries, it will influence who chooses to go to the countries/country to travel again.

Why travelers avoid certain destinations are as relevant decision making as why who choose to go to the country(countries) to travel. Perceptions of risk and safety and travel experiences are likely to influence travel decisions; efforts to predict future travel behavior can benefit to individual tourist's decision making.

As Weber & Bottorn (1989) defined risky decision is as "choices among alternatives that can be described by probability distributions over possible outcomes" (p.114). Some psychologists judge subjective perceptions of physical reality, i.e. image of a particular tourist destination, whereas value judgement refers to the way individual rank destinations according to whose attributes. i.e. attractiveness, safety, risk etc. factors to form on overall image. So, if the individual traveler had unhappy and worried and unsafe experiences to go to where the place(country) to travel during whose vacation time before. Then, this negative travel experience will influence who is afraid to go to the place (country) to travel again. Risk of place, country, destination or region means the danger is relatively high to the place, i.e. increasing in airplane accidents, crime or terrorist activity targeting citizens of potential traveler's nationality or the probability of occurrence is great , i.e. recent occurrences involving travel regions/destinations under consideration or effective actions to control consequences exist. i.e. selecting safe regions and destinations, taking extra precautions when traveling to risky destinations. These risk factors will influence the individual traveler who chooses to cancel travel plan to go to the country again.

Another interesting research, how to predict behavioral intention of choosing a travel destination, which has focus of tourism research for years, but the complex decision making process leading to the choice of a travel destination has not been well researched. The planned behavior model using its core constructs, attitude, subjective norm and perceived behavioral control, with the addition of the past behavioral variable on behavioral intention of choosing a travel destination.

Understanding why people travel and what factors influence their behavioral intention of choosing a travel destination is beneficial to tourism planning and marketing. Understanding travel motivation is the push and pull model. The idea of the push and pull model is the decomposition of an individual's choice of a travel destination into two forces. The first force is the push factor that pushes an individual away home and attempts to develop a general desire to go somewhere else, without specifying where that may be. The second force is the pull factor, that pulls on individual toward a destination, due to a region specific travel location or perceived attractiveness of a destination. The respective push and pull factors illustrate that people travel because who are pushed by their internal motives and pulled by external forces of a destination. Nevertheless, how push and pull factors guide people's attitude and how these attributes lead to behavioral intentions of choosing a travel destination have rarely been investigated. The decision making process leading to the choice of a travel destination is a very complex process. The planned behavior model is as a research framework to predict the behavioral intention of choosing a travel destination. The model based on the three constructs of attitude, subjective norm, and perceived behavioral control (Fishbein & Ajzen, 1975).

In conclusion, the factors can influence travelers who decide to choose to travel the country, which include personal safety was perceived to the highest motivation factors among the important factors which include, scenic beauty, cultural interests, friendliness of local people, price of trip, services in hotels and restaurants, quality and variety of food and shopping facilities and services. The factors include both push and pull. Push factors include knowledge, prestige, and enhancement of human relationship etc., whereas, the most significant pull factors include high technologic image, expenditure and accessibility etc. For example, Japanese travelers visiting Hong Kong. Push factors are such as exploration dream fulfillment and pull factors are such as benefits sought, attractions and good climate city. It will be the factor of future travel patterns and motivations of sub-cultural and ethic groups for Japanese choice to go to Hong Kong travelling.

How can apply (AI) digital channel (big data gathering method) predict travelling consumer behaviors?

(AI) big data digital channel can be applied to help travelling businesses to evaluate whether how much the e-ticket price and travelling package price is the most attractive or reasonable to persuade travelling consumers feel it is the most reasonable price to choose to buy the airline's e-tickets or the travel agent's travelling package product from internet channel . It helps travelling consumers to feel which airlines or travelling agents which ought change their e-ticket and/or travelling package price to let travelling consumers to choose to buy the airline e-ticket or the travelling agent's travelling package products from internet channel. It can be applied to predict whether how many travelling consumer numbers can be increased or decreased when the airline e-ticket price is variable or the travelling agent travelling package price is variable . It aims to give opinions to help any online airlines or travelling agents to judge whether which e-ticket or travelling package price is the most reasonable to let travelling consumers to accept to choose to buy which airline's e-tickets or traveling agent's package products more attractive.

Thus, (AI) e-ticket or e-travelling package price measurement technology can be preference to be applied online communication ecommerce and mobile phone internet platform aspect. As traveling businesses can enter their past e-ticket or travelling package prices data and past travelling customer number data into computer or mobile. Then, (AI) price measurement technology can gather these data to analyze these e-ticket or travelling package product prices and past travelling customer number to compare their e-ticket and/or travelling package prices variable changing range level to find their e-ticket and /or travelling package price variable difference to measure to make conclusion about every travelling package or/and e-ticket product's price variable changing will influence how many travelling customer number increase or decrease changing to choose to sell their different kinds of travelling package or e-ticket products more accurate. Then, (AI) price measurement software will help them to analyze all past e-ticket and/or travelling package price variable changing data to compare whether which e-ticket and/or travelling package price range can let travelling customers to feel it is more reasonable and attractive to influence them to choose to buy their e-ticket or travelling package product among different airlines and travel agent choices. Because any e-ticket or travelling package product's price is one important factor to influence travelling consumers to choose to buy the airline's e-tickets or travelling agent's travelling package products.

For example, Amazon publish has applied (AI) price measurement technology to help authors to decide how much every different topic of e-book or paper book price, it can attract the largest number of readers to buy. Any one author only needs to type whose book name to Amazon publish author himself/herself Amazon website. Amazon publish (AI) price measurement learning machine will help them to auto-calculate and judge how much e-book or paper book price is the most attractive and the most reasonable in order to increase reader number to buy their e-books or paper books to read. So, (AI) online price measurement machine will gather past similar book names and past every similar book readers' reading times and the number of readers to give opinions to let every author to judge whether his/her very new e-book or paper book ought charge how much price to the e-book or paper book which can attract many readers to choose to buy. Although, it is not ensure that the e-book or paper book price must let readers to feel it is the most reasonable price to choose to buy in reader's view point. However, it has other factors to influence readers' choice to buy the e-book or paper book, e.g. whether the book content is attractive to public, the author's familiarity, the book's page is enough or not to satisfy readers to read etc. factors. But, instead of all these extra factors to influence readers to choose to buy the book to read. (AI) price measurement learning machine can real give opinions to every author to let them to judge the e-book or paper book different price range whether is too high to influence readers to choose to buy to read or tool low to influence readers feel it is possible poor content book to compare other similar content books. Thus, (AI) price measurement machine can help authors to predict every reader's reading behaviors or reading experience and reading habit from online channel in short time easily. The author only enter the book name to let Amazon publish price measurement machine to check, it will follow past reader's reading habit and reading experience to judge whether the similar all book topic sale record to judge how much price is the reasonable price to attract many readers to buy the book.

Hence, (AI) can be applied to digital channel to help travelling businesses to predict travelling consumer behavior in the future. In the future, mobile/smartphone, laptop, desktop will be most frequent used ecommerce channels to develop online business. So, (AI) can be also applied to these platforms to gather data to make analysis to help travelling businesses to predict travelling consumer purchase behaviors popularly. Due to , ecommerce is popular to global, so digital online and instore channels can be one good channel to let (AI) learning machine to make platform to gather past every online travelling consumer purchase (buying) experience data to help travelling businesses to build airline or travelling agent brand personality and having a responsible, positive impact on society.

To apply (AI) learning machine technology to understand travelling customer online purchase behavior, it will raise business e-commerce successful chance: For example, (AI) learning machine can help travelling businesses to gather data to analyze to determine whether short-term or long-term signals in the online travelling consumer behavior that indicate higher purchase intents to let every online travelling business to know. (AI) learning machine can find that online users with long-term purchasing intent tend to save and click through on more content.

However, as online travelling users approach the time of purchase their activity becomes more topically focused and actions shift from saves to searches from online travelling consumption channel. Then, (AI) learning machine will further find that the brand airline and/or travelling agent purchase signals in online travelling consumption behavior can exist weakness before an online travelling purchase is made and can also be traced across different online travelling purchase categories. Finally, (AI) learning machine synthesize these insights in predictive models of online travelling user purchasing intent to the brand of airline or/and travelling agent travelling package product. Taken together, it's work identifies a set of general principles and signals that can be used to model online travelling user e-ticket and/or travelling package purchasing intent across many online content discovery applications. Thus, (AI) learning machine can help online travelling businesses to gather any online travelling users' click online travelling behaviors data to judge whether there are how many online travelling users will choose to find their online travelling business websites to make final decisions to buy their travelling package or/and e-ticket products from online channels. Then, it will give opinions to help the online travelling businesses to let it to judge whether what are the important website factors will help its online travelling business to attract many online travelling consumers, e.g. designing unattractive travelling website issue, online unattractive scene photos issue, unclear website travelling photo color issue, unclear website travelling advertisement message, contents and words impressions issue, lacking image movement frequent attractive seeing issue etc. different website factors. Thus, online digital channel will be one good choice to apply (AI) learning machine to help travelling businesses to predict travelling consumer behaviors.

Thus, (AI) big data technology can also assist travelling consumers to gather different manufacturers' data to compare what their advantages and disadvantages of their travelling package products are. Then, travelling consumers can make comparison to choose which airline or travelling agent is the suitable to whom to buy e-ticket or pre-booking travelling package in online travelling consumption market.

.

Thus, I believe that artificial intelligent "big data" gathering method can be suggested to be applied to attempt to predict travelling consumer behavioral changes in global online travelling business environment, the reasons are as below:

On the travelling consumer's beneficial hand, travelling consumers can apply this (AI) big data gathering method to attempt to gather any global airline e-tickets and/or travelling agent's package product data to be analyzed by this artificial intelligent learning system to compare human general marketing research method, e.g. survey, questionnaire, marketing plan etc. different human judgement methods to predict traveler consumption behavioral change model. Then, it analyzed all the different data to compare what are the range of the most reasonable e-ticket and/or travelling package online purchase history and sale in order to make more accurate prediction to future traveler change traveling consumption behavioral model in next month, or next half year or next year short term period traveling consumption change prediction. Thus, it seems that future AI tool can be attempted to apply to predict any industries price behavior, e.g. deciding what level of price is the attractive level to attract consumer in these industries, e.g. fuel, education, tourism, health, entertainment, etc. different product purchase. It can give more absolute price suggestion to any merchants to set their price change predict in order to increase many customer numbers to buy their products in every year, or every quarter every month, or month week, even every day etc. different sale period.

Reference

Backman and others "motivation is conceptually viewed as " a state of need, a condition that services as a driving force to display different kind of behavior toward certain types of activities, developing preferences, arriving at some expected satisfactory outcome.", 1995, p.15.

Fishbein & Ajzen, "The model based on the three constructs of attitude, subjective norm, and perceived behavioral control". 1975.

Hsu et al. "A tourist behavior model has been developed, called the expectation, motivation and attitude " (EMA) model ,2010.

ICT,WWW . "Switzerland has one of the highest population-to-computer ratio in Europe." Switzerland, 2005.

Jorea Ministry of Environment, " For South Korea environmental attitude is a major factor in decision making vis-a-vis the consumption of " green" food and services", Korea, 2015.

Korea Ministry Of Environment. Public Organizations spend 2.2 Trillon Korean Won To Purchase green Products in 2014; Ministry Of Environment: Sejoung, Korea, 2015.

Lind , Lohmann & Danielsson , United Nations Population Division, "Demographic change is said to be one of the important drivers for new trends in consumer traveling change behavior in most European countries". 2001.

Mayne, Lonnie. " Evolve of die in the age of the consumer". Entrepreneur, N.P. , 16 Apr. 2014. web of Oct. 2016.

Lee, D.; Kim, M. ; Lee, J. adoption of green electricity policies: Investigating the role of environmental attitudes via big data-driven search-queries. Energy policy 2016. 90, 187-201.

Lee, Terrence, " Tech in Asia-connecting Asia's startup system " Tech. in Asia- connecting Asia's startup ecosystem, N.p.,4 July 2016.

Weber & Bottorn "risky decision is as choices among alternatives that can be described by probability distributions over possible outcomes" , 1989, p.114.

What factors can influence travel behavioural consumption

Prediction travel behavioral consumption from traditional human's mind of tourism market research method

How to predict travel consumption? It is one question to any travel agents concern to use what methods which can predict how many numbers of travelers where who will choose to go to travel more accurately. I think that who can consider how to predict travel behavioral consumption from psychology view and computer science view both.

On the psychology view, It has evidence to support the relationship between self-identify threat and resistance to change travel behavior to any travelers, controlling for whose past travelling behavior, resistance to change if a psychological phenomenon of long standing interest in many applied branches of psychology. Past travelling behavior has been acknowledged as a predictor of future action. Such as travelling behavior that is experienced as successful is likely to be repeated and may lead to habitual patterns. Some psychologists differentiate habit between two concepts, such as goal oriented and automatic oriented both. Although repeated past travelling behavior is addition goal oriented and automatic oriented. Further non-deliberative nature of habit may make appeals to judge and to predict future individual traveler's behaviour accrately. However, repeated travelling behavior without a necessary constraint of goal orientation and automatic oriented both. So, it seems that psychological factor can influence any individual traveler why and how who choose to decide whose travelling behaviour.

On the computer statistic view, structural equation modeling is an extremely flexible linear-in-parameters multivariate statistical modeling technique. It has been used in modeling travel behavior and values since about 1980 year. It is a software method to handle a large number of variables, as well as unobserved variables specified as linear combinations (weighted averages) of the observed variable.

Whether climate change can influence travelling behaviours.

The flexibility of human travelling behavior is at least the result of one such mechanism, our ability to travel mentally in time and entertain potential future. Understanding of the impacts is holidays, particularly those involving travel. Using focus groups research to explores tourists' awareness of the impacts of travel own climate change, examines the extent to which climate change features in holiday travel decisions and identifies some of the barriers to the adoption of less carbon intensive tourism practices. The findings suggest many tourists don't consider climate change when planning their holidays. The failure of tourists to engage with the climate change to impact of holidays, combined with significant barriers to behavioral change, presents a considerable challenge in the tourism industry.

Tourism is a highly energy intensive industry and has only recently attracted attention as an important contributions to climate change through greenhouse gas emissions. It has been estimated that tourism contributes 5% of global carbon dioxide emissions. There have been a number of potential changes proposed for reducing the impact of air travel on climate change. These include technological changes, market based changes and behavioral changes. However, the role that climate change plays in the holiday and travel decisions of global tourists. How the global tourists of the impacts travel has on climate change to establish the extent to which climate change, considerations features in holiday travel decision making processes and to investigate the major barriers to global tourists adopting less carbon intensive travel practices. Whether tourists will aware the impacts that their holidays and travel have on climate changes.

When, it comes to understand indvidual traveler's behavioral change, wide range of conceptual theories have been developed, utilizing various social, psychological, subjective and objective variables in order to model travel consumption behavior. These theories of travel behavioral change operate at a number of different levels, including the individual level, the interpersonal level and community level. Whether pro-environmental behavior can be used to predict travel consumption behavior in a climate change. However, the question of what determines pro-environmental behavior in such a complex one that it can not be visualized through one single framework or diagram.

Despite the potentially high risk scenario for the tourism industry and the global environment, the tourism and climate change ought have close relationship. Whether what are the important factors and variables which can limit tourism? e.g. money, time, family problem, extreme hot or cold weather change, air ticket price, journey attraction etc. variable factors. Mention of holidays and travel were deliberately avoided in the recruitment process, so as not to create a connection factor to influence traveler's individual mind. However, the dismissal of alternative transportation modes can be conceived as either a structural barrier, in the sense that flying is perhaps the only realistic option to reach long-haul holiday destination, or a perceived behavioral control barriers in that an individual perceives flying as the only option open to whom. The transportation tool factor will be depend to extent on the distance to the destination. This can also be interpreted in a social perspective as an intention with the resources available where much international tourism is structured around flying. To increase the availability of different transportation modes, tourists could choose holiday destination closer to home.

Finally, also how to predict future travel behavioural consumption. I feel that travel agents need to predict whether any country's random daily variation of weather factor is also important to influence travel behaviour. e.g. in weather, temperature, rainfall adn snowfall with traffic accidents factors will have relationship to cause travel demand. Some scientists estimate suggest that when warmed temperatures and reduced snowfall are associated with a moderate decline in non-fatal accidents, they are also associated with a significant increase in fatal accidents. Thus increase in fatalities and temperature. Half of the estimated effect of temperature on fatalities is due to changes in the exposure to pedestrians, bicyclists and motorcyclists as temperature increase. So, if any countries have rainfall, snowfall and low temperature to cause traffic accidents, whether this accident occurrence will influence the travelers who liking climb snow hills, riding bicycle, running sports who will avoid to travel to these countries' bad weather after occurs. So, why I feel that this natural climate factor will also be one serious factor to influence travel behavioral consumption.

Market method predicts future travel consumption behavior

Whether individual habitual behaviour can influence travelling behaviour : e.g. renting travel transportation tools

Whether habit can be intended to predict of future travel behavior to people are creatures of habits. Many of human's everyday goal-directed behaviors are performed in a habitual fashion, the transportation made and route one takes to work, one's choice of breakfast. Habits are formed when using the some behavior frequently and a similar consistency in a similar context for the some purpose whether the individual past travel consumption model will be caused a habit to whom. e.g. choosing whom travel agent to buy air ticket or traveling package; choosing the same or similar countries' destinations to go to travel ; choosing the business class or normal (general) class of quality airlines to catch planes. Does habitual rent traveling car tools use not lead to more resistance to change of travel mode? It has been argued that past behavior is the best predictor of future behavior to travel consumption. If individual traveler's past consumption behavior was always reasoned, then frequency of prior travel consumption behavior should only have an indirect link to the individual traveler's behavior. It seems that renting travel car tools to use is a habit example. So, a strong rent traveling car tools useful habit makes traveling mode choice. People with a strong renting of traveling car tools of habit should have low motivation to attend to gather any information about public transportation in their choice of travelling country for individual or family or friends members during their traveling journeys.

Even when persuasive communication changes the traveler whose attitudes and intention, in the case of individual traveler or family travelers with a strong renting travel car tools habit. It is difficult to change whose travel behaviors to choose to catch public transportation in whose any trips in any countries. However, understanding of travel behavior and the reasons for choosing one mode of transportation over another. The arguments for rent traveling car tools to use, including convenience, speed, comfort and individual freedom and well known. Increasingly, psychological factors include such as, perceptions, identity, social norms and habit are being used to understand travel mode choice. Whether how many travel consumers will choose to rent traveling car tools during their trips in any countries. It is difficult to estimate the numbers. As the average level of renting travel car tools of dependence or attitudes to certain travel package policies from travel agents. Instead different people must be treated in different ways because who are motivated in different ways and who are motivated by different travel package policies ways from travel agents.

In conclusion, the factors influence whose traveler's individual behavior either who chooses to rent traveling car tools or who chooses to catch public transportation when who individual goes to travel in alone trip or family trip. It include influence mode choice factors, such as social psychology factor and marketing on segmentation factor both to influence whose transportation choice of behavior in whose trip.

How to determine future travel behavior from past travel experience and perceptions of risk and safety for the benefits to travel consumers?

How to determine future travel behavior from past travel experience and perceptions of risk and safety for the benefits to travel consumers? Why does individual traveler avoid certain destination(s) is(are) as relevant to tourist decision making as why who chooses to travel to others. Perceptions of risk and safety and travel experience are likely to influence travel decisions. If travel agents had efforts to predict future travel behavior to guess whether travelers will feel where is(are) risk and unsafe to cause who does not choose to go to the country to travel. Then, the travel agents will avoid to choose to spend much time to design the different traveling package to attract their potential travel consumers to choose to travel. The reason is because in the case of individual traveler's tourism experience, the traveler whose past disappointment travel experience (psychological risk) will be a serious threat to the traveler's health or life (health, physical or terrorism risk). The past safety or unhealthy risk to the country(countries) will influence the traveler decides to choose not to go to the countries(country) to travel again in the future.

What is push and pull factors to influence any
traveler who chooses where is whose preferable travelling destination

How to predict individual traveler's behavioral intention of choosing a travel destination. Understanding why people travel and what factors influence their behavioral intention of choosing a travel destination is beneficial to tourism planning and marketing. In general, an individual's choice of a travel destination into two forces. The first force is the push factor that pushes an individual away from home and attempt to develop a general desire to go somewhere, without specifying where that may be. The other force is the pull factor that pull an individual toward in destination, due to a region-specific or perceived attractiveness of a destination. The respective push and pull factors illustrate that people travel because who are pushed by whose internal motives and pulled by external forced of a destination. However, the decision making process leading to the choice of a travel destination is a very complex process. For example, a Taiwanese traveler who might either choose new travel destination of Hong Kong or another old travel Asia destinations again or who also might choose any one of Western country, as a new travel destination. The travel agents can predict where who will have intention to choose to travel from whose past behavior and attitude, subjective and perceived behavioral control model.

The factors influence where is the traveler choice, include personal safety, scenic beauty, cultural interest, climate changing, transportation tools, friendliness of local people, price of trip, trip package service in hotels and restaurants, quality and variety of food and shopping facilities and services etc. needs. So, whose factors will influence where is the individual travel's choice. It seems every traveler whose choice of travel process, will include past behavior. e.g. travelling experience, travelling habit, then to choose the best seasoned travelling action to satisfy whose travel needs. This process is the individual traveler's psychological choice process, who must need time to gather information to compare concerning of different travel packages, destination scene, climate change, transportation tools available to the destination, air ticket price etc. these factors, then to judge where is the best right destination to travel in the right time.

Why expectation, motivation and attitude factor can influence travelling behaviour.

Social psychology is concerned with gaining insight into the psychological of socially relevant behaviors and the processes. For instance, on a global level bad influence to global warming, it influences some countries extreme cold or hot bad climate changing occurrence, then it ought influence some travelers' behavioral decision to change their mind to choose some countries to go to travel at the moment which do not occur extreme hot or cold climate (temperature). e.g. above than 40 degree in summer or below than 0 degree in winter. Due to the extreme climate changing environment in the countries, it will cause them to feel uncomfortable to play during their trips. So, the global warming causes to climate changing factor will influence the numbers of travel consumption to be reduced possibly. This is global climate changing environment factor influences to bad or uncomfortable social psychological feeling to global travelers' mind of traveling decision. What is individual traveler expectation, motivation and attitude? Tourism sector includes inbound (domestic) tourism and outbound (overseas) tourism both incomes to any countries. According to recent article, a tourist behavior model has been developed, called the expectation, motivation and attitude (EMA) model (Hsu et al., 2010).

This model focuses on the pre-visit stage of tourists by modeling the behavioral process by incorporating expectation, motivation and attitude. Travel motivation is considered as an essential component of the behavioral process, which has been increasing attention from the travel; industry. The economic approach defines "tourism" is an identifiable nationally important industry. It includes the component activities of transportation, accommodation, recreation, food and related service. So, tourism behavioral consumption is concerned the individual tourist's usual habituate of the industry which responds to whose needs, and of the impacts that both the tourist and the tourism industry have on the socio-cultural, economic and physical environment.

However, travel motivation means how to understand and predict factors that influence travel decision making. According to Backman and others (1995, p.15), motivation is conceptually viewed as " a state of need, a condition that services as a driving force to display different kind of behavior toward certain types of activities, developing preferences, arriving at some expected satisfactory outcome." So, motivation and expectancy which has close relationship to any tourist before who decided to do any tourism of behavior. Some economists confirmed motivation and expectancy which has relations, such as expectation of visiting an outbound destination has a direct effect on motivation to visit the destination; motivation has a direct effect on attitude toward visiting the destination; expectation of visiting the outbound destination has a direct affect on attitude toward visiting the destination and motivation has a mediating effect on the relationship in between expectation and attitude.

What methods can predict future travel behavioural consumption

How to use qualitative of travel behavioural method to predict future travel consumption?

I also suggest to use qualitative of travel behavioural method to predict future travel consumption. Methods such as focus groups interviews and participant observer techniques can be used with quantitative approaches on their own to fill the gaps left by quantitative techniques. These insights have contributed to the development of increasingly sophisticated models to forecast travel behavior and predict changes in behavior in response to change in the transportation system. First, survey methods restrict not only the question frame but the answer frame as well, anticipating the important issues and questions and the responses. However, these surveys methods are not well suited to exploratory areas of research where issues remain unidentified and the researched seek to answer the question "why?". Second, data collection methods using traditional travel diaries or telephone recruitment can under represent certain segments of the population, particularly the older persons with little education, minorities and the poor. Before the survey, focus group for example can be used to identify what socio-demographic variables to include in the survey, how best to structure the diary, even what incentives will be most effective in increasing the response rate. After the survey, focus, focus groups can be used to build explanations for the survey results to identify the "why" of the results as well as the implications. One Asia Pacific survey research result was made by tourism market investigation before. It indicated the travel in Asia Pacific market in the past, had often been undertaken in large groups through leisure package sold in bulk, or in large organized business groups, future travelers will be in smaller groups or alone, and for a much wider range of reasons. Significant new traveler segments, such as female business traveler. The small business traveler and the senior traveler, all of which have different aspirations and requirements from the travel experience.

Moreover, Asia tourism market will start to exist behaviors in the adoption of newer technologies, a giving the traveler new ways to manage the travel experience, creating new behaviors. This with provide new opportunities for travel providers. The use of mobile devices, smartphones, tablets etc. and social media are the obvious findings to become an integral part of the travel experience. Thus, quality method can attempt to predict Asia Pacific tourism market development in the future.

However, improving the predictive power of travel behavior models and to increase understanding travel behavior which lies in the use of panel data(repeated measures from the same individuals). Whereas, cross-sectional data only reveal inter-individual differences at one moment in time, panel data can reveal intra-individual changes over time. In effect, panel data are generally better suited to understand and predict (changes in) travel behavior. However, a substantial proportion was also observed to transition between very different activity/travel patterns over time, indicating that from one year to the next, many people renegotiated their activity/travel patterns.

How to apply advanced traveler information systems (ATIS) to predict future travelling behaviour?

Nowadays, information can impact on traveler behavior and network performance. For example, when steadily growing levels of vehicle ownership and vehicle miles traveled information has been identified as a potential strategy towards man aging travel demand, optimizing transportation networks and better utilizing available capacity. Toward, this goal to predict further tourist behavioral consumption. Many countries, government tourism development institutes has applied advanced traveler information systems (ATIS) which travel behavior models and high-fidelity network performance models made increasingly feasible through the rapid advances in computer power. Crucial components of this problem domain are the modeling of individual tourist drivers' response to travel information and the development accurate guidance of relevance to real would trip makers. So, this advanced traveler information systems (ATIS) can assist the tourist who like to rent travelling car tools to travel in any countries own free traveler information systems service conveniently. Also, this travel information system can be intended to assist travelers to make better travel choices. e.g. this system can improve the decision making of individual traveler rather than improvements of network performance overall. So, we need to understand how tourists make their travel plans. Also, understanding decision process that lead to booking of the trip is equally important, as it allows of a potential behavior.

How does online tourism sale channel can influence traveling consumption of behaviour?

Nowadays, internet is popular, it seems that booking air ticket behavior of using internet is predicted to influence overall tourism air tickets payment method. Tourism industry has grown in the previous several decades. Despite its global impact, questions related to better understanding of tourists and whose habits. Using online travel air ticket booking benefits include booking electronic air tickets can be made from entering any electronic travel agents websites in the short time and electronic travel ticket payers do not need leave home, who can pay visa card to pre booking any electronic travel ticket from online channel conveniently.

How to analyze activity based travel demand ? Nowadays, human are concerning the traffic congestion and air quality deterioration, the supply oriented focus of transportation planning has expanded to include how to manage travel demand within the available transportation supply. Consequently, there has been an increasing interest in travel demand management strategies, such as congestion pricing that attempts to change aggregate travel demand. The prediction aggregate level, long term travel demand to understanding disaggregate level (i.e. individual levels) behavioral responses to short term demand policies, such as ride sharing incentives, congestion pricing and employer based demand management schemes, alternate work schedules, telecommuting limitation of travel agent traditionally work nature shall influence oriented trip based travel modelling passenger travel demand indirectly.

Finally, online travel purchase will be popular to influence the number of travel behavioural consumption nowadays. Any travel package products can be sold from websites to attract travellers to choose to prebook air ticket for any trips conveniently. In the past ten years, the internet has become the predominant carrier of all types of information and transactions. Regarding travel decisions, internet has also become an important sales channels for the travel industry, because it is associated with comparably lower distribution and sales costs, but also because ir adapts to hign supply and demand dynamics in this industry. Consequently, the travel and tourism industry tries to increase the internet sale specific share of sales volumes. So, internet sale channel has changed travel consumption behavioural pattern and characteristics and travel experience. For example, Switzerland has one of the highest population-to-computer ratio in Europe. It is also one of the most highly internet penetrated countries in terms of use of the WWW on a day-to-day basis, with more than 75 percent of the population older than 14 years using the WWW daily (ICT, 2005).

The reason of booking online tourism may include: convenience, fast transaction, finding traveling package choice easily, more airline seats available. So, online booking tourism will influence the traditional tourism agents visiting of sales and air tickets and travelling package numbers to be decreased. Finally, the online booking tourism market shares will be expanded to more than traditional tourism agents visits sale market in the future one day. So, the travel agents who still use the traditional tourism visiting sale channel which ought raise whose features to compare to differ to online tourism sale channel if these traditional touriam agents want to keep competitive ability in tourism industry for long term.

Actively based patterns of urban population of travel behavioural prediction method.

Actively based patterns of urban population. It is a method of motivational framework means in which societal constraints and inherent individual motivations interact to shape activity participation patterns. It can be used to predict one city or urban the numbers of travel demand in the year. It has two elements: First, capability constraints refer to constraints are imposed by biological needs, such as eating and sleeping and/or resources, such as income, availability of cars etc. to undertake the urban or city's family activities in the year. Second, coupling constraints define where, when and the duration of planning activities that are to be pursued with other individuals. So, this method needs to gather information (data) to get the relationship between activities, travel and spending work time and space time to evaluate whether there are how many families who have real needs to spend time to go to travel in the year.

What is trip based versus activity based approaches?

What is trip based versus activity based approaches? The fundamental difference between the trip-based and activity based approaches is that the former approach directly focuses on trips without explicit recognition of the motivation or reason for the trips and travel. The activity based approach , on the other hand, views travel as a demand derived from the need to pursue travel activities. So, it is better understand the individual or family behavior basis for individual or family travelling decision regarding participation in travelling activities in certain places or cities or countries at given times and hence the resulting travel needs. This behavioral basis includes all the factors that influence the why, how, when and where of performed activities and resulting individuals and household, the cultural/social norms of the community and the travel surrounding environment.

Another difference between the two approaches is in the way travel is represented. The trip based approach represents travel as a collection of trips. Each trip is considered as independent of other trips, without considering the inter-relationship in the choice attributes , such as time, destination and mode of different trips. As tours are chains of trips beginning and ending at a same location , say home or work. The tour based representation helps maintain the consistency across and capture the interdependency and consistency of the modeled choice attributed among the trips of the same tour.

In addition to the tour based representation of travel, the activity based approach focuses on sequences or patterns of activity participation and travel behavior, using the whole day or longer periods of time is the unit of analysis. Such as approach can address travel demand management issues through an examination of how people modify their activity participation, for example, will individuals substitute more out-of-home activities for in home activities in the evening of who arrived early form work due-to a work schedule change?

The major difference between trip based and the activity based approaches is in the way, the time dimension of activities and travel is considered. In the trip based approach, time is reduced to being simply a cost making a trip and a day's viewed as a combination, defined peak and off peak time periods. On the other hand, activity based approach views individuals' activity travel patterns are a result of their time use decisions with a continuous time domain. As individuals have 24 hours in a day or multiples of 24 hours for longer periods of time and decide how to use that travel among or allocate that time to activities and travel and with who, subject to their socio-demographic, transportation system and other and scheduling of trips. So, determining the impact of travel demand management policies on time use behavior is an important step to assessing the impact of such policies on individual travel behavior. The final major difference between this two approaches relates to the level of aggregation. In the trip based approach, most aspect of travel, e.g. number of trips etc. are analyzed at an aggregate level.

Consequently, trip based methods accommodate the effect of socio-demographic attributes of households and individuals in a very limited fashion, which limits the activity of the method to evaluate travel impacts of long term socio-demographic characteristics of the individuals who actually make the activity travel choices and the travel service characteristics of the surrounding environment. So, the activity based models are better equipped to forecast the longer term changes in travel demand in response composition and the travel environment of urban areas. Also, using activity based models, the impact of policies can be assessed by predicting individual level behavioral responses instead of employing trip based statistical averages that are aggregated over defined demographic segments.

Why senior age will be main travelling target?

In the past, Germany government had established tourism survey analysis to analyze survey data in order to arrive at reliable conclusions on future trends in travel behavior. To aim to find how demographic change will influence the tourism market and how the industry can adapt to those changes. The travel analysis provided data on tourism consumer behavior, including attitudes, motives and intentions. Since, 1970 year, it is based on a random sample, representative for the population in private households aged 14 years or older. Then, a continuous high scientific standard combined with a national and international users makes the travel analysis a useful tool and reliable source for tourism industry and policy decisions. It aimed to gather statistical data. e.g. on the age structure and on demographic trends, quantitative and qualitative analysis with time series data from the travel analysis. It shows e.g. not only the future volume , quite different from today's seniors, or how who will travel of family holidays will change, e.g. single parents of low, but grandparents of growing significance for tourism.

Demographic change is said to be one of the important drivers for new trends in consumer traveling change behavior in most European countries (e.g. Lind 2001). Because the growing number of senior citizens in the European Union and other industralised countries, such as the USA and Japan, looks to become one of the major marketing challenges for the tourism industry. United Nations statistics predict that the share of people being 60 age or older will grow dramatically in the coming future, and is expected to rise from 10 percent of the world population in 2000 year to more than 20 percent in 2050 year (United Nations Population Division, 2001). From its statistic, some data showed that travel propensity increased throughout life until the age of about 50 years of age and was then kept stable until very late in life 75 age. The most important results is that the travel propensity when getting older is not going down between 65 and 75 age of course, the overall development of this variable is influenced by a lot of other factors which are rsponsible for quite a variation over time. It is now possible to suggest that the general pattern of travel propensity is one of the key indicators for holiday life cycle travel behaviour, includes three stages. The growth stage tends to increase from early aduithood until 45 age old or when reaching some 80%. The next stage is stabilisation from the ages of around 50 age,until 75 age old, starting with a lower increase. Finally, the decrease stage is a slight decrease occurs once people reach the more advanced age of 75 age to 85 age old (Lohmann & Danielsson 2001).

So, it seems Germany government tourism prediction to future travellers' behaviour indicated these findings, such as on how future senior generations will travel, who had used survey data to examine the patterns of travel behaviour of a generation getting older and applied the findings to draw conclusions on the future. Also, it predicted that on the future of family trips, family semgmentation will be the travel behaviour patterns in the future. These findings together with the statistical data on demographic change allowed for a better understanding of the coming tends in family holidays. It's aim developed in consumer behaviour related to demographic change and predicted what will happen future of tourism one had to consider other influences and drivers as well, for example, trends on the supply side. e.g. low cost airlines or in travelling consumption behaviour in general whether how the past may provide a key to predict travel patterns of senior sitizens to the future.

Given the projected growth of the senior citizens market, designing specific marketing strategies to meet the prospective needs of elderly tourists will become increasingly important. It has been an implict assumption that it will be a close relationship between the travel behaviour of today's senior citizens and the those of future ones. The growing number of senior citizens in the world. e.g. China, Hong Kong, Japan, USA etc. countries. Global senior citizen tourism market will be based solely on demographic predictions about the future of the population's age structure. However, many of these seniors won't only live longer but will be fitter and more active until later in life. Many of the will also have plenty in life. Many of them will also have plenty of time and money to spend on travel. So, will these new seniors behave like today's senior citizens? Will they adopt the same travel behaviour as the previous generation or become a new market of oldies for the leisure and tourism indudtry? However, to determine the actual number of senior citizens who will be travelling and to sought to evaluate and specify certain difficult to predict the actual numbers of senior citizen to any country. However, they can be based on the implicit assumption that there is a close relationship between the travel behaviour of past, present and future seniors. But is this a valid assumption? As the reiseanalyse travel analysis survey, which was conducted in Germany every year, offered some interesting data possibiltieis. It was designed to monitor the holiday travel behaviour, opinions and attitudes of Germans and has been carried out since 1970 year, questions in the questionnaire. Data are based on face to face interviews, with a representative sample of more than 7,500 repondents, the interviews being carried out in January each year. All results refer to the average for the defined generated, which ranges generally over ten years. The group of people then at the age of 60 to 69 age is described. This corresponds to the same generation ten years ago, when they had an age of 50 to 59 age. When this methodological approach is not necessarily very sophisticated, it does have the important advantages of being cost effective.

Psychological method to predict travel behavioural consumption.

On the psychological view point, I think individual traveler's character will have those kind of personal characteristics. First, simplicity searchers value above everything ease not transparency in their travel planning and holiday making, and are willing to avoid having to go through extensive research. Second, cultural purists use their travel as an opportunity to immerse themselves in an unfamiliar looking to break themselves entirely from their home lives and engage. Sincerely with a different way of living. Third, social capital seekers understand that to be well travelled is a personal quality, and their choices are shaped by their desire to take maximum of social reward from their travel. They will exploit the potential of digital media to enrich and inform their experiences, and structure their adventures always keeping in mind they are being watched by online audiences. Finally, reward hunters seek a return on the investment who make in their busy , high-achieving lives. Linked in part to the growing trend of wellness, including both physical and mental self improvement who seek truly extraordinary and often indulgent or luxurious‘ must have experiences.

Why needs to know the personal character of individual traveler's characteristics? Because if travel agents could feel which kinds of individual traveler's character, then who can predict which kind of travel package to design to them more easily. For example, how to determine future travel behaviour from past travel experience and perceptions of risk and safety? We need to concern that the influences of past international travel experience, types of risk associated with international travel and the overall degree of safety feeling during international travel on individual's travelling experiences likelihood of travelling to various geographic regions on their next international vacation trip or avoidance of those regions, due to perceived risk. Because individual traveler's experience of safety risk degree to the countries, it will influence who chooses to go to the countries/country to travel again.

Why do travellers avoid certain destinations are as relevant decision making? Why do they choose to go to the country(countries) to travel? Perceptions of risk and safety and travel experiences are likely to influence travel decisions; efforts to predict future travel behaviour can benefit to individual tourist's decision making. As Weber & Bottorn (1989) defined risky decision is as "choices among alternatives that can be described by prodability distributions over possible outcomes" (p.114). Some psychologists judge subjective perceptions of physical reality, i.e. image of a particular tourist destination, whereas value judgement refers to the way individual rank destinations according to whose attributes. i.e. attractiveness, safety, risk etc. factors to form on overall image. So, if the individual traveler had unhappy and worried and unsafe experiences to go to where the place(country) to travel during whose vacation time before. Then, this negative travel experience will influence who is afraid to go to the place (country) to travel again. Risk of place, country, destination or region means the danger is relatively high to the place, ie. increasing in airplane accidents, crime or terrorist activity targeting citizens of potential traveler's nationality or the probability of occurrence is great , ie. recent occurrences involving travel regions/destinations under consideration or effective actions to control consequences exist. i.e. selecting safe regions and destinations, taking extra precautions when traveling to risky destinations. These risk factors will influence the individual traveler who chooses to cancel travel plan to go to the country again.

Another interesting research, how to predict behavioural intention of choosing a travel destination, which has focus of toursm research for years, but the complex decision making process leading to the choice of a travel destination has not been well researched. The planned behaviour model using its core constructs, attitude, subjective norm and perceived behavioural control, with the addition of the past behavioural variable on behavioural intention of choosing a travel destination.

Understanding why people travel and what factors influence their behavioural intention of choosing a travel destination is beneficial to tourism planning and marketing. Understanding travel motivation is the push and pull model. The idea of the push and pull model is the decomposition of an individual's choice of a travel destination into two forces. The first force is the push factor that pushes an indvidual away home and attempts to develop a general desire to go somewhere else, without specifying where that may be. The second force is the pull factor, that pulls on individual toward a destination, due to a region specific travel location or perceived attractiveness of a destination. The respective push and pull factors illustrate that people travel because who are pushed by their internal motives and pulled by external forces of a destination. Nevertheless, how push and pull factors guide people's attitude and how these attributes lead to behavioural intentions of choosing a travel destination have rarely been investigated. The decision making process leading to the choice of a travel destination is a very complex process. The planned behaviour model is as a research framework to predict the behavioural intention of choosing a travel destination. The model based on the three constructs of attitude, subjective norm, and perceived behavioural control (Fishbein & Ajzen, 1975).

In conclusion, the factors can influence travelers who decide to choose to travel the country, which include personal safety was perceived to the highest motivation factors among the important factors which include, scenic beauty, cultural interests, friendliness of local people, price of trip, services in hotels and restaurants, quality and variety of food and shopping facilities and services. The factors include both push and pull. Push factors include knowledge, prestige, and enhancement of human relationship etc., whereas, the most significant pull factors include high technologic image, expenditure and accessibility etc. For example, Japanese travelers visiting Hong Kong. Push factors are such as exploration dream fulfillment and pull factors are such as benefits sought, attractions and good climate city. It will be the factor of future travel patterns and motivations of sub-cultural and ethic groups for Japanese choice to go to Hong Kong travelling.

Bibliography

Backman, K., Backman, S., Uysal, M. And Sunshine, K. (1995). Event Tourism : An Examination Of Motivations And Activities. Festival Management And Event Tourism, 3(1), 15-24.

Fishbein, M., & Ajzen, Z. (1975). Belief, Attitude, Intention And Behaviour: An Introduction To Theory And Research, Boston: Addison Wesley.

Hsu, C.H.C., Cai , L.A., Li, M(2010). Expectation, Motivation And Attitude: A Tourist Behavioral Model. Journal Of Travel Research, 49(3), 282-296. http://dx.doi, org/10.1177/004728750 9349266.

ICT Information And Communication Technology Switzerland, 2005. ICT Fakten (ICT facts). Available from http://www.ictswitzerland.ch/de/ict%2fakten/factsfigures.asp(retrieved Dec.12, 2005) in German.

Lind, (2001): Befolkningen, Familjen, Livscykeln- Och Ekonomisk Tillvaxt. Institutet For Tillvaxtpo-litiska studier/ Vinnova/Nutek.

Lohmann, Martin (2001): The 31 st. Reiseanalyse-RA 2001. Tourism: vol. 49, no.1/2001;pp.65-67, Zagreb.

United Nations Population Division (2001). World Population Prospects: The 2000 year Revision, New York.

Weber E.U., & W, P.Bottom (1989). "Axiomatic Measures Of Perceived Risk: Some Tests And extensions." journal of behavioral decision making, 2 (2): 113-31.

However, green or nature tourism strategy may include these elements : Quality, tourism should have an impact on the quality of life for all members of the tourist process, exploitation of nature resources should be optimal and ensure their generation, balance, distribution of benefits among participants in the tourist process must be fair. So, future any kinds of green or nature tourism will need have these features in order to attract many travelers to visit any countries' green lands, e.g. they may rent cars to travel to green lands. So, developing attractive green lands will be one kind new travelling trend for green tourism in global future travel market.

There are two types of models that contribute to the better understanding of future tourism industry development, explanatory model refer to factors that cause development growth. For example, whether the travelers feel necessary to travel to different destinations, very often nice landscapes and sightseeing, pescriptive modes (e.g. life clcle explanations, physical models) examines tourism from what appears on ground e.g. large hotels facilities etc. Hence, any kinds of tourism leisure must need build these both models in order to attract travelers to choose to buy the tourism package from the travel agent more easily. It is important tourism leisure element to any one travel agent's tourism service package if it hopes to develop its tourism service success. So, the expansion of the tourist region over the natural boundaries of the city centre that occured in the first place as a result of the growth of tourism demand, is the end causing this very expansion to continue.

Butler (1980) involves a six stage evoluation of tourism, namely explanation, involvement, development, consolidation, stagnation, and post-stagnation. The last stage is further characterized by a period of decline, rejuvenation or stabilization. The applicability of the model to a given area has been assessed and judged of a tourist destination's development matched the six phases conceptually described by Butler

reference

Butler, R.W. (1980). the concept of a tourist area cycle of evolution: Implications for management of resources. Canadian Geographer, 24, 5-12.

Hence, our tourism industry is facing decline life cycle stage because COVD 19 human mouth disease has influenced many travelers feel fear to catch airplanes to travel, even they also feel to contact the potential COVD 19 human mouth disease people when they arrive the country , they feel that they may contact these sick people, instead of airplanes. So, this kind disease had influenced many travel agents reduce tourism service package number , due to many travelers' tourism leisure activities will reduce, due to travelers number reduces, they only carry cargos to transport to replace travelers COVD 19 disease influence our tourism industry is experiencing decline life cycle stage nowadays. Unless, COVD 19 human mouth attacking to lung disease can be treated by new medicine invention . Otherwise, tourism industry can not re-grow to mature life cycle stage easily.

The most used framework for examing stagnation and possible decline in tourism destinations has been tourist area life cycle model (Butler, 1980). The model has been operationalized frequently in the tourism lierature. It includes series of stages in tourism development, leadning eventually to the stagnation and post-stagnation stages. When a nature destination can either decline, however, it does not offer a systematic explanation of hoe tourism destination might avoid decline . Such as COVD 19 human mouth disease may influence travelers feel fear to catch air planes. So, even the country has beautiful nature scene to attract people to travel, althoug it is a nature attractive destination, but due to COVD19 disease occurs, it may influence this country's this nature attractive destination to enter decline life cycle stage at this moment.

Hence, tourism industry's life cycle stage , sometime it can be influenced by non predicted factor, such as COVD19 disease factor, it can influence travelers' travelling desire to be reduced suddenly from 2019 , due to they feel afraid to catch air planes to avoid to get this kind COVD 19 human mouth disease to bring lung disease when they are sitting in closed window inside air plane environment. So, COVD 19 human counth disease causes global tourism industry is facing serious decline life cycle stage. The question is that any one does not know when this kind COVD 19 disease will be treated by new medicine invention, so if this kind COVD 19 disease still can not be killed by new medicine invention, then it will continue to influence global tourism development to be improved , even any nature attractive scenes, they can not persuade any travelers to catch air planes to visit any countries to travel easily. But, however, we still need to keep our natural environment to prepare future COVD 19 diease disappears , e.g. parks are important places for the protection of ecological systems and natural resources as well as for the provision ot recreational and tourism opportunities for the public. Then, nature or green tourism can be continue to develop to attract many travelers to travel after COVD 19 disease disappears in the future.

- What are the characteristics of birth life cycle stage to tourism industry ?

Butler , R.W. (1980)'s model begins with a discovery and exploration or birth stage in which a location is discovered by a small, select group of people as a place with desirable assets often, this discovery is nature population who may see the perceived assets. As just ordinary aspects of their environment or local culture. The early tourists have very little support in the form of amenities, and typically, this is preferred and is part of a location's of being undiscovered. The early tourists, therefore rely heavily on and interact frequently with the residents of the region. This small group of early tourists is largely in dependent and shares information about a destination by word of mouth or by select affinity groups. Over time, as more people are introduced to the destination, the number of visitors begins to increase. So " word of mouth" will be traveler information to persuade them to make travelling destination choices in the tourism industry beginning. It is tourism industry's birth life cycle stage characteristics . However, internet invention can let any one see any countries' scene photos, so it is one kind of good advertisement method to introduce any countries' scene, instead of travelling magazine in tourism growth and maturity life cucle both stages.

Moreover, space tourism is at the birth life cycle stage. It needs travelers feel interest to travel space, if this kind space tourism service providers hope to implement their any space journeys in success. These factors may influence its development succeeds. Nowadays, its target market is wealthy travelers group, wealthy individual are needed, as they serve as the main consumers for space tourism . For space tourism to succeed there must be enough demand from those who are able to afford to expensive ticket. To date there have only been seven commercial space travelers, or space tourists, although they prefer to be called space flight participant, as they see themselves as pioneers and adventers as opposed to ordinary tourists. So, any future space tourism that price must need to reduce to general public, e.g. ordinary income level people, they can spend, if space tourism hopes to reach from stage stage rapidly. So, space tourism is still far to mature stage.It depends on whether how long time its any space journey ticket price can be reduced to any one can pay. So, when its customer target is not only wealthy travelers, many ordinary or common income level people, they can pay to any one space jounrney. It may mean to reach growth life cycle stage.

- What characteristics to space tourism growth stage?

When human space tourism of commericalization of activities in outer space can bring these feeling to let any one space traveler feels then, it may mean that it can reach growth stage, such as they may feel their any space journeys may bring positive impacts that outer. Space recreation can produce, in order to come up with space tourism, exploring and untravelling the hidden anystories of the space are needed. Also they can feel need drastically broadens and enrichs human's technical awareness and constructive knowledge need from any one space tourism journey package.

When space tourism reachs mature life cycle stage? What its characteristics are? When any one space travelers can feel that not only earth based attractions that simulate the space experience , they must need to catch airships to experience this different tourism experience, such as space theme parks, space training camps, virtual reality facilities , space hotels (skotel), multimedia interactive games and tele robotic moon rovers controlled from earth, but also parabolic flights, lasting up to three days or week long stay at floating space hotel, including participatory educational ,as well as sports competitions (i.e. space olympics). Hence, above these will be nay space tourism development. It can reach mature life cycle stage characteristics when any one can feel the real travelling mouth to compare to travel our earth anywhere, they can not find that they feel space tourism may be same to our earth's holiday (need to rela) or cultural (know different places or specialized tourism, e.g. expectations of adventures , even space scientists discover new experiences to expectations of adventure or get more information, scientific interest feeling. Then, at this moment, we can call space tourism has reached the mature stage. However, I believe that to develop space tourism in success. We must need to control space tourism ticket price to be reduced to general low income people. They may spend budget level. So, ticket price may be one major factor to influence future space tourism growth when it can reach mature stage. Also, it mean that whether space tourism may become another kind of popular tourism lesiure activities to use. It depends on ticket price factor, instead of its any space tourism trip arrangement factor. So, any one space tourism service provider must need long time to spend in order to implement its different strategies, e.g. ticket price, space trip arrangemet to achieve its their space tourism to achieve its their space tourism different destination package in success if they hope their future space tourism business can grow up in short time.

Airport service life cycle stage improvement strategy

Any organizations will have life cycle stage from birth, growth , mature to decline. In airport service organizations have theis life cycle stages in service aspect. Airports organizatins aim to provide safe, comfortable , even shopping environment to let passengers to stay and to wait to transfer another air planes to visit another destination or arrive the country's airport to check out or check in to enter the airport to leave. If airports have life cycle stages, what the characteristics to every stage? How to improve airport service in order to reach mature life cycle stage rapidly? How to implement airport service strategy in order to reach mature life cycle stage to the aorport organization rapidly?I shall explain as below:

Any airports need to be planned in order to raise excellent service to let passengers to let any travelers choose to travel the country whether the country can provide excellent service and facilities. It will bring indirect emotion impact to influence the travelers chooce to revisit the country to travel again. However, soft or hard element or) staff service performance or airport facility), they will influence whether the different countries travelers to choose to travel to re-visit the country again. So, learning how to keep the mature or airport service life cycle stage to stay long time, it will be one important factor to influence any airport business in success.

In the birth life style stage to airport, airport organizations must maintain the capability to provide expert advice to airport owners an matters including operational safety, during construction, environmental compatibility, and airport development standards. No other private or public organization can be expected maintain this level of proficiency. These value-added services enhance public trust when assuring consistant application of standards for the nation's airport system. So, it seems that when the new airport is built if it hopes its passenger customers can consider themselves emotion need. So, it ought concentrate on nowadays airplane landing cunways or airport transfer free service transport etc. facilities can let them to feel safe when they were walking in any airport places. If they feel anywhere are dangerous when they are walking or staying in the ne sirport, then new airport non safe or dangerous factor may influence travelers to choose the country to travel again.

Any new airports will need have good new national airport plan in order to it might operate in the near future with respect to safety areas. The plan elements may include as below:

Achieving zero accidents aim, establish standard safety areas at all commercial service airports , achieving the most minimum 85% of all passenger flights operate on runways with safe feeling, increase measure to 100% of all passenger flight operating on runways with standard safety areas after three months. Within 5 years, 95% of all passenger flights begin and end on runways with standard safety areas.

On benefits aspect, aims to mobilize work force to improve safety area performance describes realistic investment benefits. So, in any new airports birth life cycle stage, they must need to consider safety and expenditure for repair aspect in order to keep its service performance to avoid passengers have dissatisfactory feeling when they are staying in their new airports.

When the country has many travelers travel to the country , then the country's new airport passengers number must increase. It is its the new airport growth life cycle stage. These are critical success factors influence the airport, whether it can improve service performance in order to excite different countries travelers visiting the country's airport desire or grow up the visitors number successfully. The critical success factors may include: Having necessary support from internal and externa stakeholders to implement and willing to share information and identify anywhere the total airport facilities of repair needs that are both reliable and feasible projections to let passengers to feel more safe feeling when they are staying in the airport, understand its future service vision and mission, set strategic direction and goals to process/product specific objectives and decision-making across and doen the organization, define, model and prioritize planning prcesses critical for mission performance, practice hand-on sernior management ownership of planning process and allow field, personnel flexiblity in performing jobs, adjust organizational structures , an essessment program to evaluate planning process and product management , e.g. national airport system performance, create organizational understanding of the value management to customer and stakeholder current and future expectations developing human resources management strategies to support new process that solves needs planners and engineers, building information resources strategies change, especially for entering data at the source and maintains data integrity and timeliness.,establish central support group to support reengineering efforts, outreach and training efforts across the organization, phase in short-and long-term results that achieve set goals and objectives over the next two years.

Thus, when one new airport begins to feel passengers number is increasing. It ought experience the growth life cycle stage to the new airport , if it hopes that it can reach mature life cycle stage rapidly as well as keeps its mature life cycle stage to stay in this stage long time or reachs the airport service performance to the most satisfactory level in this mature life cycle stage. It must need to attempt to plan these strategies to implement in order to avoid decline life cycle stage occurs in short time. So, it explains why some new airport can experience the development to mature life cycle stage from grow life cycle stage in short time,even when it reachs mature life cycle stage. It can keep to stay in this stage long time. The reason is that it had prepared effective strategies to achieve how to improve its airport service performance aim in order to satisfy passenger needs. When they are staying in the country's airport any time. Hence, every year revising service performance is needed to any airports.

Any airports must have development processes. The question is that whether the airport needs how long time to reach growth or mature life cycle stage from birth stage or decline life cycle stage will be delayed how long to occur. The development processes may mean that the airport development life cycle stages changes that had toard a particular result or even as a series of continuous actions or operations coducting to an end (Merriam-Webster, 2013).

reference

Merriam-webster (2013). On line dictionary. Available at:

https://www.merriam-webster. com/(last accessed July , 8 2013).

Hence, any airport organizations with experience development pricess. When the new airport is built, it must be in the birth life cycle stage. Its passengers number can not increase rapidly. It needs time to grow their number. But, when the new airport operates a period, many different countries begin feel this new airport is existence in the country. They will attempt to catch airplance to visit this country airport to catch airplane to visit tis country airport to travel. If they feel this country airport service performance can satisfy their short time staying feeling or its passengers or airports visitors number may increase rapidly. It meand that this airport is experiencing growth life cycle stage. So, if the airport can attract many visitors in short time. It will reduce time to growth life cycle stage from birth life cycke stage.

So , service performance may be one important factor to inflow the airport grows. When the airport develops to the period, passengers number can not increase rapidly, it may be the airport's mature life cycle stage. Due to it's passengers number can not grow rapidly, its passengers number also may reduce. When its passengers number has significant decrease, if its reduction number is increasing more. It implies that the airport is experiencing decline life cycle stage. All any country's airport may experience whole life cycle stages. If the country's airport can not implement successful strategies, it may experience birht life cycle stage in long time because it can not grow its passengers number significantly. So, any airports need to learn how to help them to change growth life cycle stage, even mature life cycle stage can stay in long time easily. If they hope to attract many different countries passengers to visit their airports or travel themselves countries or enjoy to stay short time in themselves airports in order to grow themselves airline industry development.

- How can processes improvement management strategy influence airport service performance?

Overall processes in an airport may involve passengers, luggage, cargo, aircraft movements, ground handling, and crews . All of these operations can be systematised into processes at airport terminal. Three main types of processes can be established departing , arrival and transfer . Departure consists in catching a flight to a final or intermediate destination, arrival consists in landing and leaving the airport, and transfer consists in landing at the airport only to catch another flight to a final or an intermediate destination. Airports also deal with cargo. It involves in the movement of cargo by air, cargo fies from the shopper to the consignee through one or more airlines. However, when the airport can let them freight forwarder, being familiar with the necessary procedures how permits the airline to concentrate on the provision of air transport and to avoid time consuming details of the facilitation and landside distribution system. It will raise efficiency and improve service performance. The services product by the ground handling are crucial to the success and efficiency of the airport operations.

These services are usually provided by specialised companies. Briefly, it includes the luggage treatment, passengers carrying from plan to terminal when needed and aircraft assistance. Also, focusing on crew, there are two majoe processes, one for departures and the other for arrivals. The crew members also have to pass the security and passport controls. However, they have special channels for this. Once they reach the aircraft, the similarities with the passengers' procedure stop. Hence, they have to perform a set of activities , such as check the aircraft load sheets and help passengers to name a few. Also airport terminal operations processes for passengers and luggage, typically for departures , passengers do the check on the airline area, pass security controls, proceed to the general lounge and lastly to the gate holding area. arriving passengers are able to immediately go from the luggage claim area, but the non-passengers have to pass the passport control at first. After this passengers have to decide if they need to declare goods or not as the paths are different . Hence, if the airport can reduce all of this service processes are less complex as immigration check in-out service, liggage claim can be efficient to carry when passengers need to find themselves luggage. Then, it will reduce waste time and let they satisfy airport service absolutely. So, reducing service process time amy also help the airport to increase customers number significantly. When airport role is the middleman between airlines , cargo transport service providers and passengers, e.g. short time transport cargo service and reducing passengers check in or check out service time. then, it will let them to feel more satisfactory service to the airport.

Hence, airport capacity is as a multifactor function leaves open the exact relationship between the factors but stresses that all factors are relevant to assess airport capacity . So , understanding airport capacity and what drives the capacity usage at airports may provide an insight in the set of instructments available to optimise the use of capacity. All of these factors may influence any capacity of an airport, they may include as below:

For example, technical constraints, e.g. ATM per hour service in a runway in a combined arrival and departure fashion, when many passengers are staying at the airport, they can withdraw money from ATM easily. So, ATM number facilities service supply number and location choice to the airport factors will infuence passengers ' satisfactory level, another factor is environmental constraints, it can directly offer the wellbeing of the communities surrounding the negative emotion to passengers and communities surrounding the airprt. For this factor, the change in technology and/or operational procedures can provide more capacity in the system.

Airline business models factor, it can affect the capacity spoke model when other under a point-point one ,these models directly affect the peak hour operational capacity, particularly in big international hubs. Airlines often compete with high frequencies between destinations, thus increasing the number of movements. In addition, conncectivity also has downsides for this model: the delays in one airport might be exported and sometimes in another, due to the connectivity influencing the real capacity. This factor has been setting economic incentives or pricing models. Furthermore, expanding information systems, from one airport to multiple airports gate-to-gate concept, and the use of larger airport to redcuce frequencies.

Hence, above these factors may influence whether the airport needs how long time to reach maturiry life cycle stage when it is staying the growth life cycle stage. It depends on how its strategies implementation and how environment influence its implementation , if it hopes to achieve to reach the maturity life cycle stage in success in short time.

Finally, I shall explain life cycle cst analysis to any country pavement strategy will bring what significant influential benefits to any airports continue to develop in order to avoid to reach decline life cycle stage time in short time easily , when they are staying in the mature life cycle stage. In the construction or rehabilitation investments of highway's pavements, it is already common to perform a life-cycle analysis or life cycle cost analysis for different alternatives to airport pavements. Becauae when any airport pavements are using for a long time, every day has many airplanes need to fly to land on the pavement. It can bring significant repace influence when the airport has many airplanes are needed to land on the pavements every day in the maturity life cycle stages.

Hence, how to evaluate the repair cost expenditure budget in order to satisfy every day air planes land on the airport pavement need. In the calculations are different cost factors (including direct and indirect cost)to any airport itself pavement. Direct costs are related to the critical construction cost landing on pavement activities and are calculated with information from the airport agency and constructors that work for them. The indirect costs are related with the loss of daily revenue of the airport during work activities, such as landing on the airport pavement.

Runways are the most critical pavements area of airport , so it is critical to ensure the quality of these pavement to let airplanes to land on the airport safety, e.g. they need to be constructed with sufficient strength to carry the moving airport and have a high resistance to skidding and aquaplaining. It is most of the time accomplished with reconstructions or deep rehabilitation. Hence, predicting how much will spend on airport pavement facilities expenditure must need in every day.

However, the life cycle assessment (LCA) is a mult step procedure for calculating the life time environmental impact of a product or service is needed to any airport organizations, when they reachs maturity life cycelt stage . The complex process includes goal and cope definition in inventory analysis impact assessment. The process is vaturally iteractive as quality and completeness of information is constantly being testes. When the definition of the aim and scope of the study is done the next step is the development of an inventory, in which all significant environmental burdens during the lifetime of the product,, such as airport pavements or process , such as airplanes landing on the pavement or airplanes leaving from the pavement in the airport.

(Araujo, Oliveria & Silve) 2014 explained that life cycle snslysis of pavements are focused on the activities of extraction, production, transportation application of materials, concisely the construction of the road. Because its difficult to obtain other relevant data knowing that the use phase of the pavement is predominant with repect to energy consumption and also to gas emissions related to the atmosphere. One of the main factors for the use phase is the rolling resistance, this depends on the surface and structural characteristics of the different pavements.

reference

Araujo, J.P.C. Oliveria, J.R.M. & Silva H.M.R.D. (2011) . the importance of the use phase on the LCA of environmentally friendly solutions for asphalt road pavements. transportation research part D: trasport and environment, 32(0), 97-110. Retrieved in March 2015 from://
dx. doi.org/10.1016/j.trd.2014.07.006.

Hence, , if the airport can have good repairment or renew skills to help its pavement to improve. Then, it may bring long time benefit, such as reducing airplanes energy consumption and also to avoid gas emissions or reduce gas emissions accident occurrene, even air plane landing on pavement accident occurrence chance can reduce to the zero. so, defining the expected pavement performance time improvement strategy can influence whether the airport pavement can satisfy all airplane users how long time landing on or leaving on the airport pavement. Also it is the major factor to influence airport main function success for any airplanes arriving to the country's airport pavement or leaving from the country's airport pavement. Hence, calculating any airport pavement life cycle costs factor. It is necessary to analysis and interpret carefully the results to identfy the most economic pavement strategy in any airport's whole life cycle development stages.

CHAPTER TWO

New economic employee behavior or technology influences organizational performance

Our societies are experiencing new economic social development stage from old economic social development stage. What are the economists' opiunions or view points concern how and why our societies are experiencing new econoomic social change. What can influence to our social changes from new economic development. I shall attempt to apply some economic theories to explain why some economic theories are not be accepted to our nowadays new economic social development as below:

Firstly, the invisible hand theory changes, it is not be accepted to our nowadays new economic socical development need absolutely. It indicates that the wealth of nations marshels the theories of self interest first written about in the theory of moral sentiments into a way of looking at how societies prosper. Smith believed that real wealth was the sum of the annual produce of the land and labour of the whole country and that prosperity was based on increasing that.

He focused on the concept of natural liberty , the idea that people can deploy their resources in competition with others. This process would identify which activities were most worth doing. For example, if mining produced higher returns than the average of other activities than capital would naturally swing towards that area and away from less productive areas. It is are good example for old economic invisible hand theory.

However, our societies are changing. Smith's opinions toward the mining industry that produces the greatest value, so each worker aims for the job that will make him or her the most money.

In this case, as Smith put it, this worker " neither intends to promote the public interest, not knows how much hs is promoting it". He intends only his own gain, and he is in this led by an invisible hand to promote and which was no part of his intention. But, nowadays societies, any labours will needs to intend to help their organizations to promote the public interest, he or she needs to know how much she/she is promoting it. For this mining company example, the mining worker needs to know whether their mining tasks value is how much, when they are seeking the mining land can have how much market value for their organizations. It can gain how much profit. Because if their mining company can have high mining land value to help them to produce the good quality of mines products to sell, then they can help themselves organizations to earn high profit indirectly. Consequently, these mining worker individual wage may also be also influenced to raise.Hence, these mining workers' value is depended on whether their mining tasks can bring how much mining land value to let their mining company to sell in order to earn high or less mining sale income in this global competitive mining market.

Hence, new economy theory explaind that the invisible hand means that any labor will also need to concern or intent to promote the public interest for themselves employers, instead of doing the job to earn income, becacause when they can help their employers to promote the public interest to achieve higher social value interest to themselve organizations, then their employers can earn more profit when sale growth is influenced to raise by promoting the higher public interest. Consequently, nowadays our societies, any company's labours' wages may also be influenced to raised by their promoting interest (invisible hand method).

Secondly, the division of labour concept that is explained by Smith, he indicated the greatest improvement in the productive process of labour.... seem(s) to have been the effects of the effects of the division of labour, Smith wrote. However, it has been changing to an office or a factory , its working enviroment was seen to have difference to the division of labur view. Smith was writing the birth stage of the industrial revolution that over time would see hundreds of thousands of people drawn into mass production factories in old economic society.

BUt, nowadays our societies' manufacturing technology is improved, such as manufacturing robotic technology can assist a team of workers to cooperate to work in order to achieve high efficient productivities.Smith could see how better organized work lead to greater output by each worker, called " productivity". It is significant that his theory was based on the observation of actual economic activity rather than on irorytower supposition. He realised that one untrained worker left to his factory that makes pins, drawing out the wire, straighting it, cutting it, pointing it, grinding it. Smoith estimated that ten workers could produce 48,000 a day or 4,800 each. How to achieve a 4,800 per cent increase in productivity, he indicated three factors as below:

These three factors include:

(1) Each worker becomes more skilled in his/her particular contribution ever time,

(2) Time is saved by workers not having to swap machines and equipment as they go through each individual task as well as

(3) This encourages the design of machines that make is easier to do the work.

But, nowadays, pin factory may apply pin robotic machines to help them to increase pins productivities in short time. It implies that future division of labours or organized labours method won't be important to help pins productivities number increases. When robotic machines can replace any different pins departments part tasks efficiently, even their productive pins performance can be better than any one of the factory's different departments oin workers' tasks more easily.

Hence, in new economic society, some manufacturing industry's dividion of labour concept can not be adapted , due to robotic manufacturing machines invention. It can replace any organizations' workers tasks of manufacturing lines in any one manufacturing organizaton's team more easily and efficiently. However, in the old economic society, division of labour explains why workers on a car production line eash add some part to the basic chassis, but in the new economic society, car robots can replace different car manufacturing part tasks worker to do their different tasks on a car production line or why busy bankers do not answer the phone themselves because speaking robots may help buysy bankers to answer the phone or supermarkets do not need warwhouse workers to help them to deliver goods in warehouses, because warehouse robots can replace them to deliver goods in warehouses rapidly.

So, in new economic society, division of labour concept can not be accepted to some kinds of manufacturing industries, even service industries, due to robots can replace any workers or service staffs to do their tasks efficiently. In our nowadays society, because technology innovation, such as robotic manufacturing machine invention, it may help any organizations need many workers to worker in any manufacturing line or team. So, division of labour concept won't be adopted to any one nowadays factories or offices environment when robots can be participated to the office or factory or warehouse's working environment.

Surplus value of labour theory is Marx's economic theory. He too looks at commodities and the way the things are produced. He saw value arising from the effort, that the workers put in to produce the goods. So, the amount of labour used to make goods determined their prices over sell for the long run. Mars focused on value. In this view, the amount of labour determined the value of goods produced. For example, a machine takes five hours to make something has twice the value as make something has hours. He distinguished between use value and the exchange value that the owners of the goods could get by selling it. Marx gave opinions to indicate that a machine worker would be paid a wage to produce a box-worth of tools that would sell for a much higher price than this daily wage.

Think of supermarket checkout worker, a solicitor's assistant or a bank teller, these staffs may be paied higher salaries to compare factory manufacturing workers , office cleaners , because they can help their eomployers to bring more clients , when they can serve their clients or factory workers do not need to serve clients. So, they are different to think or judge whether their performances are excellent ot worse in order to making rising wage decision more easily.

However, it is old economic social view point to determine the surplus value of labour aspect. Inold economic view point, Marx saw that there wa a difference between what the workers were paid for their efforts and what the factory owners received as a result. Marx called this " surplus value": Th capitalists were able to keep the exta value of profits because they owned the means of production.

Capitalists therefore need to pay the workers less than the value at which they planned to sell the goods. This equation also needs to include the costs of the machinery, which Marx explains as being the value of the " concealed labour" that next in to build the machine. Their profit was the surplus divided by the sum of the labour costs (variable capitals) and machines (fixed capital).

Marx also saw that the factory owner would look the pay the minimum that the workers needed for them and their families to survive, call " subsistence wage". He said that this wage was kept to low by the existence of unemployed people ready to seek now work in society. Thus, Marx felt factory workers ar paid less wage, but service workers are paid high wage because service workers can help employers to serve clients to let they feel satisfactory service. Then clients number will be influenced to increase by whom excellent service. So, the excellent performance service staffs can increase higher salaries to compare general non-service workers.

However, in our new economic societies, surplus value of labour concept can not be accepted, because our nowadays societies, this pool was kept filled by technological , such as robots can do service tasks, e.g. shopping center front line client service tasks, security tasks, even restaurant cooking tasks, instead of warehouse, factory, manufacturing tasks. So, technological advances that reduced the need for labour to future service and manufacturing industries. This is one new service or manufacturing technological opinions or ideas to service or manufacturing labour is kust another commodity only that can be bought and sold, with its value being equal to the cost of kept is for work.

Hence, when servicing or manufacturing robots are popular ro be used to any factories, offices, restaurants, shopping centers , warehouses etc. workplaces. The service workers and manufacturing workers their wages or wages won't be have much difference, because robots may replace to do their tasks to serve their clients or manufacture any kinds of products in any organizations in any time.

It seems that service workers' wages won't be increased more easily to compare non-service workers' salaries. They may be seemed to such a commodity. When the organization decides to apply robots to replace some service or manufaturing workers to do their tasks in their teams. Hence, the surplus value of labour theory won't be accepted to the organizations when they choose robots to replace some or the department's all manufacturing workers or service workers to do their tasks.

The organization's surplus value of labour is depended whether it decides to apply robots to help it to manufacture any kinds of products or serve to their clients in nowadays new economic society.

How applying economy theories solve economic problems

The economic problem – sometimes called the basic or central economic problem – asserts that an economy's finite resources are insufficient to satisfy all human wants and needs. Economics involves the study of how to allocate resources in conditions of scarcity However, viewing economics as the study of how society allocates resources can lead to conflation of normative economic planning and empirical study of how economic agents operate in these conditions.

In mainstream neoclassical economics, it is assumed that humans pursue their self-interest, and that the market mechanism best satisfies the various wants different individuals might have. These wants are often divided into individual wants (which depend on the individual's preferences and purchasing power parity) and collective wants (which are the wants of entire groups of people). Things such as food and clothing can be classified as either wants or needs, depending on what type and how often a good is requested.

However, economists have sometimes characterized "how" to produce as a "technological problem" of efficiency whereas the allocation of what is produced is an "economic problem". In a free market, the "how" of production and allocation of resources is distributed among economic agents. In a centrally planned economy, a principal decides how and what to produce on behalf of agents. Modern economies are often welfare capitalist with various regulations, which makes the economic system more equitable while retaining the distributed free market system. Due to human wants are unlimited, an infinite series of human wants remains continue with human life.Nobody can claim that all of his wants have been satisfied and he has no need to satisfy any further want. Everybody feels hunger at a time then other he needs water. Sometime one feels the desire of clothing then starts to feel the desire of having good conveyance. When all existing wants are satisfied then new wants starts to create in mind, so the series of wants remains continue till the last moment of life. So an economic problem arises because of existence of unlimited human wants.

Problem of allocation of resources

The problem of allocation of resources arises due to the scarcity of resources, and refers to the question of which wants should be satisfied and which should be left unsatisfied. In other words, what to produce and how much to produce. More production of a good implies more resources required for the production of that good, and resources are scarce. These two facts together mean that, if a society decides to increase production of some good, it has to withdraw some resources from the production of other goods. In other words, more production of a desired commodity can be made possible only by reducing the quantity of resources used in the production of other goods.

The problem of allocation deals with the question of whether to produce capital goods or consumer goods. If the community decides to produce capital goods, resources must be withdrawn from the production of consumer goods. In the long run, however, [investment] in capital goods augments the production of consumer goods. Thus, both capital and consumer goods are important. The problem is determining the optimal production ratio between the two.

In fact, in our societies, resources are scarce and it is important to use them as efficiently as possible. Thus, it is essential to know if the production and distribution of national product made by an economy is maximally efficient. The production becomes efficient only if the productive resources are utilized in such a way that any reallocation does not produce more of one good without reducing the output of any other good. In other words, efficient distribution means that redistributing goods cannot make anyone better off without making someone else worse off. (See Pareto efficiency.) So, scientists will apply efficient distribution methods to help any countries to earn the absolute advantages when we buy and sell any kinds of products or food between ourselves countries, e.g. when US has good natural resource to grow any food, e.g. potato, wheat , vegatable, cotton , then US can export to sell to China, because China has no any farms to grow agriculture food to supply itself Chinese to eat. So, China must need to buy any agriculture food from US. Otherwise, China has cheap labor to supply to US any manufacturers to help them to manufacture their electronic products. SO, it has many US factories are built in China to let Chinese workers help them to produce their products because their wages are cheaper to compare US workers. So, comparative economic advantage will be choice to apply between US and China both countries. (Absolute advantge trade theory).

The inefficiencies of production and distribution exist in all types of economies. The welfare of the people can be increased if these inefficiencies are ruled out. Some cost must be incurred to remove these inefficiencies. If the cost of removing these inefficiencies of production and distribution is more than the gain, then it is not worthwhile to remove them.

The problem of full employment of resources
(the division of labour concept and Surplus value of labour theory)

In view of how to use available resources are fully utilized is an important one. A community should achieve maximum satisfaction by using the scarce resources in the best possible manner—not wasting resources or using them inefficiently. There are two types of employment of resources:

(1) Labour-intensive
(2) Capital-intensive

In capitalist economies, however, available resources are not fully used. In times of depression, many people want to work but can't find employment. It supposes that the scarce resources are not fully utilized in a capitalistic economy.

The problem of economic growth

If productive capacity grows, an economy can produce progressively more goods, which raises the standard of living. The increase in productive capacity of an economy is called economic growth. There are various factors affecting economic growth. The problems of economic growth have been discussed by numerous growth models, including the Harrod-Domar model, the neoclassical growth models of Solow and Swan, and the Cambridge growth models of Kaldor and Joan Robinson. This part of the economic problem is studied in the economies of development.

Needs and wants problems

Needs are things or material items of peoples need for survival, such as food, clothing, housing, and water. Everyone has a different needs and wants. Until the Industrial Revolution, the vast majority of the world's population struggled for access to basic human needs.

Wants are effective desires for a particular product, or for something that can only be obtained by working for it. While the fundamental needs of survival are key in the function of the economy, wants are the driving force that stimulates demand for goods and services. To curb the economic problem, economists must classify the nature and different wants of consumers, as well as prioritize wants and organize production to satisfy as many wants as possible.

Five bases problems of economy

In our societies , in general, our societies will have these similar problems The following points highlight the five basic problems of an economy. The problems are: 1. What to Produce and in What Quantities? 2. How to Produce these Goods? 3. For whom is the Goods Produced? 4. How Efficiently are the Resources being Utilised? 5. Is the Economy Growing?.

Problem 1:What to Produce and in What Quantities?

The first central problem of an economy is to decide what goods and services are to be produced and in what quantities. This involves allocation of scarce resources in relation to the composition of total output in the economy. Since resources are scarce, the society has to decide about the goods to be produced: wheat, cloth, roads, television, power, buildings, and so on. Once the nature of goods to be produced is decided, then their quantities are to be decided. How many tonnes of wheat, how many televisions, how many million kws of power, how many buildings, etc. Since the resources of the economy are scarce, the problem of the nature of goods and their quantities has to be decided on the basis of priorities or preferences of the society.

If the society gives priority to the production of more consumer goods now, it will have less in the future. A higher priority on capital goods implies less consumer goods now and more in the future. But since resources are scarce, if some goods are produced in larger quantities, some other goods will have to be produced in smaller quantities. Suppose the economy produces capital goods and consumer goods. In deciding the total output of the economy, the society has to choose that combination of capital goods and consumer goods which is in keeping with its resources.

Problem 2: How to Produce these Goods?

The next basic problem of an economy is to decide about the techniques or methods to be used in order to produce the required goods. This problem is primarily dependent upon the availability of resources within the economy. If land is available in abundance, it may have extensive cultivation. If land is scarce, intensive methods of cultivation may be used. If labour is in abundance, it may use labour-intensive techniques; while in the case of labour shortage, capital-intensive techniques may be used.

The technique to be used also depends upon the type and quantity of goods to be produced. For producing capital goods and large outputs, complicated and expensive machines and techniques are required. On the other hand, simple consumer goods and small outputs require small and less expensive machines and comparatively simple techniques.

Further, it has to be decided what goods and services are to be produced in the public sector and what goods and services in the private sector. But in choosing between different methods of production, those methods should be adopted which bring about an efficient allocation of resources and increase the overall productivity in the economy.

Problem 3. For whom is the Goods Produced?

The third basic problem to be decided is the allocation of goods among the members of the society. The allocation of basic consumer goods or necessities and luxuries comforts and among the household takes place on the basis of among the distribution of national income. Whosoever possesses the means to buy the goods may have then. A rich person may have a large share of the luxuries goods, and a poor person may have more quantities of the basic consumer goods he needs.

Problem 4: How Efficiently are the Resources being Utilised?

This is one of the important basic problems of an economy because having made the three earlier decisions, the society has to see whether the resources it owns are being utilised fully or not. In case the resources of the economy are lying idle, it has to find out ways and means to utilise them fully.

Problem 5: Is the Economy Growing?

The last and the most important problem is to find out whether the economy is growing through time or is it stagnant. If the economy is stagnant at any point inside the production possibility curve, it has to be moved on to the production possibility curve PP whereby the economy now produces larger quantities of consumer goods and capital goods. Economic growth takes place through a higher rate of capital formation which con?sists of replacing existing capital goods with new and more productive ones by adopting more efficient production techniques or through innovations.

All of these economy problems will be our societies often causes to anyone feels need to solve problems in order to achieve our societies can have enough resources to satisfy our every day living.

● rational consumer theory

The Consumer Problem

It seems that economic problems and consumer problems are similar, I feel that it is possible , economists can attempt to apply any economic theories to solve some consumer problems in some suitations. They can find the accurate solutions when they can apply the suitable economic theories to solve the suitable consumer or economic problems in our societies. I shall indicate that how economists can apply the suitable economic theories to attempt to solve some consumer problems in our societies as below:

Consumer theory is concerned with how a rational consumer would make consumption decisions. What makes this problem worthy of separate study, apart from the general problem of choice theory, is its particular structure that allows us to derive economically meaningful results. The structure arises because the consumer's choice sets sets are assumed to be de?ned by certain prices and the consumer's income or wealth. The consumer's problem is to choose that is most preferred or, equivalently, that has the greatest utility.

The assumption of perfect information is built deeply into the formulation of this choice problem, just as it is in the underlying choice theory. Some alternative models treat the consumer as rational but uncertain about the products, for example how a particular food will taste or a how well a cleaning product will perform. Some goods may be experience goods which the consumer can best learn about by trying ("experiencing") the good. In that case, the consumer might want to buy some now and decide later whether to buy more. That situation would need a di?erent formulation. Similarly,if the agent thinks that high price goods are more likely to perform in a satisfactory way, that, too, would suggest quite a di?erent formulation. Agents are price-takers. The agent takes prices p as known, ?xed and exogenous. This assumption excludes things like searching for better prices or bargaining for a discount.

● Demand And Supply Elastic Theory Solves Consumer Problems

What is economy rule predict consumer behaviour? Why and How does economist can apply economy rule to predict consumer behaviours? I shall explain the reasons as below:

Why does economic principle be the best to predict consumer behaviour. It may include these two reasons: The first focuses on the substantive domain of study, in this interpretation , economics is a social science devoted to understanding how the economy works. The second definition focuses on methods: economics is a way of doing social science, using particular tools. In this interpretation the discipline is associated with formal modelling and statistical analysis rather than particular hypotheses or theories about the economy. Therefore, economic methods can be applied to many other areas besides the economy, everything from decisions within the family to questions about political institutions.

Demand and supply principle predict public transport tool passenger behaviour

Economists need to use the right economic ideas to predict consumer behaviour. So, Misuse the wrong economy ideas to predict consumer behaviours. It will do more wrong judgement to evaluate or predict why and how and when the country's consumer behaviours will change. It is every economist needs to consider issue. For example, the economy idea application of economic supply-demand principles to public transport. Different fares would give commuters with more-flexible hours the incentive to avoid peak travel times. They would allow passenger traffic to spread out over time, reducing the pressure on the public transport system when enabling even larger total passenger flow. IT aims to reduce traffic congestion, increased public-transport use, reduced car-bon emissions and cause air pollution and generated considerable revenue for the country's transport system. So, if the country can apply supply and demand economic principle to attempt to predict how many passengers number needs to catch transport tools to go to work or go to school or other activities. Then, it can predict how many bus, ferry, taxi, train, underground train, tram etc. different public transport tools to satisfy future public transport passengers' needs in society. So, this demand and supply principle is the comparative best rule to predict any kinds of public transport passengers' road needs, when they need to either go to school, go to office, go to leisure or shopping etc. different kinds of activities. So, applying the demand and supply principle to predict road and sea public transport passengers can help the country to reduce air pollution when they feel that they can find any public transport tools to catch any time conveniently , then it can encourage them to reduce car purchase desire. When many people choose to catch public transport tools, then it will reduce many cars number on the road. Then, air pollution will reduce as well as any public transport tools' income will also increase as well as traffic jam will also reduce. When the country can evaluate how many people choose to catch bus or taxi or ferry or train or underground train, or tram or train etc. different kinds of public transport tools, then the country can predict the more accurate public transport tools number to every kind of public transport tool to satisfy their journey needs. e.g. whether underground train or train or tram need to decrease or increase the frequent times or number to catch the volume of passenger in busy or non-busy time; or whether bus company has need to increase how much buses to catch the city location passengers when they are living in the city. Moreover, supply and demand principle can help any public transport tools to explain why their passengers number reduces in the year, it may due to fare charge is unreasonable, feeling uncomfortable to sit on the seat or air condition is poor in the transport tool environment, or there are no more seats because many there are much time is full passenger and no seat vacancy to provide to them to sit .

So, supply and demand principle can help any kinds of public transport tools to find whether which is (are) the factor(S) can influence the current or last year passengers number reduce. Then, they can concentrate on improving their weaknesses to raise their service quality . So, supply and demand principle can also help they to evaluate whether what their weakness are in order to improve to increase passengers number. They can do questionnaires to enquiry their passengers' response to evaluate whether which areas of services that they feel unsatisfactory. So, the different kinds of service satisfactory feeling to the passengers number data will be the main source to help the kind of public transport tool to analyse and conclude the results more accurate, then they can make the more accurate judgement to improve the of service. For example, the questionnaires indicate that the many passengers feel the bus fare is reasonable, but many passengers feel they can not find any seats to sit easily. So, it implies that the bus firm ought buy more buses or enlarges bus size and increases more seats in the enlarged buses. Then, it does not reduce its fare but it needs to find solutions to let passengers can find seats to sit in every bus more easily. But, if the questionnaires indicate that there are many passengers feel its fare is higher or unreasonable to compare other kinds of public transportation tools. Hence, it can avoid to spend more expenditure to increase bus number to the city, if the city has many passengers , they still choose bus to catch, but they feel its fare is too higher to compare other kinds of public transport tool. Then, it only needs to reduce its fare , it ought help it to increase passengers number. Hence, demand and supply principle is the most suitable economic method to evaluate any kinds of public transport system passenger needs in any country nowadays.

- Supply and demand and price elasticities principle predict oil energy user behaviour

The another case is that demand and supply principle can predict oil buyer behaviour to find whether what factors can cause the oil buyer individual need reduces. For example , a rise in production costs increases market prices and reduces quantities demanded and supplied. Or when, energy cost rise, utility bills increases and households fid extra ways of saving heating and electricity. But, others are nor. For example, whether a tax is imposed on the producers or consumer of a commodity, say oil has nothing to do with who ends up paying for it. The tax might be administered on oil companies, but it might be consumers who really pay for it through higher prices at the pump. Or the extra cost might be imposed on consumers in the form of a sale tax, but the oil companies might be forces to absorb it through lower prices. It all depends on the " price elasticities" of demand and supply. With the addition of extra assumption, this model also generates rather strong implications about how well markets work. In particular, a competitive market economy is efficient in the sense that it is impossible to improve one person's well-being without reducing somebody.

● Demand and supply principle can misuse to predict consumer behaviour when the two firms participate advertisement to promote their products in the same time

Why can demand and supply principle misuse to predict consumer behaviour when the two firms participate advertisement to promote their products in the same time ? I shall explain as below: Assume that two competing firms must decide whether to have a big advertising budget. Advertising would allow one firm to steal some of the other's customers. But when they both advertise, the effects on customer demand cancel out. The firms end up having spent money needlessly.

We might expect that neither firm would choose to spend much on advertising, but the model shows that this logic is off base. When the firms make their choices independently and they care only about their own profits, each one has an incentive to advertise, regardless of what the other firm does. When the other firm does not advertise, you can steal customers from it if you do advertise, when the other firm does advertise, you have to advertise to prevent loss of customers. So, these two firms end up in a bad equilibrium in which both have to waste resources. This market can not apply demand and supply principle to predict consumer behaviours because they depends advertisement to promote their products. If these two firms advertise their products in the same time. Then , it is not possible that if one firm increases it price and it will cause its customer number loss, due to its advertise can help it to attract customers to consider its product from television or radio or newspapers or magazine promotion channels. So, I suppose that these two firms decide to increase their price, when they advertise their products to let customers to know in the same time. They will not lose their customers or reduce their customers easily. Because their customers can be persuaded to choose to buy their products to compare other similar products in preference. So, their increasing price will not influence their customers number lose easily. It explains that demand and supply principle is not right to this case, so demand and supply principle can misuse to help them to predict consumer behaviours when they advertise their products in the same time. Also, demand and supply principle is not suitable to them to predict consumer behaviours when they advertise their products in the same time. They will do wrong prediction to their consumers purchase desire when they advertise their products in the same time.

ON conclusion, using these demand and supply and price elasticity techniques, economists derive specific prediction for how consumers choose which products to buy, how households save, how firms invest, how workers search for jobs, as well as for how these actions depend on the particulars. They can help them to predict job and consumption behaviours more accurate, it depends on whether the situation is right, such as both competition firms participate to advertise their products in the same time case, it is not right to apply above economic principle to predict consumer behaviours. They will get wrong prediction when they apply this principle to predict consumer behaviours.

However, demand and supply principle can predict below any one of these cases. I shall indicate as below:

The problem of need-based scholarships: Most systems for providing college scholarships are based on some definition of financial needs, with scholarships generally being given only to those students who must need financial help in order to attend school.

Is need, rather than academic ability, the best basic on which to choose those students who are to be encouraged to attend college? Which way of choosing who gets aids is the more just? Which is the more efficient ? Is the overall educational level of society increased more by giving financial aid to bright students or to needy students? Presumably the aid offers more leverage to needy students, since they all need the money in order to attend college, whereas, many of the bright students would attend college in any case. But is a smaller number of bright students the more important addition?

So, the school can apply demand and supply principle to predict whether how many parents feel need financial assistance and evaluate how much financial amount is the right to borrow. It aims to calculate how many parents feel real financial need and how much to lend to them in order to let these students to get the most fair financial assistance.

Assuming the school wish to use need as a basis, how does the school determines " financial need"? Is need a function or parents' income? What, then , does the school about children of wealthy parents who are living independently of them and get no aid from parents? Should they be punished for their parents' wealth? But if they are given aid, won't all students, in order to get aid, claim to be independent of their parents?

Is need solely a matter of family income, or should not the school takes a family's financial obligations into account? Does not it make more sense to give aid to someone whose parents must put night more children through school than to someone from a family of five or one only with the same income? But in a possible parallel situations, should a family that carries mortgages on one or two large homes get preference simply because they do not have much money left to spend on college? Does doing this reward ? Is there a difference between the case of night children and the case of the large mortgage? How should parents who are not married , but are living together and supporting their children jointly be counted? Most parents are supporter to their children , although they are married in possible.

So, the school needs to gather all these data to evaluate how many parents are not married or married or living with their children together, how much salary they earn as well as every family has how much children as well as whether they have mortgage for their houses. So, these number will be the financial education assistance demanders, but it does not represent their real financial needs. It is possible that someone does not feel any financial need, although their children apply financial assistance to your school. Then , your school needs to evaluate whether how much financial assistance can lend to every real financial need student family. It can not exceed your final financial expenditure budget (supply) , when your financial expenditure is not enough. SO, demand and supply principle can be applied to research this school real family financial demand to lend to the real financial need families and evaluate whether the reasonable financial amount to lend to every child family to study in your school.

- Supply and demand principle explains Why has it relationship between immigration to US these two regions immigrant number and wage?

A fascinating and important example of supply and demand, full of complexities, is the role of immigration in determining wages. If you ask people , they are likely to tell you that immigration into California or Florida US, surely lowers the wages of people in those regions. It is just supply and demand analysis of immigration. According to this analysis, of these to these two regions in US. Immigration in to a region shifts the supply curve for labor to the right and pushes down wages. Why has it relationship between immigration to US these two regions immigrant number and wage? Careful economic studies cast doubt on this simple proposition, however, a recent survey of the evidence concludes:

The effect of immigration on the labor market outcomes of natives is small in US. There is no evidence of economically significant reductions in native employment. Most analysis, finds that a 10 percent increase in the fraction of immigrants in the population reduced native wages by a most 1%.

How can we explain the small impact of immigration on wages? The main mistake is to forget how mobile the American population is and that the impact of immigration on wages, we must examine the effect of new immigrants when the strength of the local economy and the number of native-born residents in a city are unchanged, that is

, when these other things are held constant. Unless you exclude the effects other changing variables, you can not accurately predict the impact of immigration. The same principle holds in doing a supply0and demand analysis of any market. As much as possible, when you are examining the impact of a supply or demand shift, you must try to keep all other things constant.

Rationing by prices theory

By determining the equilibrium prices and quantities of all inputs and outputs, the market allocated or rations out the scare goods of the society among the possible uses. Who does the rationing? A planning board? Congress or the president? BO, the markplace, through the interaction of supply and demand, doe the rationing. This is rationing by the purse.

What foods are produces? This is answered by the signals of the market price. High oil prices stimulates oil production, whereas low food prices drive resources out of agriculture. Those who have the most dollars votes have the greatest influences on what goods are produced. All of these considers how demand and supply to the market.

For whom are goods produces? The power of the pursue indicates the distribution of income and consumption. Those with higher incomes end up with larger houses, more clothing, and linger vacations. When the most urgently felt needs get fulfilled through through the demand curve.

Even, the how question is decided by supply and demand. When corn prices are low, it is not profitable for farmers to use expensive tractors and irrigation systems, and only the best land is cultivated. When oil prices are high, oil companies drill in deep offshore waters and employ novel seismic techniques to find oil.

IN sum , any thing needs through demands, interact with costs of goods, as reflected in supplies in our economic world. Hence, demand and supply theory ought be the most accurate method to help any businesses or governments to predict their shareholders behaviours when they will change as well as how and how their behaviours change.

New Economic Consumer Choice Theory Solves Consumer Problems

What is 'consumer choice theory'?

'Consumer choice theory' is a hypothesis about why people buy things. Put simply, it says that you choose to buy the things that give you the greatest satisfaction, while keeping within your budget. At the heart of this theory are three assumptions about human nature?

The first assumption is that when you shop, you choose to buy things based on calculated decisions about what will make you happiest. In economics language, this is known as utility maximisation (Economists really like to put quite simple concepts into long complicated terms.)

Secondly, the theory assumes that no matter how much you shop, you will never be completely satisfied. In other words, you will always be happier consuming a little bit more. This is known as the principle of non-satiation.

Thirdly, even though you always get more happiness from more consumption, the amount of pleasure you get from each good decreases with the more you consume. So if you eat two ice creams rather than one, you get more overall pleasure, but the second ice-cream won't be as satisfying as the first. This is known as decreasing marginal utility.

Consumer choice theory has influenced everything from government policy to corporate advertising to academia.But the theory has been criticized for not being the most accurate description of how people actually make choices. A whole new branch of economics, called 'behavioral economics', has emerged essentially to use findings from psychology to disprove the assumptions behind consumer choice theory. This has also led others to argue that consumer choice theory is less about describing how we do actually behave, and is more about describing how people should behave.? In other words, by portraying people as self-interested shopaholics, economists are saying that is it okay and natural for us to be avid consumers.

Consumer choice theory can be applied to solve consumer problems during the country can have economic growth , the reasons may include as below:

The scenario leading to inflation starts with poor growth. Forget about everything that comes next and focus on that most important factor. Because it happens that the scenario leading to a budget crisis also starts with poor growth, and the scenario leading to a long-term unemployment crisis starts with poor growth, and a scenario leading to a begger-thy-neighbour trade crisis starts with poor growth, and so on. So a very important question is: what can be done to improve the prospects for economic growth? In particular, what is the right countercyclical approach to take to best situate the economy for future growth? I shall indicate during US, Amera's economy growth occurs, then economists can attempt to apply customer choice theory to solve US itself country's consumer problems more easier.

In no small part, the question comes down to interpretations of charts like the one at right. On the one hand, long and deep downturns seem to have almost no effect on the long-term rate of growth. On the other hand, in the long run we're all dead, and those who live during an extended period of economic weakness suffer for it. Meanwhile, it's also difficult to see where high debt levels influence the long-run rate of growth, at least where this chart is concerned.

During to the medium-term growth stage, is the bigger threat to American growth rates a market revolt against American debt levels? Or is it structural unemployment stemming from the slow, jobless recovery? Or is the cyclical shortfall in public investment? Or something else entirely?Of course, there's no real reason one has to choose a problem to address at the expense of others. More aggressive monetary expansion could make the finding of a solution to all these problems easier, but the Fed is unwilling to oblige me on this score. It may well be concerned that lack of fiscal discipline will lead to increasing inflation expectations, making its job harder (but then fiscal problems are treaceable to growth). If that is the worry, however, one has to ask why the Congress has been unable to strike a deal for $20 billion in stimulus this year for $80 billion in fiscal tightening in a year or two (fill in whatever amounts you wish). But the outlook for the American economy vis-a-vis any number of potential crises will hinge on growth, and growth will hinge on the ability of private business to exploit promising opportunities as they arise. And the question is: what's likely to hurt that ability most? High interest rates? Lack of consumer demand? A shortage of adequately prepared workers? Right now firms appear to be most worried about demand shortfalls. So how much can you boost demand without making the primary fear high interest rates? A lot, if the expansion is on the monetary side.

- How to spply consumer choice theory to predict Consumer Behavior Marketing at Apple Computer

During US economy growth, Apply computer applies consumer choice theory to solve its computer buyers' choice problems among different kinds of brand computer competitors. Have you ever wondered why Apple is so successful? They were not the first company to invent the personal computer, portable music device, the tablet, the smartphone, software to download music, or the set-top box to name a few. Apple has amassed a brand loyal following like no other brand backed by significant sales, market share, and profitability. So, how does Apple do it? What's the secret behind their success?

Marketing using consumer behavior insight is how Apple succeeds. Even though Steve Jobs and Apple, did not use consumer research in the initial development of most products, consumer behavior plays a huge role in their marketing and ultimately the success of the company. Once a consumer purchases a product or downloads iTunes Apple has access to data the company leverages. Apple uses this information to gain significant insight into the consumer and what drives purchase behavior.

Consumer behavior marketing is an essential ingredient in the current business climate. The companies that apply this type of marketing well have a distinct competitive advantage that distances them from their rivals. Consumer behavior research is the primary driver at the core of any good strategy. Research provides actionable insight and ensures business success.

If you answer no to the following questions, this post is for you?

Are you applying consumer behavior marketing currently?

Have you conducted consumer behavior research within the last two years?

Do you have consumer behavior marketing in your marketing plan with well-defined marketing strategies and tactics?

Are you achieving the maximum results for your organization?

Every business has a target audience and consumer behavior marketing provides the fundamental methods for understanding your target. Consumer behavior research provides the underlying element that drives quality

strategies and ensures business results.
"Marketing is understanding your buyers really, really well. Then creating valuable products, services, and information especially for them to help solve their problems."

The organizations that have an intimate understanding of their target audience possess a competitive advantage over those that do not. Establishing a one-to-one relationship and thorough knowledge of your target audience is a core responsibility for business in the 21st century and beyond. Regardless if you are B2B, B2C, B2G or a hybrid organization you have a target audience. The information in this post can be applied to any business type. This post focuses on Apple (B2C) employing consumer behavior marketing as a critical ingredient for their success.

Hence, Apply computer shops have several computer teachers to teach any visitors how to use its laptops, hen they enquire its any computer salespeople. Due to its salespeople had been trained to learn how to use the different kinds of laptops. So, anyone enquires them, they can answer their enquires concern any computer questions immediately. Then, they will feel Apple laptops are the first choice to compare other kinds of laptops brands. It is one salespeople answering strategies to persuade any Apple computer visitors to feel its any laptops are the first or preference choice to compare its competitors in this computer market, so customer choice economic theory is the most suitable strategy to solve Apple computer's customer individual purchase decision problem.

● Microeconomics Models and Theories solve customer problems

Microeconomics is concerned with the economic decisions and actions of individuals and firms. Within the broad church of microeconomics, there are different theories that emphasise certain assumptions and expectations of economic behaviour. The most important theory is neo-classical theory, which places emphasis on free-markets and the assumption individuals are rational and seek to maximise utility. However, there are many critiques of the neo-classical model, arguing economics is more complex with issues of market failure and irrational behaviour.

Pre-classical microeconomic theory

Before, Adam Smith, economics was more disparate with no commanding overall theory. Philosophers like Aristotle and Plato made references to issues in economics such as division of labour. The dominant ideas, pre-classical economics, were based on theories of mercantilism – the idea a nation should try to accumulate gold.

Classical microeconomic theory

Classical microeconomic theory was developed by Adam Smith (Wealth of Nations, 1776) and later economists, such as David Ricardo The essential aspect of classical microeconomic theory include:
Adam Smith mentioned the 'invisible hand of the market.' He noted how when people act out of self-interest, markets tend to provide goods and services which are demanded by the population. It needed no central price setting, but market forces responded to changes in demand and supply, e.g. a shortage pushes up the price and causes demand to fall.
Smith also investigated topics such as the division of labour, specialisation and economies of scale. The early classical economists emphasised the importance of costs to firms and consumers.

Utility maximisation

An important development of classical economics towards the end of the nineteenth century is the concept of utility maximisation. The concept of utility was developed by philosophers/economists – Jeremy Bentham and John Stuart Mill. In microeconomic theory, it was believed a consumer will buy goods depending on the marginal utility (satisfaction) they get from the good. This theory assumes consumers are rational and seeking to maximise the satisfaction they get.

Neo-classical theory

Neo-classical theory is a modern re-interpretation of classical economics of the nineteenth century. Neo-classical theory places importance on markets, but developed new ideas, especially regarding utility and rational choice theory. Elements of neo-classical theory.
1. Market distribution of goods and services.
2.R ational choice theory. This is the idea individuals hold rational preferences and make rational choices; seeking to maximise their outcomes – be it profit, wages, consumption or investment.

3. People act independently and make use of available information.
4. Marginalism. In neo-classical economics, more emphasis was placed on concepts of marginal utility and marginal cost. We make choices depending on satisfaction we get from one extra unit of a good.

Economists such as Carl Menger, William Stanley Jevons and Marie-Esprit-L?on Walras. and Alfred Marshall developed ideas such as diminishing marginal utility. Many of these neo-classical economic theories were brought together in Alfred Marshall's very influential textbook, Principles of Economics. (1890)
?Note there is some blurring between classical economics and neo-classical economics.
?Neo-classical economics has also come to mean 'orthodox economic theory. To a large extent, it has incorporated new developments in microeconomics, such as theories of market failure, market structure and econometrics.

Theories of Market failure

Neo-classical economics has become associated with a belief in the efficiency of markets. However, microeconomic theory has also incorporated the criticisms and limitations of free-markets. Monopoly. Adam Smith was well aware of the problem of monopolies and how firms could use their market power to set excessive prices. Imperfect competition. In the 1930s, Joan Robinson developed a model of imperfect competition, an awareness many markets were somewhere between monopoly and perfect competition often assumed in neo-classical economics. Externalities. Developed by Arthur C.Pigou in The Economics of Welfare (1920) this is the awareness production and consumption decisions can have harmful (or positive) effects on third parties. Therefore, a free market can lead to overconsumption of demerit goods and negative externalities.Game theory. An awareness, decisions are not linear or simple, but the interdependence of agents influences what we decide to do.

Behavioural economics

The most important trend in recent decades in economics is the greater emphasis placed on aspects of behavioural economics, which uses many insights from related fields such as psychology.

Disputes rational choice theory. The essential element of behavioural economics is that it argues individual agents are often not rational and often do not seek to maximise utility.

Behavioural economics examines how agents can be influenced by biases, and make decisions not predicted by neo-classical economic theory. Behavioural economics can explain the irrational exuberance of booms and busts.

Econometrics

In the post-war period, economics became increasingly mathematical with economists attempting to use mathematics to explain models and theories. Econometrics looks at economic data and seeks to extract simple relationships. The basic tool is the linear regression models and can be used to try and predict consumer spending and demand for labour.

Heterodox models of microeconomics

Heterodox models differ substantially from microeconomic foundations of neo-classical economics. Schools of thought include

Marxist economic theory

Karl Marx developed an alternative perspective on economics. He focused on the surplus value created under the capitalist economic system. To Marx, the invisible hand of the market would be better described as the invisible hand of capitalist exploitation of workers. Marx claimed workers did receive their full labour value but were compensated for their necessary labour only – enabling capitalists to profit from the surplus.

Institutional economics. The role of society and institutions in shaping economic behaviour. For example, Thomas Veblen looked at theories of 'conspicuous consumption' and noted how the desire for social status could drive much economic theory. Institutional economics could be seen as a forerunner for later behavioural economics.

Environmental economics Argues traditional economics wrongly places value on increasing output. The most important thing is creating a sustainable environment which maximises living standards. So, manufacturers need to consider how to manufacture their products , but pollution can not be raised as the same time, because human will face to raise cost of living and living experiences to be poor , even food shortage, water pollution , air pollution , death rate raises when technological productivities brings pollution to our natural environment. Hence, environmental economoic theory is the most suitable to solve manufacturers' pollution problem.

Buddhist economics/non-profit goals. Like environmental economics, this questions the assumption higher incomes and higher output are desirable. The theory of hedonistic relativism suggests higher incomes do nothing to increase happiness levels, and traditional economics can encourage society to pursue materialistic goals which actually create more problems of stress, conflict and environmental degradation.

Some of the basic models you might find in A-Level economics :

Price Discrimination
Perfect competition
Price Mechanism
Monopoly
Oligopoly and kinked demand curve
Game Theory Pricing strategies
Market failure
Behavioural economics

ON conclusion, any macro economy theories can be applied to find the most reasonable methods to solve any customer problems in societies by economists as above. So, I believe that any economic and customer and social problems can be solved by economic theories in our society.

.Developed countries low skillful labour
market wage grows up causing
factors

Nowadays, there are many countries still have low wage labours, even developed countries, such as US, UK , these countries have many workers can not earn high or unreasonable wages to be paid the same wage level to any developing countries, such as China, India normal workers wages level, e.g. arehouse, clearner workers. Why do these developed countries still have unfair or unreasonable or low wages level? What are the reasons cause these developed countries employers treat them to pay their wages in these low skillful jobs in the low wage level and the wage growth is slow. I shall indicate the demand and supply theory to explain these low skillful level workers' low wage level causing reasons as well as the division of labour concept and surplus value of labour theory to explain why developed countries, such as US, UK , they still have low skillful labor market wage grows up or increase workers number labor market environment suitation as below:

The first factor is excess labour supply. In economic view, demand and supply theory as well as division of labor theory and surplus value of labour theory may be applied to explain why developed countries' low skillful workers' normal wage level grows up slowly nowadays in long time. Why do many developed countries still have many low skillful workers to earn the unreasonable low wages level to same to the developing countries? For example, Amazon e-commerce profit firm in US, UK warehouses still pays the same low wage level in these countries, these developed countries' low skillful level workers' wages are the same low level to the developing countries' e-commerce profit firms' warehouse low skillful level workers' wages, such as Hong Kong, China. Their UK, US warehouse picking up or delivery warehouse workers' wages are paid about US$28,000 per year in UK, US Amazon warehouses. Their wages are same to the developing countries' e-commerce firms' warehouse wages level in general. Although, they are working in US, UK developed countries, but these low skillful labours wage level can not be higher than the workers' wages in developing countries in general. Whether the reasons are due to that their low skillful level warehouse jobs, such as picking up or delviery job nature factor or other factors to cause their low pay. However, I feel that their warehouse picking up or delivery job nature is not the main factor to cause these developed countries' low skillful level workers' low pay wage and slow growth reason. I believe that the main factor is analyzed by economic view, it means that these developed countries, such as US, UK , they have more excess number of low skillfil level labour supplies, but there are less employers number, they need to employee low skillful level of workers in their low skillful level job market in developed countries.

Hence in labour supply and demand view, due to these developed countries employers do not need to worry about whether they will have shortage of low skillful of labour supply. So, they pay the common low level of wage to same to the developing countries' low skillful level workers. These developed countries employers will stilll have many low skillful level workers apply their jobs to do in themselves countries job market. In economic view, when supply is more than demand, such as this developed countries' low level skillful labour market case, there are many low skillful level workers need to find jobs or apply jobs to do in these developed countries, but there are less employers need to employ low skillful level workers in these developed countries in the same time. So, it must case that their general wage level can not increase rapidly easily in long time.

So, developed countries' low skillful labour market seems same to developing countries' labour market situation. If workers in developed or developing countries are underpaid and exploited, a profit -seeking businessperson would be able to reap immediate profits by hiring the workers away from their current occupatons ans re-employing them elsewhere in any time easily. They won't need to worry about whether they would feel difficult to find any low skillful level workers to work when their age level is low level in general.

Why has wage growth been grown slowly in developed countries, such as US, UK? Although, developed countries have low unemployment rate, many people can find any kinds of jobs to work very easily. But, it is not possible due to there are many employers feel need to create or increase many low skillful job positions. Otherwise, it is due to there are many people need to seek jobs to do. So, the job seekers number is increasing, but the job position supply number is not increasing , even is decreasing in these developed countries. So, there are lot excess labour supply and less job demand in developed countries, such as US, UK. Hence, it explains why their wages can not raise rapidly as well as low unemployment rate in these developed countries, because there are less job positions demand from these developed countries' employers as well as US, UK are low population country. So, their low skillful level job position competition is also low. Then, it causes low unemployment ratio and low wage level as well as slow raising wage growth effect in these developed countries nowadays.

It means that it has stagnant wages in these developed countries. In fact, country -specific answes don't explain why low wage growth is a global phenomenon whose training for the future and career developement were simply not their problem. So, wages slow growth and low level paid to low skillful labour issue is a global labour market phenonmenon in developed and developing counties nowadays. It is very popular to many employers, they can provide in-house training to teach their low skillful knowledge level workers to learn their related-job knowledge to prepare their career development. So, the developed countries' low skillful level workers can learn any tasks knowledge to prepare to do their new jobs when their new employers provide on-job-training . So, they do not need afraid that they do not learn how to do any kinds of low skillful jobs . It will bring another effect, developed countries employers won't have comparison to whom has owned or had not owned any kinds of task knowledge to prepare to do their tasks when they are employed in beginning. Because every low skillful employees or workers will have in-house training or on-job training learn chance to help them to raise the kinds of low-skillful tasks knowledge level. SO, any low skillful workers must have the same in-house or on-job training learn treatmen from their new employers. Then, their wages will not be influenced to be either higher or lower when they enter their new firms to work in beginning. Their wages level must be the same level, none of reasons are whether they are proficient or low skillful level workers. This is another main factor to influence their wages slow growth in developed countries nowadays.

The another factor may be refugee immigration to the developed countries. Because when there are many refugees can apply to emigrate to these developed countries to live, such as US, UK. Then, they will increase the low-skillful labours number to supply to their domestic labour market. Then, it will increase the labour supply of low skillful level to developed countries' domestic workers supply market because these are many low skillful level of refugees workers , they compete to them to find any low level skillful level jobs to do. So, it brings the effect of excess low skillful worker supplying , when these developed countries employers demand to the low skillful workers number does not increase rapidly. So, in economic view, when the supply exceeds to demand, such as these developed countries , low skillful labour market case, refugee immigration brings excess low skillful workers number increases and employers' low skillful level workers demand number does not increase. So, it explains that why these developed countries low skillful level workers' wages can not grow up rapidly.

The another final factor is that technological development can replace manual low-skillful workers. For example, when (AI) artificial intelligence, robotic technological invention may replace low skillful level workers to manufacture or deliver or pick up jobs in warehouses or factories. So, it explains that developed countries employers do not need any manual workers to help them to do above these simple jobs. So, such as Amazon's UK, US warehouses can apply robotics to replace present workers , it can fire them easily. When any developed countries low skillful workers' employers feel that they do not need to worry about the low skillful level workers number will decrease, even they can apply other mtehtos to replace them in any low skillful level job positions.

On conclusion, in economic view, excess low skillful level workers number supply as well as low demand of low skillful level workers number , due to immigration number increases, robotic technological substitute workers' skillful invention, the low skillful level jobs position need reduces, but domestic low skillful levle workers number increases etc. these factors can cause the developed countries' low skillful workers wages grow up slowly nowadays.

CHAPTER THREE

Explaining technology or employee behavior influences organizational performance

Engagement (Building good organizational culture) Strategy solves Hill Wood Medical Centre organization international different culture difficult cooperation problem

● How and why can engagement strategy solve medical organizational departments difficult culture cooperate problem ?

Organizational cultures and subcultures will influence Hill wood Medical Centre organizational performance and commitments. The subcultures may take precedence over the organizational culture for individual employees and thus gain their commitment. Hill wood medical centre can therefore focus on the relationships of both organizational culture and subcultures to satisfy staffs need to serve patients in happy work environment. Organizational culture includes leadership style and job satisfactory measurement. Hence, employees' commitment was examined in relation to the level of consent to and conflict with managerial strategy. Although, managerial strategy is not the same as leadership, the attributes and skills required in leadership could be seen as an essential part of managerial strategy. Organization culture(s) has (have) a causal modelling approach to examine the determinants of organizational commitment and labour turnover. Organization culture(s) can include a variety of variables , e.g. age, pre-employment expectations, perceived job characteristics and the consideration of leadership style, which all influence organizational commitment indirectly via effects on job satisfaction. I supposed that Hill Wood Medical Centre existed relationship of organizational culture and subcultures to influence staffs feel satisfactory and commitment. Also of interest is the relationship of these variables with leadership style, job satisfaction and subject characteristics, such as age, level of education to its staffs in this hospital.

In Hill Wood Medical Centre organization, its organizational culture was the hospital cultures and subcultures which refer to the culture of the wards or work units or operation rooms to every department staff commitments refer to nurses team and medical service chief medical officer team and surgeons team and administrative department etc their different departments' individual staff's commitments. There is a culture relationship between this medical centre organization commitments and it was measured with administration department and operating rooms and wards department etc different departments' subcultures as well as surgeons and nurses and doctors and administration staffs etc different teams' subcultures. More specifically, it is expected that such as Hill Wood Medical Centre organizational culture could be more supportive and innovative to its different departments, such as wards and surgeons operating rooms and administrative office etc different departments subcultures.

Thus, I believe there is a strong relationship between this medical centre organizational cultures and subcultures and commitment and characteristics of this organizational overall culture, such as corporate values and beliefs commitments and performance to Hill Wood Medical Centre organization. However, I think this medical centre's bureaucratic work practices organizational cultures often result in negative employee commitment due to its supportive work

environment could not result in greater commitment and involvement among employees. For example, these different departments needed to met Sharon Lawson, administrator of Hill Wood Medical Centre to discuss how to solve their departments problems in their meetings in that day, but Sharon Lawson could not had any suggestions in these meeting in that day. It seemed that this medical centre had negative culture and subcultures to get negative results due to who needed to spend time to wait Sharon to meet them and the administrator could not give any suggestions to solve their department problems on that day. Such as Holly from state health department told Sharon the general inspection needed to be improved, e.g. kitchen needed cleanliness and inspectors felt this medical centre needed to allow patients access to drug supplies, but this state health department representative had requested inspection before six months and Helen controller asked Sharon about the new computer hardware who requested six months ago and Helen told Sharon who needed it now for billing efficiency to office use, but Sharon decided to make request to board for computer hardware purchase next meeting and some surgeons were drunk to work in operating rooms, who caused danger to patient's life to cause some patients complained these surgeons, but Sharon did not solve whose complaints at that day immediately and medical staffs were discussing why the medical centre had not purchased one upgraded piece of standard diagnostic equipment used in body scanning $700,000 cost, but Sharon had not enquired whose reasons clearly to decide to buy the equipment next year, but doctors did not understand why Sharon could not purchased this year. Then the nurses agreed to give Sharon a week to investigate the situation

and attempted to resolve it and a meeting was scheduled for next week to review the situation.

Finally the medical centre's attorney needed to wait for twenty minutes to discuss about what steps were to be taken to solve with surgeons, Dr Chambers who was complained about drunk wine work in surgeon operating rooms issue, but Sharon had no more time to meet whom to discuss on that day. Hence, it seemed that this medical centre had not good culture and subcultures in its organization, such as Sharon had not enough time arrangement to meet them to discuss their departments' problems on the same day. It seemed that Hill Wood Medical Centre had no good organizational culture and subcultures to cause staffs conflicts and administration department also wasted much time to handle departments' meetings only. If Hill Wood Medical centre culture and subcultures could be changes, such as every department could attempt to discuss how to solve their problems before who met the administrator . Then I believe that who could give reasons or ideas to support their view point to persuade Sharon made final decision to shorten their meeting time. Hence, this medical centre seemed that it's subcultures and culture were negative.

I supposed that it's nurses team subcultures tended to identify more cooperation closely with different teams, such as surgeons operating rooms team, doctors team, wards team etc departments to compare the administration department. It meant nurses teams' subcultures needed often exhibit greater loyalty and commitment to these departments in the Hill wood Medical Centre organization. Thus, it seemed that it needed better subcultures in nurses teams to share different departments' job to reduce staffs conflicts to serve patients satisfactory. However, Hill Wood Medical Centre organizational culture and subcultures could influence staffs' job satisfaction and commitment positively or negatively due to this medical centre cultural variables could influence their feelings , such as the amount of reward, flexibility of work schedule and balance of work and home life etc. Hence, Hill Wood Medical Centre culture could cause those intrinsic factors to influence every units staffs' feelings of job satisfaction. In relation to educational level and organizational commitment, it seemed that educational level was negatively relative to this Hill Wood Medical centre, such as it could permit surgeons were drunk to work in operating rooms often, it was danger to every patient life during surgeons were drunk to work . Hill Wood Medical Centre overall culture was from low to top level communication channel and bureaucratic work organizational culture was often in negative employee commitment, such as all departments needed to wait the administrator to arrange meeting time to solve their departments problems in the same day. However, much decisions could not get solutions from the administrator.

It seemed that this Hill Wood Medical Centre's bureaucratic organization cultures and subcultures caused Sharon had arranged more meetings on that day to influence who had not enough time to do their departments' duties on that day efficiently due to who only concentrated on handling meetings issues on that day. I think Sharon Lawson who did not know how to arrange what kinds of job duties and meetings which were more important which ought to handle on that day or what kinds of job duties and meetings which were not more important to handle on the same day. Hence, who could not get any discussion result in these meetings on that day due to Sharon, administrator had not enough time to negotiate their departments to solve problems successfully in meetings. In conclusion, this medical centre organizational cultures and subcultures seemed that which were not positive to staffs' commitments and job satisfaction. Such as its different departments needed to spend much time to wait administrator to arrange meetings to discuss their problems, but who did not make any decisions in their meetings. The administrator would influence different departments overall work efficiency and effectiveness to be poor. So, it ought need to change its organization culture and subcultures to raise its different departments‘ efficiency and effectiveness as soon as possible.

● suggestion engagement strategy influences to medical centre departments' staffs build kindly culture efficient cooperative method

Describe the culture or cultures at Hill wood Medical Centre ? Are these subcultures ?

How would you recommend that Sharon administrator measure effectiveness at Hill wood Medical Centre?

The medical centre performance effective evaluation meant to measure whether the degree to its overall organization was improving or deteriorating. The measurement combines quantitative and qualitative analysis and efficiency trend to get the degree of effective result. On the quantitative analyses measurement, e.g. medical errors occurrence rates ; patients medical treatment health rates. On the qualitative analysis measurement, e.g.acquiring executives who communicated a culture of quality through personal supportive polities and investment of resources, such as the degree of diagnostic equipments effectiveness, the degree of staff quality improvement and the degree of health information technological effectiveness and the degree of every patient's service satisfaction etc. Performance measurement effectiveness is well established throughout medical and health care industry, of which include the core areas of finance, operations, clinical care and information technology services as below:

Finance is an organization often measures the efficiency of its accounts receivable, i.e. timely collection of payment for services rendered, such as this Hill Wood medical centre can collect how much payment for services from patients per week and it earns how much profit or loss per week. Operating is an organization needs the lengths of time to take for a patient to receive an appointment in the practice or measures individual patient whose satisfaction with the care received, such as the satisfactory degree of Hill Wood Medical Centre every patient how who feel to every doctor, physician, surgeon and nurse whose service performance and personal attitude to whom. Clinical care is an organization measures how often care is delivered in accordance with evidence based guidelines or how effective that care is in improving every patient outcome, such as whether Hill Wood medical centre had how many doctor and surgeon and physician and nurse numbers who could treat every patient to be health to satisfy who don't feel sick or hurt again after who left this hospital. Information technology is an organization widely integrated into health care settings to support for performance measurement, such as whether Hill Wood medical centre needed to buy how many diagnostic equipments to use to body scanning for surgeons or needed to buy how many computers to office to use to achieve the best performance.

This Hill Wood medical centre needed these processes to measure its quantified numbers to a health care service provided to on behalf of or by a patient that was needed on scientific evidence of efficiency or effectiveness, so it could quantify a specific system, e.g. getting a test done or a service performed and it's outcome could measure to quantify every patient's health status resulting from its nurses and doctors and surgeons and physicians whose health care. Thus, in the clinical area, Hill Wood medical centre could measure every patient outcome to compare to every care standard, such as every patient's test value to measure effectiveness. Measurement effectiveness is central to the concept of this Hill Wood medical centre quality improvement, it provides a
mean to define what medical centres or hospitals actually do and to compare that with the original targets in order to identify opportunities for improvement. On clinical care and operational measure aspect:

Hill Wood medical centre ought to establish standardized and systematic procedures for problem solving to able to test and implement major practice changes. Such as clinical guidelines or care maps for specific conditions or procedures, department specific quality plans with short and long term goals, improved educational and training materials for clinical staff error reduction, hand washing and infection prevention, education materials for patients regarding full prevention, information technology that reduced medication errors and improved data collection etc these changes. To decide whether how much change criteria it ought need to change it's measurement effectiveness was depending on the nature of the change and the rate of acceptance and adoption of staff. It aimed to resistance to change in culture from surgeons and physicians and nurses and doctors; measured how much limited resources were available to use or maintain quality related equipment investment, such as office equipments or operational rooms diagnostic equipments of numbers as well as whether how to make the patient complaint numbers to be reduced to achieve zero tolerance to any staffs as well as whether departmental quality plans could achieve special goals effectiveness measurement as well as whether training could be achieve continuous quality improvement to staffs measure

effectiveness as well as organizational structure change could be raised staffs service performance efficiently, such as whether creation was needed on service quality and addition staff and responsibilities were needed for quality improvement

as well as whether patient care redesign and more training was needed for aides and multi disciplinary leadership teams change. Establishing organizational culture and subcultures of service quality measurement effectiveness aspect as below:

. Setting how long time to achieve short term and long term attainable goals and celebrated successes to individual staff and individual units involved in reaching their goals.

. Keeping the individual unit staff involved in problem identification and problem solving time spending. It aimed to raise everyone to feel much valuing expecting all to participate

to solve any problems in the most shorten time.

On finance and information technology measure effective aspect:

Effective organizational culture and subculture change could encourage every unit leader and peers to be patient, but recognized that changing took time and continuing to keep quality improvement to measure whether it needed how much time to balance quality and financial goals and considering investments, such as how many equipment numbers were needed to buy to provide to office and operational room units to use to raise office productive efficiency and effectiveness as well as operational rooms service efficiency and effectiveness to measure to achieve quality improvement from a short and long term perspective to this Hill Wood medical centre. It aimed to evaluate whether new policies were bringing equipment into operating rooms or office to use was needed or was not needed . I recommend Sharon, administrator needed to indicate these qualitative performance effectiveness measurement questions included:

.What barriers did this medical centre face in implementing the strategies or achieving success?

.Did it overcome those obstacles and if so, how?

In conclusion, to measure effectiveness of this medical centre whether how it could achieve quality improvement for success. I recommend Sharon, administrator needed to consider what should be the indicators to include implementation of aggressive quality targets for performance indicators as well as how to decide tightening of recruitment and standards and enhanced respect for all staffs in enhancement of quality improvement processes to shorten time to solve problems in

efficient manner and hoped to decide new investments in quality related information technology combined with the number of staffs input numbers efficiently and effectively.

Thus, the four core areas of performance measurement was one quality improvement models of high performing effective measurement to Hill Wood Medical Centre.

What do you think some of the effectiveness criteria might be?

I think some outcomes of effectiveness criteria to this Hill Wood medical centre, it might be the practice changes appeared to have resulted in improved outcomes for patients. In

addition to major improvements in the combination quality measures which based on morality, morbidity and complication rates, such as below:

Process/ operations effectiveness criteria: faster receipt of test result, faster patient flow, easier and more efficient data sharing and recording, fewer medication errors. So, I think it could measure the doctors and nurses and surgeons and physicians who serve to every patient's performance whether what effectiveness criteria to these staffs from their every serving patients' satisfactory level. Health related effectiveness criteria: calculate the reductions in morality rates, e.g. the surgeon reducing numbers were drunk to work in operational rooms every month and the patient health numbers every month.

Work environment and reputation effectiveness criteria: increase in patients satisfaction and staff satisfaction numbers and morale improved status numbers every month in this medical centre. If it could increase the numbers of patients satisfaction and staff satisfaction and morale improved status numbers, it would have greater ability to improve service quality to surgeons and doctors and nurses in this medical centre.

Bottom line effectiveness criteria: the effective measurement of decreasing or increasing costs per medical centre units and length of stay for certain conditions and increased or decreased patients admission numbers and market share numbers every month. I think it lacked enough equipments for office to use and diagnostic equipments numbers were needed to be upgraded to use in body scanning because the departments leaders needed to met to Sharon, administrator to permit to buy those equipments urgently. It seemed this medical centre service effectiveness criteria would be poor due to there was not enough equipments to provide to these units to use possibly. Hence, if this medical centre could raised the quantitative and qualitative effectiveness criteria as above, it would change positive outcomes to motivate these units doctors, surgeons, nurses, physicians and administrative individual team leaders and their colleagues to strengthen the service quality improvement process to this Hill Wood medical centre. However, I think this Hill Wood medical centre performance was poor from the above effectiveness criteria analysis. Performance must be defined in relative to explicit goals reflecting the values of various stakeholders.

On conclusion, when the international medical center can have one excellent engagement (good organizational culture) strategy, it can solve international medical staffs whose cooperative challenges more easily. This medical centre internal stakeholders were such as patients, doctors, nurses, surgeons, physicians etc and external stakeholders were patients, debtors, banks, Government shareholders etc. This medical centre performance might be defined according to the achievement of specific targets of either clinic to patient services or internal departmental operations. Targets might relate to traditional hospital functions, such as health treatment, care and rehabilitation as well as administration, ambulatory patient delivered services and health care networks. Following this medical centre evidences which indicated the poor performance of effectiveness criteria, such as Sharon, administrator lacked enough time to meet some department leaders to help them to solve problems successfully on that day, so it caused who needed to make another meetings to discuss their problems again. It seemed the administrator wasted their time to do other important duties on that day efficiently and effectively. I think Sharon, administrator was not one effective administrator in this medical centre. If who could not change whose management attitude to co-operate with other department managers(leaders), then who could cause poor subcultures to different departments to build to this medical centre overall organization culture and who also influenced other department performed ineffective and inefficient results due to Sharon, administrator who did not know how to arrange time to meet them everyone efficiently.

In conclusion, I think if this medical centre hoped to reduce doctors and nurses and surgeons and physicians and administrations etc staffs frequently conflict and maximized work effectiveness of its departments. Sharon administrator had responsibility to change whose personal work attitude to adapt their subcultures to co-operate with different departments. Otherwise, this medical centre would not be maximize effectiveness and would increase staffs conflicts to cause staff turnover numbers to be increased seriously.

England NHS public hospital patient price structure of marketing strategy

1. What do you understand by the concept of a pricing model? Critically discuss their relevance to a public sector service ,such as the NHS.

A price model reflects the fact that companies can generate revenue through a variety of combination of the basic price and prices charged for optional additional items. Some price models may be sustainable by giving away a product at very low price initially, but then charge higher prices for essential items that are needed to make the product function. Sometimes, the dominant pricing model in a market is challenged by a new entrant, with the result that consumers' expectations are changed. The price model can occur in perfectly competitive market or non perfectly competitive market. A perfectly competitive market characteristics include there are many producers supplying the market, each with similar cost structures and each producing an identical product. No single supplier on its own influence the market price because it is not monopoly, water and electricity is managed by government to control the public utility company which can not charge high fee to every householder user at the reasonable price ; both buyers and sellers are free to enter or leave the market and there are no barriers to entry or exit and there is a ready of information for buyers and sellers, for example about competing alternatives, e.g. oil products and stock markets where shares are bought and sold are exist in perfectly competitive market. In perfectly competitive markets, firms are price taker and their ability to set prices is limited by the level of demand and supply within the market they serve. If the total demand go up, all other things being equal, the going rate of prices in the market for their product will rise. Likewise, if there is a drop in total supply for whatever reason (e.g. because of bad weather, there will be further pressure for prices in the market to rise. The final price paid in the market will reflect the balance between supply side and demand side factors.

The model of perfect competition presented the forces of competition may be ideal for consumers because the tendency of market forces to minimize prices and/or maximize firms' outputs. But in such markets, suppliers are forced to be price takers rather than price makers. in a perfectly competitive market, firms are unable to use marketing strategies to affect the price at which they sell. At a higher price, buyers will immediately substitute identical products from other suppliers. Lower prices would be unsustainable in an industry where all firms had similar cost structures. Otherwise, an non perfectly competitive market, firms are able to use marketing strategies to affect the price at which they sell. Such as UK medical service market , private hospitals and public hospitals and clinics which can raise their service fee to their patients to follow their patients demand due to their doctors and nurses service performance, medicines quality and price and patient beds supplies factors to influence their service charges to their patients in UK. Hence, NHS needs to provide different and excellent medical service to its patients to make them to feel it's service is better to other private hospitals and clinics if it wanted to apply price model to its car parking or hospital phone system service charge to its patients because it is a public sector medical service organization. It ought not charge extra service fee to its patients in its hospitals. If it charged extra service fee, such as car parking and hospital phone system service which are same or higher or lower than other private hospitals or clinic , which need to ensure which medicine quality, doctors and nurses performance which are better than private hospitals and clinics and its patient beds need have enough supply to any patients when who feel need to sleep in its hospital. Because NHS image is a non profit medical organization to any UK poor patients, who choose NHS medical service are due to its medical service charge is cheaper than private hospitals and clinics and who feel it can provide free car parking and free hospital phone system service.

A market is defined here need not be a physical location where exchange takes place (as happens in retail and wholesale grocery markets). A market in the economist's sense refers to all individuals and firms who wish either to buy or sell a specific product. A market is defined in terms of products or service and geographic description, so the UK soft drinks market refers to all individuals in the UK who seek to buy soft drinks and the suppliers to that market. The UK medical service market structure can describe as the number of consumers, such as patients and medical providers , such as private hospitals and public hospital , such as NHS (National health service) and clinics; the barriers that exist to prevent new private hospitals or clinics or public assistance hospitals from entering the UK medical service market (or prevent UK patients do not prefer to choose NHS medical service); the extent to which the supply medical services is concentrated in the UK small number patients normally and the degree of collusion that occurs between patients and/or private or public hospitals or clinics medical service providers in the UK medical market. Governments often seek to regulate the prices of key products and service, such as electricity and telephones and public hospitals medical services, so it is important to understand how firms can reconcile the sometimes conflicting approaches of market forces and regulation, such as NHS public sector medical service in United Kingdom. Of course, if NHS public sector medical service planned to charge some non major service fees, such as car parking and hospital phone calling service to its patients and hospital visitors and staffs which are same to private hospitals, it needs to consider pricing model should never be seen as an isolated element of hospital's marketing decision making. It needed to consider its service performance of its doctors and nurses, its social responsibility of public medical service image whether it is better or worse than private hospitals that it had created and NHS 's distribution strategy whether it's patient beds supply numbers are enough to patients and whether it's medicine quality and supplies and prices which are reasonable to compare to private hospitals or clinics in this medical service market in United Kingdom. Private business organization with a broad range if products or services are often price different with their portfolio in quite different ways. They may have developed a price model, which describes the way that it uses pricing of its portfolio to maximize its overall revenue. Hence, one product or service may be charged at a very low price, on the assumption that it can raise higher price if many clients choose to buy its product or consume its service. In some sectors, a number of different pricing models co-exist. For example, in the emerging multi-channel television broadcasting market, some channels are provided free of charge to users, but make revenue from selling advertising space, when others charge to users, either on a monthly/annual basis or a pay to view basis. The idea of a pricing model is familiar to private sector organizations, but do they have a role to play in the public sector? In the UK, pricing models are increasingly being discussed and developed for services which have previously been considered a vital service and available freely to all.

Adrian, P.(2012) showed that the National Health Service (NHS) has a long and proud tradition of providing health service to all, according to an individual's need, paid for out of general taxation, according to individuals' means. Pricing has historically had very little role to play in the NHS. However, from the mid-1990 year, individual NHS trusts began exploiting charges for ancillary services as a means of boosting their revenue. One of the first targets for charging was users of hospitals' car parks. Trusts argued that providing car parks was not central to the mission of NHS trusts, and conveniently, government was encouraging more people to use public transport and leave their cars at home. Critics argued that patients were essentially captive and public transport was not a realistic alternative for most people. However, it showed that at one hospital in London, a patient who attended A&E on the advice of her GP, was charged UK$3.75 for the first two hours' use of the hospital car park and UK$7.5 thereafter. She was ten minutes over the two hour period and therefore had to pay higher charge. She also questioned the fact that charges were reduced to UK$1 per hour after 6:00 PM, when many hospital departments were closed. For private sector service, a lower evening price, when there is not much demand from customers, and plenty of spare capacity, it quite common. But is it right that a hospital should only charges lower prices at the not busy time when much of the hospital itself is closed? If lower prices are designed to stimulate additional demand, it this a realistic prospect when many hospital departments are only available between 9:00 AM to 5:00 PM? Another source of revenue exploited by many hospital trusts from the use of bedside telephones by patients. Many trusts entered agreements with private telephone service providers which allowed incoming and outgoing patient calls only through the officially appointed system, which used a premium rate number.

A proportion of the revenue was retained by the hospital. Conveniently, hospital trusts pointed to evidence that mobile phones could harm sensitive medical equipment , and therefore used this to eliminate competitive pressure from patients' mobile phones, forcing them to use the hospital's own telephone system. The ethic of hospital telephone pricing was challenged by the House of Commons Health Select Committee, which accused some trusts of using excessively outgoing call, adding to patients' costs, and boosting hospital revenue. It cited a hospital in Essex where people wishing to telephone patients were being charges 49p per minute at peak time and 39p off peak. By comparison , a typical household rate for a long distance phone call was around 7p in the peak and 2p in the off peak. The select committee also expressed doubts about whether a ban on mobile phones in hospitals was actually a result of possible interference with medical equipment and recommend visitors should be able to use mobile phone within certain areas of hospitals. So, it seems that UK private hospitals patients phone calling service fee is below than householder phone calling service fee and it is not every patient must need to use phone when who stays in hospital as well as the visitors should able to use mobile phones and who should not use hospital phones within certain areas of hospital, who will not interference with medial equipment. Otherwise, by banning mobile phones, had private hospitals been more concerned about creating a monopoly environment for pricing their telephone service, than any possible risk to their equipment? However, I think National health service (NHS) which is one public government assistant hospital, it can not be same to private hospital to charge unreasonable car parking fee or hospital phone service fee to its patients, due to these ancillary services is not hospital main income source and it is one non profit hospital, it needs to provide the fair and non expensive medial charges to its poor patient segment because who are not rich, so who will prefer to choose NHS medical service to compare to choose private hospital services in United Kingdom.

National health service (NHS) is a privatization, fragmentation and market competition of health care provision supposedly to cut costs and improve the efficiency of the health service in England. The NHS was set up in 1948 year to be a free and accessible care, publicly owned and funded sector service in England. NHS needs to consider to redefine its relationship with health service, limiting the quality and quantity of care it can expect to receive, how it access that care, who is delivering if and even how it is paid for. The result will be poorer, fragmented services with larger differences in quality and access. Services/treatments will cost more and the public will increasingly have to pay for aspects of its care that used to be free at the time of treatment. Traditionally privatization has been through the sale of public assets and services to private owners through the mass sale of shares, e.g. the sale of telecoms, railways, energy or water services. These companies than own the services and are able to make profits from them like any other are able private businesses. In the NHS until now, this model of privatization is taking place through a combination of the reduction of the role of government in regulating health provision, the transfer of services to the private sector through commissioning from any qualified providers, such as independent sector treatment care centers, outsourcing of parts of services to the private sector, the creation of market mechanisms for the distribution of funding within the NHS (e.g. commissioning, payment by results mechanisms, the purchaser-provider split and so called patient choice policies). The use of private finance initiatives that use private money to build new buildings and infrastructure and then the state has to pay, the creation of foundation trusts that are run much more like private businesses and have the ability to raise funding through private patients that pay for services, allowing services to become not for profit organizations, such as social enterprises, cooperatives or mutual and thus leave public ownership, limiting access to certain services previously provided by the NHS. Provided healthcare tends to cost more. It requires a large bureaucracy to operate, with huge transaction costs that come with contracts, billing and litigation. In general, as the proportion of private spending on health care rises, so does the overall cost.

The creation of healthcare market can also impact upon the continuity of care people receive. There is always the threat that the private sectors or other providers who take on a service that doesn't secure the expected financial returns may cut losses and withdraw from the provision of that service. NHS is under increasing financial pressure. For example, surgery like hip and knee replacements are more expensive areas of care, the results cause the loss of training opportunities for junior doctors expenditure spending and other health professionals as ever large shares of routine surgery and medical procedures are diverted away from the NHS. Centers for research and medical innovations are also threatened. This can lead to service being out. NHS hospitals will therefore fail financially and be pushed into greater debt. This could lead to hospital mergers, closure or the private sector coming in to run the service on profit making contracts. NHS will bring poor health care service if it will not increase its service charge price to patients. The poor service will be caused, such as permanent damage may have been inflicted on patients with serious conditions due to the lack of follow up care after treatments. In a second worrying example dangerous delays affected the patients of a privatized out of hours. A competitive market system leads to greater rationing and gradually drives patients to take on more responsibility for funding their own care. It seems this already in the privatization of long term care and dentistry. Patients may soon have to top up the cost of their hospital care in the same way that many already do for community health services. The concern is that the NHS will provide a less comprehensive range of treatments. For the private sector, the aim is to make a profit from every contracts, which is not the same as providing the best service . For example, Southern Cross, where the need to make profit lead to the rapid closure of care homes, leaving old people with no home. Hospital people with learning disabilities and challenging behavior were subject to physical and psychological abuse. Privatization will lead to fragmentation of the health services. This is a process on a commercial footing and redesigning the system along market lives. With different organizations delivering different service in different locations, it is also likely to lead a new health service with some area receiving much better care than others, hardest, leading to greater health inequalities. Fragmentation of services leads to worse clinical outcomes as staff have less opportunity to work in a fully integrated dynamic multi disciplinary team. Patients with complex needs can be particularly considerable.

The impact of privatization on current NHS staff, who are transferred from NHS employment to non NHS organizations would be changed terms and conditions at the time of transfer. These terms and conditions could be changes at some time in the future, staff would no longer be covered by the national negotiating arrangement in the NHS, meaning they would not be entitled to any future pay uplifts or agreed charges to the change terms and conditions of service . If staff moved from this employer to another outsourced community service, who would lose their entitlement to access the NHS pension scheme and would be treated as new staff rather then former NHS staff, the new service provider could argue that the service who will be providing is so different that they will not be requiring staff to transfer. Those staff will than be made redundant. In conclusion, NHS is one public medical service non profit organization. It's pricing model ought be public service price model, such as no price discrimination and non competitor based pricing aim. It may be difficult or undesirable to implement a straightforward price-value relationship with individual of public services for a number of reasons: Such as NHS public sector medical service pricing can be actively used as a means of social policy, subsidized prices are often used to favor particular patient segment groups, such as car parking fee charges to visitors or hospital staffs only as well as hospital phone system service charges to visitors only or prescription medical service charges favor the very ill and unemployed patients and low income patients and students patients.

2. What factors should influence the level of charges at an NHS car park?

Principles for fair hospital car parking, such as NHS is important because its car park service represents the hospital reputation. Charging for car parking is often necessary, but needs to be fair, providing a travel plan for users of all types of transport, controlling parking fairly, with concession for those whose health conditions or work commitments mean they have to park frequently or at anti social hours, showing car park and transport costs and how charges are invested, thinking about the environment and how transport can reduce the NHS 's impact , being open and involve patients and the public. It is important to get car parking and transport policy and it is communication, right to ensure fair access, good patient and staff experience and to protect hospital organization , such as NHS reputation. Clinical and social changes as car ownership to patients, staff and visitors to hospital sites has increased. For services with rural or urban , as public transport infrastructure is less convenient and reliable . When for specialist treatment, some patients need to travel greater distance and modern hospitals have often been located on the edge of population centres.

Car parking is also a factor in patient's experience of using healthcare. When much progress has been achieves to improve the patient environment inside the hospital, including cleanliness and new buildings, patients frequently report dissatisfaction with transport and parking arrangement. Visitors concerns both cost of car parking and also the availability of space for people with an essential need, illustrating the competing demands that managers need to balance. Patient experience is an important objective for hospitals; poor experiences can undermine confidence in clinical quality and stress can be worsened by poor transport and parking policies. Car parking can have a major impact on the local and national reputation of the NHS hospital . As patient choice increases, reputation and loyalty will be key drivers for provider's commercial sustainability. It seems car parking is one important factor to influence patients who choose hospital more than location/ transport/ easy to get to/ reputation of consultants factors. Ensuring that patients can access hospital when they need to is an important part of healthcare delivery. Many patients who need to travel to hospital by car, either because of mobility or illness, a lock of alternatives or through choice. However, providing a car park is not the only component of a travel plan. Access to healthcare should be considered in terms of service planning, decisions on location of services, building design, access routes and the other transport modes. One of the factor of the current changes to the way that NHS hospital services are delivered is that healthcare should be localized where possible. In many cases, people who used to have to travel to hospital are being treated in community health centers. The NHS hospital can also ensure services are accessible. Most notably, ease of access has recently been improved by reducing waiting times and by enabling patients to choose and book their appointment at a time and location that is convenient to them. Another of factor is whether NHS hospital had or had not ran a bus service from a nearby park and ride car park that runs every 15 minutes. The service has proved popular and is now run by the UK country council.

The hospital is been to extend the shuttle service to the other three park and ride car parks which serve the city. The other factor influences NHS hospital charge includes the control parking fairly with concessions for those whose health conditions or work commitments mean they have to park frequently or at anti-social ours. In order to ensure that those patients who really need to access hospital by car are able to NHS often need to ensure that car parking space is available on site. Space is usually constrained, NHS hospital is in city or town center with high land costs and planning constraints. Charging some patients, visitors and staff to park can manage demand for space when ensuring that those who really need to park are able to access services. Where charging is required to manage demand, the overriding principle should be to ensure that where possible those patients who have the greatest need to park are prioritized. Where managing demand is a reason for charging for car parking, there may be scope for varying rates for different times of the day and the week, for example, increasing charges for non essential users in peak hours but applying a minimal charge at night when there is less reason to ration space. As well as prioritizing car access for those with greatest needs restrictions on car parking may also be required to deter non hospital traffic, particularly where NHS hospital is located in controlled parking zones, near shopping centers or other facilities that might need to illegitimate required use of NHS hospital grounds. In these cases , NHS hospital may be required to be charge the same as local car parks to avoid abuse by non visitors. However, alternative arrangement could also be explored, including day permits for people with appointment. NHS car parking fair policies should need to be fair application. This is often a cause of concern for patients and visitors.

Concessionary schemes and season tickets should be well publicized and available, since a patient may not known in advance low frequently who will need to attend a clinic in the next month. Penalty charges, or towing away should only be applied extreme circumstances with a presumption of good faith that no patient or visitor chooses to stay in hospital longer than necessary and may how on arrival how long who will have to wait for treatment. Running a car park can be expensive. These are maintenance, security, insurance and running costs and the NHS hospital has to pay for the space the car park uses. Costs are particularly high where land prices are high or there is increased risk of crime. At the same time, patients and the public rightly don't expect healthcare to suffer to pay for parking. The transport costs of non car owners are not subsidized by the NHS budgets to provide subsidized free car parks . To make car parking fee would be to penalize those using public transport. Therefore, fair charging is often the most sensible answer to adopt these two demands. Climate charge and pollution and congestion factor also have health impacts. Reducing car dependency is also a public health objective in order to reduce traffic accidents and increase physical activity.

These NHS organizations have a number of environmental and health reasons to seek to encourage people to use other modes of transport. Parking charge together with the expansion of alternative bus an cycling options to encourage a modal shift from cars to alternative transport. Patients , visitors and staff need to be made aware of these aims. NHS hospital can achieve a travel plan to develop to its car parking with the aim of during a period of busy time reducing single occupancy car journeys by 15% over three years, ensuring tat patients and visitors do not have to search for a space for more than ten minutes at peak times, encouraging the number of direct bus routes to the site to increase reducing staff parking spaces per employee by 10% as staff numbers grow. Car parking charges were introduced as part of the plan with certain categories of staff on exempted from charges (night and weekend staff, disabled staff, volunteers, car sharers and tenants of residential accommodation. From an environmental perspective, NHS travel plan supposed to reduce numbers of cars arriving at the site and the numbers of bus car raise. It aims to improve bus services to cause air pollution at the busy car parking period and cycle parking spaces and improved cycle facilities have encouraged staff to commute by bike. Additionally, a park and ride scheme aims to reduce car traffic of the NHS hospital in the busy time.

Moreover, it is absolutely wrong to charge cancer patients regardless of income, for unavoidable parking costs. From a staff point of view, NHS hospital car parking is an indirect tax on healthcare. However, most unions also support the aim of reducing car usage, as long as policies are fair. Because NHS hospital needs to develop transport policies for patients requiring regular cancer treatment. This approach has potentially negative publicity into a positive image to public. These ought be free parking for the duration of a cancer patient treatment or as often as is needed. So, price structure strategy will be needed to this UK hospital to solve nowadays challenge.

● Outsourcing service Strategy solves Unversity cost raising challenges

If you are studying at a university or college, critically reflect on the pricing strategy that it has adopted for ancillary services.

The development of a costing and pricing strategy will provide an university staff with greater access to price information, thereby providing a more accessible platform from which to base negotiations with commercial organizations. As prices will be informed by cost, the university will be seeking to apply pricing strategies that maximize university as opposed to maximizing income. In fact, any universities is education industry which is different to common businesses which provide service or product to raise price when client numbers are increasing easily. Due to if an university which planed to increase school fee to charge students, which needed have unique courses to attract students to choose to study and its lecturers educational experiences and education methods needed to make student to raise learning interest and feel the courses are useful to choose to study the university subjects, so who shall compare the university subjects to other universities subjects, then to evaluate their school fees and lectures educational experiences and qualifications to decide whether who ought to choose the university or another university to study. So, I believe that the university can not raise its school fee easily if it has no more confident its subjects and lecturers which can make students to study to feel more satisfactory till to graduate. Otherwise, it will reduce student admission numbers if it still increase school fees, due to it has not researched what the subject contents are students who like to learn. Hence, any universities can't increase its school fee easily.

However, university ancillary services have primary paths to reduce internal cost to raise competitive advantages, such as services differentiation, low internal cost or internal span structural advantage. I shall recommend these price strategy to adopt to reflect some university ancillary service (non major) service. The pursuit of a service differentiation strategy to an university advantages. The university needs truly understanding its unique core service (value) and then focusing resources on its ancillary services. An implicit part of having a focused price strategy is not only defining what the university is going to invest in, but is also clearly articulating what the university is no going to do. For example, if the university investigated its students did not like to eat some foods taste, which ought to change some foods taste which could satisfy its students eating needs in its university canteens. Even the university could charge cheaper student parking fee to compare outside public car parks when they park their cars in university parks from the morning to afternoon studying busy time. It could only permit students to park their cars in its students private car parks. Hence, university staffs and visitors could not permit to drive whose cars to park in university private student car parks, so university staffs could park whose cars in university staffs car parks as well as visitors could park whose cars in university visitors car parks. However, who also needed to pay cheaper parking fee to compare outside public car parks to buy car park tickets to park their cars in university staffs and visitors both car parks in any limited time. Even, the university book shop could sell lower second hand books and new books prices to compare other private book shops to attract students to choose to buy studying books from university bookshops. However, if the university tried to pursue too many areas of service differentiation, which was likely to invest too broadly and thus reduced the return on investment for previous capital possibly because it needed time to research whether which aspects of it needed to change to adopted students tastes to satisfy their needs, then it needed time to change its services and it also needed time to evaluate whether it's changed services which can satisfy its students demand to make decision to raise its service prices. Hence, it ought concentrate on changing one aspect of ancillary service to ensure it's changing was right to adopt students' taste to attempt to raise service price. Then, it could attempt to evaluate whether what ancillary services which needed to change to achieve price raising possibility. University recognizes that focusing on the core is hard to do, given the history and culture of university. But the worst case scenario for an university is to be relatively expensive and completely undifferentiated. Whether will who pay high school fee per year to go to an university that is completely undistinguished on any ancillary service?

An university looks to areas where which can make cuts and achieves efficiencies, an university should start farthest from the core of teaching and research ancillary services. Cutting from the outside in and building from the inside out. Growth in programs and research, increasing faculty and student demands and increasingly compliance requirements have all contributed to the growth of administrative costs. The reasons are often very legitimate. But as new programs are added, old programs often are closed down in some university ancillary services, e.g. unimportant administration internal service . The resulting breadth of campus activities creates too much complex it for staffs to manage with any efficiencies of scale in university. Units don't trust one another or the center to provide ancillary services. Data center management is a good example of fragmentation on campus. At the university, the central information technology group managed fewer than half of the servers on campus in its data center. For the servers located in the colleges, fewer than half were managed by college information technology groups, the rest were considered hidden at the department or faculty level. Despite the internet data and security risk of having too many unmanaged serves on campus in the university's central information technology department. In similar cases, outsourcing data centers would be a good solution. Third party data centers could provide more solutions, higher levels of securing, greater flexibility in capacity and lower cost than internal solution. Redundancy, an university is an many other campuses, it was managed at the department level, there were no product standards and each department negotiated its own vendor contracts. A sample of purchase order showed that the same item was being bought for as much as e.g. 36% more in some departments than in others. By centralizing end, standardizing more if its procurement to expect to save more expenditure. An university hierarchy, most campuses have too many middle managers. Before it reorganized , an university has average spans of control (the number of employment). Campuses engage to save cost. An university campuses engage in too many activities that require to broad a skill set to effectively deliver in house. Take information technology application management for example, not only does it need to support classrooms and research needs across a diverse set of disciplines (history, music, law, engineering, biomedical science etc. different subjects), it also has to cover functions (finance, human resource, research, administration, student registrar, libraries and student services etc. functions). It weren't enough, information technology also has to serve industries beyond the core academics, including bookstores, retail food, debt cards, total museums, publishing houses. A single IT group would have a hard time managing all it that well, given the expertise required, leading to either poor service delivery, sub scale and costly delivery.

Outsourcing more of non core activities would reduce campus complexity and cost. Third party provides have greater scale capability and skill because the outsourced service is their core business, enabling them to deliver the same or better service at a lower cost. In order to reduce aministrative costs without diminishing service and perhaps even enhancing it's campuses will need to subscale operations by creating shared service or outsourcing improve processes by eliminating low value work and automating much. Better manage university assets to whether it is real estate, physical assets or intellectual property, a number of activities where partnership with third party providers would allow for financial relief and improved performance. Hence, an university can also invest its intellectual property to build its build to raise its market value for long term to raise its sale price for long term.

In conclusion, an university can attempt to use these two kinds of price strategies to adopt to reflect to its ancillary services. Such as the first is competitors price strategy, the university can set its students and visitors and staffs car parking fee by examining what its competitors such as, it's close public car parks are charging their car parking fee services whether they are similar in terms of the university car parking service characteristics fee to satisfy its parking car users' needs as well as the university can set its canteens meals price by examining what its competitors, such as it's close private outside restaurants meals price whether they are similar or different taste and low meal price to attract students or staffs or visitors to choose to eat their meals . The another is demand based pricing strategy, the students are prepared to pay represents the upper limit book numbers to the university's every year studying books. Such as the university book shops can decide every years different subject second hand or new teaching books price to follow the students demand. For example, if the subject second hand or new teaching books supply numbers is less than the student demand numbers, the university can raise the subject books sale price. Otherwise, if the subject second hand or new teaching books supply numbers is more than the student demand numbers, the university needs to reduce the subject books sale price, even it needs to reduce their prices to be lower than outside other private book shops marketing price to sell in the year. Hence, it seems that any universities can adapt price strategy to reflect to their services or products prices.

- Outsoucing service strategy can help this university to solve staff management challenge.

When you are one university entrepreneur how you manage university leaders to raise excellent management performance. Frances Workman could own those above personal trait leadership characteristics to do this Willard University president job successfully. For example, Frances workman has been president of Willard University for less than two years. Frances had been an excellent speaker and used every opportunity to speak to citizen groups as well as who also worked hard to build good relationship with the major politicians and business leaders and who managed to maintain favourable relationship with most. Frances had proved to own a trait leader's personality ability, such as intelligence and verbal fluency, self confidence and interpersonal skill. Frances was an achievement drive leader, such as France could lobbied legislature and the Willard Universitycoordinating board for a larger share of higher education budget dollars. In the result, Frances could build favourable image to efforts to increase funding for Willard University within two years, as well as Frances president, could build a positive image to people and let them to build a positive image to people and let them to build a positive image of Willard University . The results of whose efforts included an increase in enrolment of more in the last year.

This occurred when most other colleges enrolments were also decreasing as well as $2 million dollars outside funds were donated to Willard University and faculty morale was higher in the first year. Hence, Frances could judge and adapt and dominance and was tolerance for stress to deal new issue to achieve this Willard University aim successfully within two years. It proved that Frances owned trait leadership style. However, Frances was seemed to be employee centre leadership style president, it meant a behavioural leadership style that emphasised employees' personal needs and the development of interpersonal relationships and a employee centre leader frequently delegated decision making authority and responsibility to others and provided a supportive environment, encouraging interpersonal communication. For example, Frances president, concentrated on handling external matters and who delegated the responsibility for daily internal operations to whose three major vice presidents. Hence, Frances could build concentrate on building positive image to public people and let them to build a positive image of Willard University. Finally,Frances could help Willard University to increase student enrolment numbers of more in the last year and $2 million outside funds were donated to Willard University and faculty morale was higher in the first year. Otherwise, this occurred when most other college enrolments were also decreasing. Thus, it proved Frances Workman leadership skill was successfully. Secondly, based on information provided, Alvin Thomas was lack trait theory of leadership style personal characteristics, who was not such as self esteem and dominance, whose ability was not such as intelligence and non verbal fluency, non judgement, non adaptability, non enthusiasm, non achievement drive, lack self confidence , non tolerance for stress and non interpersonal skill. Hence, Alvin Thomas lacked trait leadership style to do Eastern State University president successfully. For example, Alvin Thomas had been president as Eastern State University about three years, who was not as popular externally as Frances and who was not a particularly effective speaker. Hence, it proved Alvin Thomas was not a verbal fluency and lack interpersonal
skill president.

suggestion of solvable method:

Based on the information provides, describe France's and AI's leadership styles.

Leadership means the process of providing general direction and influencing individuals or groups to achieve goals. Formal leader can be formally designated by the organization or informal leader can provide leadership without such formal designation. Leader needs to lead group, team and social processes can directly or indirectly affect behaviour in organizations. The behaviour of leader has positive effects to link between leadership and organizational performance and who needs have developed a vision as well as specific goals to whose organization. Leadership styles (traits) that have been identified as important include flexibility and creativity, especially because of the importance of innovation to leader whose organization. Firstly, based on information provided, France's was belonged to trait theory of leadership style, trait leadership style includes those personality characteristics, leader was such as self esteem and dominance; leader's ability was such as intelligence and verbal fluency, judgement, adaptability, enthusiasm, achievement drive, self confidence, tolerance for stress and interpersonal skill. Frances Workman could own those above personal trait leadership characteristics to do this Willard University president job successfully. For example, Frances workman has been president of Willard University for less than two years. Frances had been an excellent speaker and used every opportunity to speak to citizen groups as well as who also worked hard to build good relationship with the major politicians and business leaders and who managed to maintain favourable relationship with most. Frances had proved to own a trait leader's personality ability, such as intelligence and verbal fluency, self confidence and interpersonal skill. Frances was an achievement drive leader, such as France could lobbied legislature and the Willard Universitycoordinating board for a larger share of higher education budget dollars. In the result, Frances could build favourable image to efforts to increase funding for Willard University within two years, as well as Frances president, could build a positive image to people and let them to build a positive image to people and let them to build a positive image of Willard University . The results of whose efforts included an increase in enrolment of more in the last year. This occurred when most other colleges enrolments were also decreasing as well as $2 million dollars outside funds were donated to Willard University and faculty morale was higher in the first year. Hence, Frances could judge and adapt and dominance and was tolerance for stress to deal new issue to achieve this Willard University aim successfully within two years. It proved that Frances owned trait leadership style. However, Frances was seemed to be employee centre leadership style president, it meant a behavioural leadership style that emphasised employees' personal needs and the development of interpersonal relationships and a employee centre leader frequently delegated decision making authority and responsibility to others and provided a supportive environment, encouraging interpersonal communication. For example, Frances president, concentrated on handling external matters and who delegated the responsibility for daily internal operations to whose three major vice presidents. Hence, Frances could build concentrate on building positive image to public people and let them to build a positive image of Willard University. Finally,Frances could help Willard University to increase student enrolment numbers of more in the last year and $2 million outside funds were donated to Willard University and faculty morale was higher in the first year. Otherwise, this occurred when most other college enrolments were also decreasing. Thus, it proved Frances Workman leadership skill was successfully. Secondly, based on information provided, Alvin Thomas was lack trait theory of leadership style personal characteristics, who was not such as self esteem and dominance, whose ability was not such as intelligence and non verbal fluency, non judgement, non adaptability, non enthusiasm, non achievement drive, lack self confidence , non tolerance for stress and non interpersonal skill. Hence, Alvin Thomas lacked trait leadership style to do Eastern State University president successfully. For example, Alvin Thomas had been president as Eastern State University about three years, who was not as popular externally as Frances and who was not a particularly effective speaker. Hence, it proved Alvin Thomas was not a verbal fluency and lack interpersonal skill president.

A path goal leadership theory focuses on several types of leader behaviour and situation factors as well as Directive leadership behaviour is characterized by implementing guideline, providing information on what is expected, setting definite performance standards and ensuring individuals follow the rules. Participative leadership behaviour is characterized by sharing information, consulting with those whose who are led and emphasizing group decision making. However, Alvin Thomas was seemed to be job centre leadership style president, it emphasises employer tasks and the methods used to accomplish them. A job centre leader supervises individuals closely , provides instructions, checks frequently on performance and sometimes behaves in a punitive manner toward them. For example, who did not spend much time dealing with the external affairs of the University, who delegated much of that responsibility to one vice president. Hence, who spent much of whose time working on the internal operation of the University and less of whose time working on the external affairs. Although, who delegated much of responsibility to one vice president to assist who to do external affairs, but Eastern State University's a large number of students still without adequate faulty and it was not involved in externally funded research as well as although, who spent much time dealing with the internal operation of the University and who was committed to develop a quality University, but who did not change the administrative structure of the University within three years. He seemed to lack leadership skill. For example, who planned to give responsibility to one vice president and who had high performance expectation to them, set ambitious, goals and reviewed every significant decision made in the University and replying heavily on whose vice president to implement them effectively and who developed planning system and maintained good relations with University board. Hence, who often needed to supervise whose every vice presidents to deal external affairs closely and provided instructions, checked frequently on their every performance within those three years. But, Eastern State University student enrolment numbers declined slightly by almost 300 students and Eastern State University record was removed from American association of University professors, externally funded research had increased by approximately by $2 million dollars during the previous year, even faculty morale was declining and most faculty members did not believe who had an important voice in the administration of the University. However, who spent much of his time working on the internal operation of the University, but faculty morale was declining and most faculty members did not believe who had an important voice in the administration of the University as well as who could not lead to the one vice president and who also could not provide instructions and checked whose performance how to deal external affairs correctly. Hence, it implied that whose leadership skill was not successful within these three years.

What are the important factors that the leaders of Willard and Eastern must consider in order to be effective?

The important factors that the leaders of Willard University and Eastern State University must consider in order to be effective as below:

Outsoucing service strategy can help this university to solve staff management challenge. The Eastern State University president, Alvin Thomas both were as their organizations‘ chief executive officers who were very important given the substantial influence design Universities strategies and overseeing Universities’ implementation to lead their vice presidents to deal internal or external affairs efficiently and effectively. Frances Workman and Alvin Thomas both presidents needed to develop a vision for their Universities‘ units or groups led, who also needed to manage Universities limited resources under their direction to include financial capital, but especially human capital, e.g. vice president and administrator position numbers and who also needed to build valuable interpersonal relationships (social capital) with University staffs and good University images (goodwill) to let current and future students and parents to fell those two Universities goodwill existed in global education market. Hence, both Willard University and Eastern State University both presidents needed to provide effective leadership that could enhance associates productivity, e.g. Improving lecturers’ teaching methods and skills and improving office administrators and service staffs whose service performance to manage human capital well and built and maintained relationships both with whose Universities‘ different organizations(departments) with internal associates and other leaders ,e.g. vice presidents and externally with alliance partners and colleges and universities.Those two university presidents ought need to criticize if their universities didn’t meet their goals or their university teams have a losing reason. Hence, these two university presidents needed to revise their performance to find why their universities could not achieve their goals and they needed to discuss any meetings to attempt to find any solutions from university boards every year. These two university presidents (leaders) needed to provide direction and to influence all universities staffs during who begun to do their new jobs and during who were doing their new jobs, who needed to attempt to do these activities effectively, e.g. providing useful information (guidelines) to assist vice presidents how to carry on dealing their external and internal affairs, resolving conflicts, motivating followers, anticipating problems, developing mutual respect among groups (university departments)members and coordinating groups (departments) activities and efforts. It aimed to revise what presidents do activities were not effective and then they could know what activities who needed to change to discuss with vice presidents to find solutions more effectively.These two university presidents also needed to build leader member relations, it meant the degree to which a leader was respected and was accepted as a leader and had friendly interpersonal relations. If these two presidents could build friendly interpersonal relations to their colleges, such as vice presidents, administrators etc senior staffs. It would increase these staffs confidence and assistance to these two presidents further the years. Thus, if these two universities’ presidents could attempt to change their management attitude to their colleagues (staffs), special senior position staffs, then I believed that they could lead their universities‘ different teams (departments) to work more effectively.

In fact, not all people in positions that call for leader behaviour, e.g. management positions. A manager who follows rules and fails to provide direction to and support for whose associates is not acting as a leader.The measuring the effectiveness of leaders factors include productivity, job satisfaction, absenteeism, turnover rates of staffs being led. Thus, the presidents of these two universities needed to consider how to lead whose staffs to work effectively in order to achieve their universities' aim every year. Otherwise, these two presidents would be only a manager role who only followed universities' rules to work, but who did not provided direction to and supported to their associates effectively. Hence, who would not acting as a leader role. Any leaders who need have leadership traits characteristics include that driver refers to the amount ambition; leadership motivation refers to a person's desire to lead and influence others; assuming responsibility; leaders with honesty are truthful what they say and what they do; leaders must be confident in their actions and showing that confidence to other; leaders who posses a high degree of intelligence are better able to process complex information and deal with changing environments and these two presidents(leaders) of this two universities needed to prepare management knowledge of the domain in which who were engaged allows who to make better decisions and prepared to anticipate future their universities internal and external issues and understood the implications of their colleges, e.g. vice president actions easily.

Compare and contrast France's and AI's effectiveness as leaders of their respective Universities .

In fact, Willard University president Frances Workman ,whose leadership was more effective than Eastern State University president Alvin Thomas performance. The reasons were that Frances had worked in Willard University for less than two year, who could deal external issues and internal structure of the organization, administrative component effectively. For example, Frances had started a new alumni club to help finance academic needs, such as new library facilities and higher salaries for faculty and staff successfully. In addition, who lobbies legislative and the university coordinating board for a larger share of higher education budget dollars. In the result, her favourable image to efforts to increase funding for Willard University. Frances could concentrate on handling external matters and who delegated the responsibility for internal operations to her three major vice presidents.However, before Frances arrival, this university had several presidents, but none of whom could manage university's internal affairs effectively. Due to the lack of leadership resulted in low faculty morale, which affected student enrolment to cause university had a poor public image. Otherwise, after Frances arrival, who could build a positive image to people and let them to build a positive image of Willard University. The results of whose efforts include an increase in enrolment of more in the last year. This occurred when other colleges enrolments were also decreasing. Hence, Willard University had a serious competition to it's competitors and $2 million dollars outside funds were donated to Willard University and faculty morale were higher in the first year. Otherwise, another Eastern State university, had Alvin Thomas as president who had been president about three years longer than France's working period and who was not as popular externally as Frances, who was not a particularly effective speaker and did not spend much time dealing with the external affairs of the university, who delegated much of that responsibility to one vice president, who did work with external groups but in a quieter may than Frances did and who spent much of his time working on the internal operation of the university. However, who led this university poorly and the Eastern State University had these problems which included a large number of students without adequate faculty; it was not involved in externally funded research. Although, who was committed to develop a quality university, but who did not change the internal operational administrative structure of this university from his one vice president successfully. In fact, State University still had more students than Willard University, but its student enrolment declined slightly by almost 300 students after Alvin Thomas started to manage this university. Although, Alvin Thomas had high performance expectations to staffs, set ambitious goals and reviewed every significant decision made in the university and replying heavily on whose one vice president to implement them effectively and who developed planning system and maintained good relations with university board. However, State University record was removed from American association of university professors, although, externally funded research had increased by approximately $2 million dollars only during whose three years working periods; but faculty morale was declining and most faculty members did not believe who had an important voice in the administration of the university. Hence, Alvin Thomas who could not lead faculty staffs built confidence to continue to serve this university and who could not raise public had confident its lecturers whose educational quality and performance.

What did each do well?

The Willard University president, Frances Workman who performed more well to compare another Eastern State University president, Alvin Thomas as below:

France had performed as an excellent speaker and used every opportunity to speak to citizen groups as well as who also worked hard to build good relationship with the major politicians and business leaders and who managed to maintain favourable relationship with most. Hence, who could build favourable image to efforts to increase funding for Willard University within two years. Frances knew whose strengths, so who concentrated on handling external matters and who delegated the responsibility for daily internal operations to whose three major vice presidents.

In conclusion, who was an effective leader to lead three vice presidents and the student numbers were also increasing largely and Willard University and faculty morale was higher in the first year during Frances had worked in the university within two years.

The Eastern State University president, Alvin Thomas could not perform well within three years. Although,who did not spend much time dealing with the external affairs of the university and who delegated much of that responsibility to one vice president to deal external affairs, so who could spend much of whose time working on the internal operations and less of whose time working on external affairs. However, Eastern State University's a large number of students still without adequate faculty and it was not involved in externally funded research and who did not change the administrative structure during Alvin had worked in the university three years. In the result, student enrolment numbers declined slightly by almost 300 students and university record was removed from American association of university professors, even faculty morale was declining and most faculty numbers did not believe who had an important voice in the administration of the university. Hence, who only knew how to delegate to give responsibility to only one vice president to deal internal operations and who concentrated on dealing external affairs alone. However, externally funded research had increased by approximately by $2 million dollars during the previous year. In conclusion, Alvin Thomas could not lead whose teams to deal external affairs and internal operations effectively to compare to Frances Workman, who only helped university to give funded research $2 million amount increased, but who could not build good university image and raised department administration efficiency effectively within these three year.

What could each have done to be more effective?

I should recommend these methods to raise these both university presidents Alvin and Frances whose leadership who each could have done to be more effectively. It would be divided internal operations and external affairs two aspects:

On the dealing external affairs hand, they needed have clear external marketing and communication strategic plan. It aimed to create marketing, communication and branding strategies that maximize demand for these two universities' degree course programs to persuade many external parties (donors) to donate more to support them. First, they could oversee the editorial direction, design and production of all publications, universities web properties, social media initiatives, advertising and media with a goal of creating dynamic and engaging materials that reflected the key brand attributed of these both universities.Second, they needed to lead crisis and issues management planning and rapid response messaging to deal strategic counsel on reputation and issues management to senior leadership.

Third, they needed set strategy for marketing, communication, advertising and promotions to ensure that all messages from their universities were accurate, consistent and presented a image and they needed to built partner with university leaderships to generate innovative ideas and solutions to engage donors. Fourth, they needed to oversee the development and execution of their strategies for their universities' interactive and social media programs and supervised the development and deployment of web/social media sites aimed at enhancing their universities' brands and reputation as well as they needed to lead a diverse team of web producers, graphic designers, project managers, marketing and editorial writers, media specialists to provide mentorship to staffs both in terms of departmental strategies. Aimed to increase donation chances and student numbers for long term.Fifth, they needed to cultivate strong working relationships with staff faculty and students across their universities and they also needed to raise the value of the Willard University and Eastern State University and effective studying market to present whose universities' history (stories) to know.They could attempt to use these communication medias (channels), social media e.g. university magazines, radio or television advertisements and other forms of digital communication. Proven success at developing and implementing online and social media strategies to enhance visibility and engagement and loyalty.The most important, their vice presidents also needed to appreciate for their universities' history, achievement and aspirations of Willard and Eastern State Universities and the ability to effectively articulate whose presidents' vision to diverse external audiences as well as who also needed to have ability to synthesize complex information and produced marketing and communication materials that addressed a wide variety of goals and objectives as well as they also needed to have excellent judgement and creative problems and solving skills including negotiation and conflict resolution as well as who also needed have confidence to project credibility to the media and other strategic stakeholders.Moreover, these two university presidents needed to prepare enough resources to provide, e.g. strategies, media communication channel, excellent leadership skill and effective human resources. The, these two presidents(leaders) could have more ability to attempt to perform more effective for their job duties.

These two universities presidents' fundraising responsibilities were creation and communication of a vision for their universities. Thus, they should temper whose ideas and goals to match the overall fundraising potential of their universities. The fund donors wanted to know about their presidents' vision and their universities; strategic direction along with the resources their universities needed to get.

Conversations between these presidents and prospective major donors and who would focus on what the donors wanted whose gift to accomplish. It is important to listen to the donors rather than drive hard. Fundraising included not only such factors as having a clear vision for these two universities and strategic priorities that would be reason with prospective donors and afforded sufficient fundraising potential, but also possessing a professional staff with the expertise and budget to get job along and a commitment was from the president of their time and energy to lead the campaign to successful completion. Seeking external fundraising counsel was often very useful to these two universities. Hence, these two presidents should also recognize that the long term nature of donor relationships was that who existed between the donor and their universities, not with these two presidents personally due to these presidents, academic deans, faculty members and professional fundraising staffs were agents role acting on behalf of their universities. On the dealing internal operational affairs hand, If these two university presidents were going to spend most of their time leading, then who needed to recruit others to do the managing. They needed to put together a group of managers to every university departments, e.g. administration, marketing and communication, finance and accounting ,student service, education etc departments. It aimed to let every department had a manager (leader) to lead their teams to adopt every department sudden changing in any time. After appointed these staffs, they must be delegated to deal as much of the problem solving. Moreover, their universities' committee chairing also needed to be delegated to avoid to deal extra internal operations with detail and caused to have too little time to perform the key function of setting the target and motivating people for their main duties. To lead change successfully, these both university presidents needed an effective decision making structure that could respond rapidly to internal and external affairs and pressures. It meant making the decision making structures needed to become less hierarchal and complex. Many changes were failure because the vision and the strategies were not adequately communicated to the staffs to get whose commitment and support to achieve organizational success effectively.They also needed effective communication strategy for their universities, normal methods of communication,internal newspapers, meetings with deans and heads of universities which were all important. Moreover, they also needed to visit other universities and departments regularly, held informal meetings with small groups of senior staffs, recruits and other natural groupings.These two universities also needed to considerate how to evaluate staff performance to compensate them to feel fairly.The new systems of appraisal method, including 360 degree assessment for senior management and promotion which together linked the work of individuals much more directly to their key university objectives also be needed to be achieve. So, these two universities needed to appraise individuals and units and vice presidents were needed to motivate by recognising and rewarding achievement and who were not compensated not only by praise and status but also by money and these two universities also needed to allocate resources which would always be scare to units and to individuals on a performance related basis.Assuming to these two universities academic were responsible for academic affairs when their presidents and administration practiced a centralized management of all resources and planning decision, it meant that their universities' departments needed to share and allocate their duties clearly. So, new ways were needed to facilitate this process of change possible and to avoid the risk.

The introduction of a supportive evaluation system, aiming at identifying not only areas of excellence, but critical situations as well, in order to get possible solutions for their whole universities' departments as well as the introduction of a new goal oriented approach in administration and the linkage of the expansion of the administrative staffs to goals.I suggested that their universities' organizations of the administrative structure needed a clear definition of functions and responsibilities to match the newly focussed objectives and general development plans, such as there would be no faculties, but quite large academic departments whose heads would report to vice presidents directly. Hence, university heads needed to change their duties, as the vice president was responsible for academic affairs and external relations as well as the chef executives (presidents) was responsible for finance, human resources and other internal management activities. For example, one of the largest tasks was to devise a combined programme of undergraduate and postgraduate courses.It was also necessary to plan and implemented new administration systems for finance, human resources, student records, libraries, computer systems websites etc. It meant that these would be in overlap of some services and staffs. It was decided that the new reorganizations would have two heads for an interim periodand to follow a process, e.g. offering job sharing or alternative jobs to staffs displaced. It aimed to reduce their universities' expenditures. They then had to be challenged to consider realistically what the new department should become, what was needed to make that new vision become reality and what might need to realise the vision and ensured it made an impact externally. The reason of this new vision needed to be considered immediately was that it provided a structure, a focus to planning and stopped development where staffs were focus on the negative aspects of change. There was a range of internal and external relationships that had to be managed reorganization. If the department was viewed as the internal structures, their universities themselves presented a whole range of relationships for the department to negotiate. Then there were the further external alliances and partnership outside their universities that needed to be developed.

In conclusion, if these two universities presidents could reorganize their universities' internal departments operational structure and built clear goals and objectives to let internal departments to know as well as who could change personal attitude and found consultants to assist them to promote their image to let public had more confidence to their universities' education and courses quality. Then, their donations and student enrolment numbers would be caused to increase further possibly.

Building effective organizational international communication strategy solves broadcasting television department cooperation challenge

● upward communication strategy solves
broadcasting television department
communication challenge

When you are one television company entrepreneur, how you manage your television film and movie teams work efficiently. KBTZ was a large television station in United States. It was one of the largest revenue producers in its entertainment market and employed more than 180 staffs and it was as the local television leader in the use of sophisticated electronic equipment. The station's physical plant was planned to accommodate the new equipment and to boost its image at the leader in the entertainment market. However, its organization development caused much problems to need to solve.

On the one hand, due to external pressure to cause organization change, such as entertainment market competition needed to have high technological new equipment to purchase to provide to different departments to use, e.g. cameras, films etc. equipment. Hence, different department staffs needed to learn how to use these equipment to raise productive performance quality. On the other hand, due to internal pressure to cause organizational change, such as reducing aspiration performance factor was caused poorly in KNTZ organization, which meant gaps was occurred between what an individual, unit or organization wanted to achieve and what it was actually achieving in KTZ organization. Due to KBTZ television station's operational department ,engineering department, programming department, sales department, news department etc. departments which every department individual staff, work group, division or overall KBTZ organization was not meeting its own expectations to adopt KBTZ new organization changes as well as television programming needed new productive tactics to change new strategies and processes often caused follow poor performing individual staffs, units and KBTZ whole organization, which might reduce aspiration levels instead of making changes sufficient to increase performance. Because KBTZ large television station often compared itself with other television stations in the entertainment industry , when comparisons with similar others suggested that better performance was possible. However, KBTZ staffs could not adopt organizational change development suddenly, so it caused many different departments felt difficult co-operation together in KBTZ television station organization. In fact, American television station entertainment industry was encountered by life cycle forces, it meant the natural and predictable pressures that built as to KBTZ television station organization grew and that KBTZ television station must hope to continue growing.

Hence, KBTZ television station was at elaboration stage, it meant KBTZ needed for balance, focused on efficiency and innovation, formal procedures existed and empowered low level

managers and associates in its organization if KBTZ still wanted to keep its large television station position in United States. However, KBTZ 's large television station's physical plant planned to accommodate the new advances equipment to provide different departments staffs to use and to boost its image as the leader in the United States entertainment market. It would cause its staffs feel difficult to adapt to adjust efficient and effective co-operation between departments due to it's planning change caused a process involving deliberate efforts to move KBTZ television station within its organization undesirable state to a new and more desirable state during KBTZ 's organization development was carrying on. Hence, due to its organization development change it would cause these basic problems at KBTZ organization as below:

suggestion of solvable method:

As I was the KBTZ consultant to meet with Valerie Diaz, president and general manager, who explained the key problem as:

The first problem was the high stress to which KBTZ 's manager and associates who felt about time deadlines in television problem, e.g. when it's precisely six o'clock , KBTZ news department staffs must be on the air with the news. All of the news material, local reporting, news, interviews must be processed, edited and ready to go at six o'clock. This news department staffs felt difficult, due to who could not have any half prepared material extended deadlines to cause lose the KBTZ 's audiences. This situation caused a great deal of conflict and turnover increased, such as a number of well qualified and motivated employees were leaving KBTZ television station. The news department's employee turnover was about 35% which was too high as well as KBTZ also had trouble hiring qualified people who fit their culture and

these new qualified staffs feel difficult to co-operate with KBTZ staffs to cause conflict. It seemed to be team conflict problem.

The second problem was that business manager felt difficult to manage different departments, due to who previously worked in sales and in the general manager's office, but who lacked management training and this was whose first managerial position to help in managing whose departments.

It seemed to be personal difficult management problem.

The third problem seemed the news department and business office and programming department indicated who felt the new director who lacked leadership ability to manage any departments, such as new department managers and associates felt extreme dissatisfaction with the department head, new director who had very negative attitudes toward their overall work environment , new director lacked leadership ability to let news department managers and associates communicate easily. Moreover, news department associates also complained of very low reward, including pay, promotion opportunities and managerial praise and who also complained of constant criticism, which was the only form of managerial feedback on performance. Hence, it implied the new director did not attempt to solve any departments staffs difficulties to adopt new organization change to cause their dissatisfaction and conflict and complaints occurrence to whom. It seemed to be new director personal leadership problem and news departments staffs team communication and individual dissatisfaction problems.

The fourth problem was operations department manager who complained another departments, such as news department staffs, who were confused all of the time and engineering groups, staffs were lazy and who did like cooperation to influence operational department performed ineffectively, due to these groups needed to co-operate to work together. So operations manager suggested me (KBTZ 's consultant) dismissed chief engineer and shaped up (reorganized) the news groups and the engineers groups . It seemed to be difficult co-operation occurred between operations department and engineering and news both departments problem.

The fifth problem was chief engineers who complained the unreasonableness of certain people in other departments. For example, the difficulty indicated that whose team engineers could not immediately repair some malfunctioning equipment in their area and it could take several hours just to determine the cause of the failure. It seemed that engineer department lacked enough engineers and equipment were provided to them to work from operational department . It caused team conflict problem.

The sixth problem was the program director complained the station was missing a lot of opportunities in other areas, e.g. news and sales, the chief engineer was incompetent and operations managers were difficult to motivate low level managers to make any decisions or took any responsibilities . It seemed the program director who felt dissatisfactory to other departments personal performance problem.

The seventh problem was the promotion manger who expected a little training to provide in how to deal with people, innovation and communication problems. It seemed that promotion manager felt difficult to adopt new organization change problem.

The eighth problem was sales department representatives complained who ought to increase salaries due to whose good sale performance. It seemed that sales representatives‘
dissatisfactory problem. Finally, the business office and programming department also made one survey to indicate individuals in these departments to have generally positive attitude, such as job satisfaction, but who had two important negative attitude in whose working environment. In general, these low and middle level staffs whose negative attitude of task environment major problem indicated who thought that whose department heads and the general manager could handle downward communication better , it meant that the middle and low level staffs felt the top level managers lacked effective communication to them as well as these were several comments about being underpaid relative to other station employees.

Although, the survey indicated the managers and associates whose high satisfaction, but who also believed that the negative factors led them to be poorly motivated. Such as some low and middle level associates reported that who were not sure who was top level immediate manager , since both the assignments editor and the assistant news director gave them assignments. It seemed that who lacked communication between departments to influence who did not know who had actual authority to give job to them to do.

It would cause difficult to co-operation to finish every job between department. If the assignments needed to finish urgently, who would influence any news, entertainment programmes could not been finished before the time deadlines. It seemed to be team communication problem. The another problem was that, some low and middle level associates also reported that creativity (thought to be important in the jobs) was discouraged by the director's highly authority management and structured styled as well as new director personal work attitude was not good style. It seemed that this new director had unsuitable personal management skill to lead this KBTZ different departments to follow whose guidelines to finish their jobs daily, to cause these departments ' staffs felt dissatisfactory to this new director's personal work attitude . It seemed that this was new director's personal management attitude problem. Moreover, this business office and programming department's survey also indicated these departments existed these problems in KBTZ television station organization.

Firstly, although most of operation department associates were satisfied with their jobs and reported pride in their departments and only some associates felt satisfactory about their operations department manager (head). All other some associates tended to feel overworked (reported a 74 hours workweek) and thought the department head expected too much and who also thought who were underpaid relative to their task demands and criticized managerial feedbacks on their performance and the department head never prised position performance and who only regarded them for poor performance and who also reported concern over the conflict with engineering group

, but who believed operations and engineering department conflict, whose departments' leaders (managers) should be resolved. It seemed that this operations departments manager could not manage some departments staffs to work in normal hours to cause them to feel unhappy to work and they also felt underpayment and unreasonable feedback on the performance problem. Anyway, the engineering department many associates were very dissatisfied with whose jobs and who had conflict to operational department and who also believed engineering department head did not support them and who lacked department meetings to receive feedback on their performance from the chief engineer. It seemed that this engineering department's chief engineer who performed more poor to compare to operations department manager to cause
many associates felt dissatisfactory to him. Otherwise, the survey indicated that only promotion department associates had positive attitudes and their job satisfaction were high and everyone viewed their task environment positively and who had only few negative attitudes were primarily directed toward the ineffectiveness of the news department . It seemed that promotion department had none any problems, so its associates could criticize the another news department ineffectiveness result confidently.

Finally, the sales department's colleagues could not responded to the survey to indicate whether what kinds of problems who felt .Due to sale department head was the KBTZ television station manager's son family relationship , so who could not respond to complete this survey whether whose feelings to this sales department manager was satisfactory or was not satisfactory to him, it would cause who lost their job if who responded whose actual feelings to me (consultant) to know at that day possibly.

Which organization development techniques should I consider using and why?

As I was KBTZ television station consultant, I should apply these organization development techniques to solve this company problems. Organizational development techniques included relationship techniques, such as T-group training,
team building, survey as well as structural technique, such as management by objective and supplemental organizational processes. The news department problem, such as high stress to this department managers and associates. It was respect to time deadlines in television problem. The department's staffs must be on the air with the news. All of the news material , local reporting , news , interviews must be processed, edited and ready to go at six o'clock. So, this news department staffs often worried about extended deadlines or who only half prepared material or who lost the audience, it caused conflict and a number of well qualified and motivated employees would leave this KBTZ television station organization and KBTZ also felt trouble hiring new qualified people could adapt KBTZ organization's culture to help KBTZ organization to raise competition in this USA entertainment market. On the other hand, due to news department staffs who were confused all of the time, so it also caused operations department manager who felt difficult co-operation with to cause operations department and news department would be often conflicts about news department extended time deadline issue. Even, program department director also complained the station was missing a lot of opportunities in other areas, e.g. news and sales. I should use organization development technology, relationship technique T-group training to solve this news and operation departments cooperation problem, which meant news department would implement group exercises in which individual focused on their action, how others perceived their actions and how others generally reacted to them, so participants often learnt about unintended. Hence, this news department managers and associates who could divided several groups, it aimed to focus on their individual action, e.g. local reporting group, news report group, interviews group, news material preparing group. So, these every group members (staffs) who could perceived whose individual group action and reacted to another group individual member action, such as news material preparing group individual member could focus on gathering news material preparing job duties, then who could gave news material to news report group individual member to prepare to analyse materials to prepare to report.

Another interviews group individual to prepare how much time needed and what places should be choose and who to be interviewed to prepare every day different news to let audience to watch six o'clock news programs in television every day. Then, who could gave local reporting group individual member to analyze their every individual interviewing
record to produce every local reporting.

Thus, T-group training benefit was that participants, such as KBTZ news department's material group individual member, local reporting group individual member, news production group individual member, interviewed group individual member who could often learnt about why unintended negative consequences were caused of certain types of any group individual member's behaviour to cause to extend time deadlines or to cause only extend time deadlines or to cause only half prepared material due to very few time was enough to prepare precisely at six o' clock to ready to go before this news department all groups must be processed to edit. Hence, group member which needed to finish whose identified group job, e.g. interview group members who only needed to focus on carry on training how to make date and time appointment to meet individual in the beginning to till to how to prepare what kinds of interview questions would enquire and every interview was planned which needed how long time to finish. Hence, such as interview group individual member could review whose every interview progress to aim to achieve to shorten time to perform the better news programs quality to provide to television audients to watch at everyday six o'clock news time. Hence, the news department's every group member could give chance to enquire survey feedback from every team leader (manager) to review their everyday news job to investigate whether whose group performance would cause unintended negative consequences to influence other group performance to be poor, such as investigating the day's news extended causing was due to the day interview group's individual member who could not organize overall interview procedure to arrange time to finish effectively or other group's individual member to cause. Hence, relationship technique T-group training method could review whether which group(s) to cause the day news extended deadlines or found whether which group(s) caused overall team which could not prepare all material to finish the day news watching at six o'clock . It was one fair method to measure whether which group staffs were qualified people or whether which group staffs were not qualified people to co-operate in this news department.

Other problem was about business department head, business manager seemed that who lacked management training to prepare to do this position, such as who previously worked to do this position, such as who previously worked in sales and in the general manager's office only. Hence, who must need to provide training to prepare to know how to manage KBTZ 's television station organization different departments, such as news department, sales department, operations department, engineering department, program department, promotion department efficiently. As I was KBTZ 's consultant , I felt KBTZ could provide relationship technique of survey method to assist whom. If every departments could get survey, then this business manager could obtain enough dates to meet all units to discuss problems easily. Then, when who collected all departments' problems from this survey, KBTZ could use structural technique of management by objectives method to assist him (business manager), it meant a management process in which individuals (different group members) negotiated whose group daily task objectives, such as engineer group member could negotiate how much equipment who needed to repair urgently and how many equipment who could repair and gave reasons why who could not repair some equipment in that day. All departments might have task objectives to measure whose every group members performance to revise what factors caused whose performance to be poor in order to correct

to achieve every department's group member could raise work efficiently. Thus, this management process needed spend much time to revise every department's group individual negotiate task. For example, the business manager needed to meet engineering group leader (chief engineer) and members(engineers and technicians) to discuss whether how many equipment who needed to repair and whether how many equipment who needed to repair and whether how many equipment who felt who had no much time to repair this week, then next week, this business manager would enquire these engineers to revise whether what reasons occurred to cause who could not repair all machines last week.

As this engineer department individual member technician who had negotiated task objectives to let whose chief engineer and engineering manager to know whether who felt that who could finish task to repair how many machines every week, then they could meet to attempt to explain what factors caused them could not repair all equipment further week. Hence, this business manager could used the same management by objectives structural technique method, such as every department individual member needed to negotiate task objective to finish every week, then who needed to meet whose department manager to revise what factors influenced their work efficiency, e.g. news department material group could meet to discuss task objective about how much time and how many staffs who needed to prepare to gather any related material to report this week ; interview group could meet to discuss task objective about how much time and how many staffs who needed to prepare to organize any effective interview procedure to prepare individual interview this week ; news edited group could meet to discuss task objective about how much time and how many staffs who needed to be edit for daily news this week. Thus, this business manager could know all department's every group individual task objectives per week clearly, then who could meet them to attempt to find whether what factors which caused any department's group individual member who could not achieve whose last week objectives efficiently and effectively.

The new director seemed have unsuitable personal management style to lead whose different departments to work together to cause their dissatisfaction to him in this KBTZ television station organization. For example, the news department felt this new director lacked leadership ability to led news department managers and associates communicate easily. Moreover, news department associates also complained of very low reward, including pay, promotion opportunities and managerial praise and who also complained of constant criticism , which was the only form of managerial feedback on performance. Hence, it implied the new director did not attempt to solve any departments staffs difficulties to adopt new organization development change to cause their dissatisfaction and conflicts and complaints occurrence to whom. I should suggest this new director as a leader who needed to find method to help different department leader(manager) to lead whose associates to feel this KBTZ organization must earn more beyond the past by providing a rationale for change currently and let them to feel guilt and poor anxiety about this KBTZ organization chose not to change and create a sense of psychological safety to them to concern the change, such as news department associates who complain of low reward, including low promotion opportunities and managerial praise and who also complained of constant criticism feedback on performance.

It seemed that who would also complain about low reward, low promotion opportunities and managerial praise and unfair feedback on performance to this new director , even who had good personal managerial style to lead all departments to work. A reason was why these departments, such as news department colleagues complained as above issues because who felt the new director could not adopt to work due to KBTZ sudden change to cause who should be de-commit and dissatisfactory form the status. Hence, this new director needed to let who to know KBTZ organization would cause poor anxiety and guilt to them in the future if KBTZ organization did not change at this moment as well as this new director might create of psychological discomfort to these departments to let them to know that organization would loss from its television competitions, even it would dismiss who if KBTZ television station should not choose to change at this moment, such as the negative outcomes would be made and KBTZ 's managers and associates would suffer if changes were not made. Moreover, this business manager also needed to remind every department members that as well as who also needed to downward members to know this who individual would need to change to adopt this new organization change culture to every department in large meetings. Even, this new director also needed to let every department manager (leader) to know how this change process needed to carry on and every department manager also needed to implement evaluation systems to track every department's group individual expected behaviours and work performance whether whose work were more efficiently or whose work were not more efficiently during this KBTZ organization was carrying on changing at the same time. Hence, every department manager could create efficient reward systems that reinforce every department's group individual's expected behaviours and who could also ensure that whether the hiring and promotion systems which could support all departments colleagues new demands. Especially, news departments felt low reward dissatisfaction. Hence, it could measure whether who ought to raise reward or who ought not to raise reward of their work performance to evaluate more efficiently and effectively. In conclusion, this KBTZ organization leader (new director) ought attempt to let all departments staffs to know why it needed to change organization style and what would be the disadvantages to any departments colleagues if it decided not change at this moment. Then, I believed that department staffs complaints would be reduced and who would feel more fair to pay reward after who knew how who needed to do whose task to adopt this employer to feel satisfactory.

- film producing entrepreneur downward communincation strategy solves team cooperation challenge

When you are one film producing entrepreneur, how you manage your actor teams to work efficiently. Helen Reardon is the producer and director of the film, Going North, based on a novel, the best seller list for 16 months and who is considered to be one of the best directors in Hollywood, who already has two Academy Awards to whose credit and many hit motion pictures.Tom Nesson is a promising young actor, his most recent film, the western express was well received on the box office. Because his current popularity, who was chosen to play the leading male part in Going North film.The next days, Tom won't work in about 10 minutes later, who explained that the makeup people were show in getting his makeup on. No one questioned this, any who began where who had staff off yesterday. However, Helen dissatisfied Tom's performance to play his role action during this movie was carrying on.Hence, who had argued. In result, Helen enquired president in the studio executive offices to demand who either dismissed Tom Nesson, actor or dismissed who self.

The studio executive did not want to lose either Helen, producer and director of film or Tom actor or both. Neither had a history of being difficult to work with. They were not sure what was causing the problem. This movie seemed to be causing all kinds of problems. e.g. strike and the disagreements between wardrobe and set design. They obviously needed to examine all of the circumstances involved to the making of the film. I supposed to use these communication networks to give reasons why causing problem between Helen and Tom. Communication occurs at several different levels and the communication that occurs among individuals or groups of individuals. This is referred to as interpersonal communication.

Networks serve various purposes in organizations and which can used to regulate behaviour, promote innovation, integrate activities and inform and instruct group members. Network also differ in the extent to which who are centralized or decentralized. In centralized networks, all communications pass through a central point or points, so that each member of the network communicates with only a small number of others.Traditional organizational hierarchies, where subordinates communicate to their boss who are centralized networks and all units must communicate with a central headquarter, which then simultaneously coordinates all the units. In decentralized networks, many people or units can communicate with many others.

However, wheel and Y networks are more effective in accomplishing simple tasks and these structures promote efficiency, speed and accuracy by channelling communication through a central person as well as the circle and all channel patterns networks are more effective for complex tasks and communication among all parties facilities the use of group resources to solve complex problems. As this case indicated that Tom won't work in about 10 minutes later, who explained that the makeup people were show in getting his makeup on. No one questioned this, any who began where who had staff off yesterday. Helen and Tom have encountered communication network difficulty. I shall suppose this film producing firm organisational structure is a traditional organizational hierarchies, where subordinates communicate to their department supervisor, e.g. marketing staffs who needed to communicate to marketing manager during who had any problems, then who needed to wait marketing manager to tell to the studio executive president to let him know, so who needed to spend much time to wait studio executive president(central contacting person) to help who to solve problems. Hence, it seemed this movie firm any department staffs who needed spend much time to wait their managers to tell whose problems to studio executive president to know to help them to solve, but who must need to wait whose managers had enough time to help them to deal their problems, then whose conflicts would be solved easily.

The most important influence, the conflicts were between the marketing department and design department and makeup department which would influence Helen, producer and director and Tom, actor whose team co-operation to become more difficult because whether this movie could finish before schedule due date, it must need all departments could cooperate efficiently. Otherwise, any departments' conflicts would influence other teams working performance to be poor in directly, such as Helen, movie of director and Tom, actor whose conflict could be influenced by makeup department and marketing department and design department whose conflicts indirectly. Helen Reardon , the producer and director of the film knew that Tom, film actor went to work in about 10 minutes later next day. However, Helen decided not attempt to enquire makeup department supervisor to explain why the matter had happened directly. Otherwise, who decided to complain Tom's performance to studio executive office directly.I suppose this film producing firm had adapted the wheel and Y networks communication, but these structures are promoted efficiency, speed and accuracy by channelling communication through a central person when the organization structure is simple and there are less staffs work to less departments in its organization. Due to Helen and Tom and studio executive office lacked communication before Tom already did this actor. So, Helen could not know the makeup department would encounter what kind of problems easily.Due to this film company's organization structure was caused complex , but it still adapted the wheel and Y networks communication structure and these structures are promoted efficiency, speed and accuracy by channelling communication through a central person only. Hence, there were not any makeup staffs could inform to Tom that Helen, film producer and director did not like any staffs worked lately. However, Helen did not meet Tom and the makeup department manager to discuss what actions who demand Tom needed to do to satisfy whose team cooperation together before Tom began to work clearly.Moreover, Helen also dissatisfied Tom's performance to play his role action during this movie was carrying on to cause who had much argument. In result, Helen decided to enquire president in the studio executive offices

to demand who either dismissed Tom Nesson, actor or dismissed who self.Thus, it caused the decision of Helen who enquired the studio executive office president to demand who either dismissed Tom , actor or dismissed who self directly because the studio executive and makeup department manager and Tom, actor and Helen, producer and director of the film between of them lacked effective communication before Tom, actor began to work in first day. If they could spend time to discuss what Tom needed to do to achieve their demand from Helen, producer and director of the film and makeup department, manager before Tom began to do this film. I believe that Tom and Helen problem won't be caused easily.

suggestion of solvable method:

What do you suppose is really causing the problem between Helen and Tom? Explain?

I should recommend this film company needed to adapt the circle or the all channel patterns communication network in its organization. I suppose this film company had many movies to produce at the same time and it was needed more staffs to finish different films in the limited time and it caused the management staffs would not have any time to discuss what kinds of staff problems would encounter in different departments easily.Moreover, it lacked downward communication to low level staffs and studio executive president had not met the makeup department manager and Tom, actor and Helen, producer and director of the film to discuss what their demands were before Tom began to work in the first day. However, studio executive presidents ought communicate to subordinates (actors, producer and director of films, makeup department managers), to provide job instructions, information on organization policies and performance feedback to let them know. Downward communication would be the best way to inform associates about the film company organization's goal and about changes faced by it because this film company had encountered its different departments' conflicts, such as makeup, marketing, design departments as well as staff's individual conflicts, such as Helen, movie director and Tom, actor whose conflicts.

In conclusion, this movie company indicated that Helen, director of the movie complained to studio executive president because who felt dissatisfaction and disagreement Tom, actor' personal behaviour and poor role performance. Hence, this team two staffs who could not build good co-operational relationship to work together to cause whose conflicts in this movie team work because who lacked effective communication before Tom started to work first day.

Discuss the problems between set design and wardrobe and those with the market department.

After few weeks, problems began to arise. Arguments came between the set design staff and wardrobe. They felt that the sets and costumes didn't match. Some thought colours clashed at times. Each group blamed the other, whether whose fault it was. Later, makeup department staffs explained who were being asked to work unreasonable hours. The makeup staff claimed that who had an informal agreement with studio management about the hours they would work and that this agreement had been forced.The problems between set design and wardrobe and those with the market department occurred because they lacked horizontal communication which took place between associates at the same level, e.g. the set design staff and wardrobe staffs felt that the sets and costumes didn't match and some thought colours clashed at times and each group blamed the other, whether whose fault it was. It implied these departments had organizational barriers to communicate effectively to cause these two departments felt difficult cooperation and dissatisfaction and argument occurred, e.g. message/work overload, noise, time pressures, breakdown in the communication network and team cooperation barriers.It also implied these departments had individual barriers to effective communication, e.g. status differences, consideration of self interest, poor listening skills, lacking discussion time etc. In result, it caused conflicts between departments.Later, makeup department staffs explained who were being asked to work unreasonable hours. The makeup staff claimed that who had an informal agreement with studio management about the hours they would work and that this agreement had been forced. This problem occurred that it implied this film company lackedenough staffs to provide to makeup department to cause who being asked to work unreasonable hours (overtime) and were given unreasonable salary as well as who felt unfair because this movie firm had forced to them to choose to do overtime job forced.

In conclusion, due to design and wardrobe and those with the market department lacked effective communication to discuss whether what furniture design and colour tools to which design department would accept, so it caused market department supplied the design tools to make design department to feel dissatisfactory and it would influence this movie procedure to be late finished finally. Moreover, the makeup department staffs felt unhappily to be enforced to work overtime from management. Some makeup would strike or late to work, who would cause Tom, actor could not have enough time to make up facial and wore dresses to perform during Helen, director of team arrived every time. Thus, some makeup department staffs would strike who should also influence director Helen and actor, Tom whose team cooperation effectively in the beginning.

Could any of the problems in this case have been prevented?

If so? How?

The studio executive offices presidents obviously needed to examine all of the circumstances involved to the making of the film in order to prevent these problems occurred.The first problem referred as below:

Helen Reardon is the producer and director of the film, Going North, based on a novel, the best seller list for 16 months and who is considered to be one of the best directors in Hollywood, who already has two Academy Awards to whose credit and many hit motion pictures.Tom Nesson is a promising young actor, his most recent film, the western express was well received on the box office. Because his current popularity, who was chosen to play the leading male part in Going North film.The next days, Tom won't work in about 10 minutes later, who explained that the makeup people were show in getting his makeup on. No one questioned this, any who began where who had staff off yesterday. However, Helen dissatisfied Tom's performed to play his role action during this movie was carrying on. Hence, who had argued. In result, Helen enquired president in the studio executive offices to demand who either dismissed Tom Nesson, actor or dismissed who self.

The studio executive did not want to lose either Helen, producer and director of film as well as Tom both. Neither had a history of being difficult to work with. They were not sure what was causing the problem. This movie seemed to be caused all kinds of problems. e.g. strike and the disagreements was between wardrobe and set design. They obviously needed to examine all of the circumstances involved to the making of the film. Communication must occur at several different levels. On one level is the communication that occurs among individuals or groups of individuals and this is referred to as interpersonal communication.Networks serve various purposes in organizations and staffs need have suitable networks arrangement to integrate activities and inform and instruct group members. Networks also differ in organization extent to which staffs are centralized or decentralized in any organizations. In centralized networks, all communications pass through a central point or points, so that each member of the network communicates with only a small members.

The problems of this movie firm could be prevented as: Firstly, the personal conflict had been occurred between Tom, actor and Helen , director of this movie, I recommend this film company needed to adapt the circle or the all channel patterns communication network in its organization. I suppose this film company had many movies to produce at the same time and it was needed more effective to finish different films in the short time. Hence, the studio executive office would not have any time to discuss what kind of staff problems would encounter in different departments easily. I also suppose management staffs lacked downward communication to low level staffs, presidents had not met the makeup department manager and Tom, actor and Helen, producer and director of the film to discuss what their demands were before Tom began to work in the first day. However, studio executive presidents ought communicate to subordinates (actors, producer and director of film, makeup department managers) to provide job instructions, information on organization policies and performance feedback let them know. Downward communication is the best way to inform associates about the film company organization's goal and about changes faced by it. The reason is why downward communication is frequently deficient in this regard because this film company had been complained about personal conflict and department conflict during this movie began to produce.If this film company studio executive president who could attempt to enquire whether what Tom and Helen would encounter any conflicts before Helen decided to accept Tom to do this movie actor, I believe that their team co-operation could work more effectively.Secondly, the two teams' conflict had been occurred between market and design departments, it was due to design department felt that the sets and costumes did not match and colours clashed conflict due to market department did not discuss with design department before market department began to purchase materials.

The problem between set design and wardrobe and those with the market department occurred because they lacked horizontal communication which takes place between associates at the same level, e.g. set design staff and wardrobe staffs would feel that the sets and costumes didn't match and some thought colours clashed at times and each group blamed the other, whether whose fault it is. It implied these departments had organizational barriers to effective communication , which included these problems existed to cause dissatisfaction and argument occurred in these two departments, e.g. work overload, noise, time pressures, breakdown in the communication network and team cooperation barriers.It also implied these departments had individual barriers to effective communication, e.g. status differences, consideration of self interest, lacking decision time, poor listening skills etc.Thus, these marketing department which ought need to contact design department to enquire whether what kinds of furniture design and colour which design department would accept, then their conflict would not influence Tom , actor who started t perform those job at the first day.

Thirdly, the one group conflict had been occurred within makeup department,Later, makeup department staffs explained who were being asked to work unreasonable hours. The makeup

staff claimed that who had an informal agreement with studio management about the hours they would work and that this agreement had been forced. This problem occurred that it implied this film company lacked enough makeup staffs to cause who being asked to work unreasonable hours and unreasonable salary and who felt this firm had been forced to them to choose to do overtime job because the makeup studio management had an informal agreement to demand them to do this overtime job. Finally, they felt makeup department manager refused their demand, so they would decide to complain studio office executive president directly.

If, this movie company's the makeup department manager could spend time to meet this studio executive president directly to discuss how to solve staffs shortage issue before who decided to give overtime to makeup department staffs. It meant that makeup department manager ought not tell whose makeup teams who must need to work overtime for this movie enforcedly. Otherwise, who ought enquire studio executive president's ideas how to solve this staff shortage problem immediately. Then, it would reduce makeup team's conflict due to makeup management could give discussion chance to makeup team and studio executive president both immediately.

How can the problems now be solved?

Due to this film company had communication conflict difficulty. It was without good internal communication within every individual department, e.g. makeup, marketing departments etc. then it was no good external communication between different departments, e.g. design and marketing departments, so it caused personal and group conflicts. In addition, it was possible to image this film company organizational communication could not without conflict because its staffs had different opinions, so their staffs who would not accept other staff's different opinions easily. In fact, this film's organizational communication was necessary for conducting in an effective manner, e.g. studio executive office president needed to spend some time to communicate with makeup department whether what who felt dissatisfaction as well as this movie Tom actor and Helen movie producer and director needed to meet studio executive office president to discuss why their conflict had caused and how their conflict could solve together.Any effective communication is required and is not only for maintaining human relations, but is also for achieving practical experience to show individual or group communications are needed to reduce departments or personal conflicts in this movie firm within organization.However, the makeup department conflict and management team conflict as well as Tom, actor and Helen, director of this movie and studio executive president individual conflict as well as the design and wardrobe department and the market department both group conflict which had those similarities as it was a necessary process, participants (individuals or groups) were actually or apparently influenced by another individual party or group parties and their conflict would influence this movie productive process. In fact, this movie individual or group conflict was a process where it's these staffs deliberately made an effort to prevent efforts of other staffs with an opposing action, which would result in frustrating other department staffs to achieve their goals or satisfied those interests. For example, this movie firm's marketing department horizontal conflicts occurred between employees within the same department, such as marketing manager needed them to work overtime to influence their personal interests due to this movie firm had scared human resource and finance resource in this department. I shall recommend these methods to solve these problems in this movie firm as below:

This film company studio executive presidents can hold different planning meeting with all major parties, e.g. the first parties Tom, actor and Helen, producer and director of this film as well as the second parties makeup department manager and makeup staff represents as well as the third parties, the design and wardrobe department manager and the market department manager. Hence, these department parties can spend some time to discuss their individual and group conflicts about their dissatisfaction and complaint to attempt to give opinions to negotiate in meeting fairly. The film company top management level , studio executive presidents who can enquire these parties' dissatisfaction and complaint directly and who can attempt to give opinions to negotiate these parties to reduce their leaving chance to threaten this film producing process, e.g. design and wardrobe department needs to discuss how to arrange any colour and furniture design to satisfy marketing department needs and executive presidents in their meeting; and the actor, Tom and the producer and director, Helen and executive presidents can spend time to discuss how to solve their conflict in their meeting. This movie firm executive presidents can arrange meeting to discuss with makeup department's staffs how to either increase makeup department staff salaries to let them to accept to do overtime job or it could choose to employ more right numbers staff to reduce makeup department staffs overtime or it could adopted makeup department staffs' any opinions in order to reduce their overtime.

In conclusion, of this movie firm management could have downward communication to spend some time to discuss how to solve every teams' conflicts together immediately , I believe that their conflicts would solve immediately.

Fair compensation strategy solves factory workers and baseball players cooperation challenge

I shall assume fair compensation strategy can be applied to schools. When one school students need to cooperate to finish one assignment. Although school students do not need salary to compensate their performance for finishing the assignment when they need to cooperate to do the assignment together. But, school assignment result will be such as one salary compensation to pay to this assignment MBA team. So, the work hard student must earn higher assignment mark result to compare the poor student.

In this university MBA A-team students team, the dimensions of diversity were responsible for the conflict were as the different groups of these five students should be treated equally that rewards should be based on merit (university project result) and decision maker (team leader) should be blind to the sex or ethnicity of MBA students to arrange their different roles and job duties to carry on doing this business plan project in their university. Hence, workplace diversity management can apply to this university MBA students diversity management. Workplace equal employment opportunity is similar to this university MBA A-team five students equal roles and duties opportunity as well as workplace organization decision maker is similar to this university .MBA A-team students team leader who needs to decide either employees or MBA A-team student team

members to pay attention to characteristics like sex or ethnicity to determine if who affect employment consequences or to arrange university MBA A-team five student members every role and duty to finish this business plan project. In workplace, every employer needs special actions , such as hiring the ethnic minority candidate when applicants appear to have equal qualifications, are considered appropriate requirements to remedy the effects of past discrimination and thus attain equal opportunity.

Thus, this university ought feel that it was such one employer, it needed to help A-team to choose one MBA student for A-team leader from whose prior working experiences and qualification. Then, it needed to give reasons to these other four A-team student members to explain why it felt this MBA student was the best right applicant for their A-team leader. University professor Bowell group advisor might give probation period to this student leader if this A-team four members complaint this team leader who could not serve in the executive function to assign and oversee everyone's work and gave the presentation at end of project. Then , professor Bowell this team advisor might suggest them to select another new leader, so this A-team would not be disbanded easily. As this university selects the right applicant for every position. It needs committee to assist its selection processing. If the dean determines that the committee lacks diversity , it can be reconstituted by including persons from other departments or even other universities. The search committee chair must review information from candidates to ensure that minority and female and male applicants are in the pool.The dean's office reviews applications of diverse candidates of none of them appears among the search committee's choices of candidates to be interviewed, the committee must provide an explanation. Finally, the university team advisor ought be similar to an employer who needs to choose who are the top student candidates (employees) to make A-team (job offer) from their educational background, working experiences. It aims to reduce dimensions of diversity were responsible for the conflict.

Describe which barriers to effectively managing diversity were present in this situation?

Diversity can be defined as a characteristic of a group of people where differences exist on one or more relevant dimensions such as gender. First, faults can be present in situations characterized by diversity. Faults occur when two or more dimensions of diversity are correlated. For example, if all /most of the young people on a cross-functional task force represent marketing when all/most of the older individuals represent product engineering, then a fault is said exist. Faults merge multiple identifies (e.g. young and marketing focused) to produce barriers to effective collaborations within a group. Research on this phenomenon is relatively new, but has produced findings suggestion poor group outcomes. It can be applied to this A-team university team members conflict what barriers are to effectively managing diversity were present in this situation.

The barriers to effectively managing diversity were present in this situation , it is possible that this A-team group members who have different educational and working backgrounds to cause barriers to effectively managing diversity in this situation. For example, Rebecca is a young marketing manager for a large and high end Italian fashion company. She hopes this university MBA course can help her to be promoted to an executive position as well as Aran is 52 year old founder and CEO of an management consultant firm. He hopes this university MBA course can help him to retire from his consulting firm earlier and become an in house information system consultant to a large multinational firm. When she knew Aran promoted him to be this A-team leader because he had the most experience and he should serve in the executive function. Thus, he would assign and oversee every member's work and he would also give the presentation at the end of this project. Although, Aran have more confident to give reasons why he is the best person choice to be this team leader to manage every member and he also give useful suggestion that Cameron, an internet entrepreneur who heads his own small but successful company who will be in charge of analyzing the financial feasibility of their project, developing the marketing plan, and evaluating the technical operations and the other members need to assist him. However, Aran is one managing consultant and Rebecca is one young marketing manager. Aran's educational and working experience is related to information system, but Rebecca educational and working experience is related to marketing field. Thus they have different expertise and skill. Rebecca feels that she has marketing field experience and she is younger than Aran. So, she have more ability than Aran to attempt to do a team leader to manage this A-team members how to produce marketing plan and report and presentation effectively. In conclusion, because these five students have different educational and working experience in their expertise field, so they feel themselves has ability to attempt to be team leader or attempt to do their job duties who prefer to choose by themselves. It will cause difficulty to any one team leader to manage diversity in this A-team members effectively and successfully.

● Factors cause electronic assemblies factory workers team poor performance

When you one electronic assemblies factory entrepreneur, how you manage your workers team work efficiently. The best ways evaluate to measure what factors are seemed to be influencing this company electronic assemblies products manufactory factory workers team performance.

The First factor, we need to know what kind of methods which can be used to measure team performance, then, we can follow these measurement methods to judge what factors are seemed to be influencing this team performance more actually. Effectiveness and efficiency are the best ways to evaluate team performance. Efficiency is oriented towards successful input transformation into outputs. Effectiveness measures how outputs interact with the economic and social environment and it is being used to reflect overall performance of the team. This company electronic assemblies products manufactory factory team of workers could be evaluated team performance in terms of effectiveness. It's main focus is to achieve team's mission, goals and vision, such as whether how many workers could attempt to finish to wire eight assemblies an hour to meet their one client, Pacific electronic company to know how many assemblies of numbers had been finished to wire currently in order to meet whose Pacific electronic company client shipping schedule or not. At the same time, which value these electronic assembly workers whose performance in terms of their efficiency which relates to the optimal use of resources to achieve the desired output, such as whether how many worker numbers and machine tool numbers would be needed to provide to wire assembly numbers to finish in order to meet whose Pacific electronic company client shipping schedule or not. However, this team performance would have this question ,such as whether there was a difference if this team was effective yet inefficient. Hence, this team would face unprecedented challenges (factors) which were seemed to be influencing team performance. The first factor was such as, it's client Pacific electronic company needed shorten time to finish wire assemblies which was the main factor to influence performance, such as this team workers would feel difficult to increase to wire eight assemblies an hour from three assemblies an hour, so who would feel anxiety to meet the shipping schedule to finish whose job and quality of assemblies production could not be satisfied to Pacific electronic company client possibly.

The second factor was such as, this company factory and office team management structural relationship. Usually, high team performance has strong upper management and human resource standards which had been set in place. Because of high team performance expectation, right staffs were being hired to fulfil the positions in order to employees were well aware of the performance measurement and the importance achieve the excellence in their duties. Due to a high degree level of employee involvement needed to be in the team production process, the entity was awarded with staffs commitment which reduced rotation level and the cost associated with the hiring and training process. Hence, employees who were devoted to the team were well aware of necessary knowledge and skill and experience to create unique solutions for clients. Training can be an essential tool for maintaining and improving the productivity of staffs and relevance of skill. The ongoing shortages of labour and skill, the company should be taking action to reduce the impact of staffs scarcity by training staffs who already had employed.

Development opportunities were provided to motivate staffs by providing them with skill and knowledge enrichment . At the same time, a better skilled, more motivated workforce would help boost competitiveness, improved productivity and increased profit margin. Moreover, this company lacked good team communication relationship, such as Bill, factory team supervisor who only knew whose same workers of team, such as some of workers Dennis and Steve and Jack who would feel difficult because whose workers were supposed to wire three assemblies an hour normally with five years, but who were supposed to do eight assemblies an hour to sudden meet one client, Pacific electronic company client schedule to finish confidently as well as who would feel dissatisfactory, due to whose wages did not increase much more to pay for performance to the optimal compensation currently and these workers lacked enough training to face this sudden change to face this client's demand. Thus, it was possible that to influence whose team performance to be poor due to who could not adapt this sudden change from this client's demand. Due to Bill, electronic factory supervisor had not communicate to face to face to contact to enquire whose workers whether what reasons to cause who would feel difficulties if who needed to increase to finish wire assemblies and attempted to find solved methods due to sudden clients‘ demand. Hence, Bill could not have knowledge and skill to judge whether the reasons were either the numbers of workers or machines were not enough or both to cause that they would feel difficulties to increase their speed and effort to finish up to eight wire assemblies of numbers to meet this clients' current schedule sudden change demand at this moment.

The third factor was whether this company had effective strategic approaches to this team. A high team performance which maintains five major approaches: They include strategy, customers, leadership, processes and structure , values and beliefs. Strategic approach takes the team to a higher plan of maturity with a vision where the entity is going; customer approach strives for loyalty; leadership approach is associated with management knowledge to transfer the strategy to employees (teams) level and which will have a direct impact on their behaviour and beliefs and teams‘ processes and structure and high performance team will strive for implementing innovative policies to support team strategy; the last model is value and belief which translates into team ability to implement the strategy. In fact, this team lacked effective strategic approaches, such as Mr Martin, office manager did not told Bill, electronic factory team supervisor how to lead whose team to a higher plan to maturity with a vision where the entity was going, such as team lacked training or team lacked enough numbers of worker and machine to provide to increase to produce up to eight wire assemblies of numbers to meet this client's schedule shorten change demand to cause this team lacked evaluation to measure every worker individual effort to judge whether who ought have effort to already to finish more wire assemblies of numbers and who ought increase their wages due to they had more effort to raise more productivity to produce eight assemblies or more numbers. Hence, it caused the effort workers did not like to increase the productivity to meet this client sudden change easily due to who felt unfair treatment to compare the other less effort workers in this team.

However, the Pacific electronic company client would lose confidence to Mr Martin office manager if who could not accept Dave, shop of supervisor suggestion either to add some more incentive bonus to these workers to raise whose productivity or providing training or providing more machine and worker numbers to attempt to assist current workers ability to meet the client's schedule. Otherwise, it would cause this client did not choose to find its help next time again. The important factor was whether this factory supervisor and shop supervisor and office manager who had effective communication to predict how to solve any sudden clients' order change trouble between of them. However, I think that, Bill factory supervisor lacked effective leadership to whose workers team in this factory, such as it seemed that some workers; Dennis, Steve and Jack who responded to Bill factory supervisor who felt difficulties to wire eight assemblies an hour suddenly. In fact, some of them had confidence to finish who told lie to Bill because Bill, factory supervisor could not be a good leader to know how to lead whose team to wire assemblies efficiently and effectively daily. Thus, Bill's leadership would have a direct impact on team workers behaviour and team performance poorly if Bill could not change whose leadership skill and who needed to facilitate workers team performance rather than to direct the team, due to who was a formal leader to their team. The company lacked value and belief with translated into team ability to implement the strategy, such as Mr Martin, office manager could not communicate with Dave, shop of supervisor and Bill, factory of supervisor by face to face contact to discuss whether how who could raise to produce wire assemblies of numbers during any clients‘ sudden shorten schedule occurrence before, so it caused this factory workers team had not more confident to increase to produce more eight wire assemblies of numbers one hour due to this clients' schedule sudden shorten change. Otherwise, if who could often to discuss to suggest any methods to raise these factory team productivity, this factory leader, Bill would have enough time to plan already how to lead whose factory team workers to co-operate to raise productivity efficiency and effectively in this shorten schedule.

suggestion method:

Identify the team norms and goals. Are they compatible with organizational objective?

● What factors seem to be influencing team performance?

I felt that some of this electronic company factory team norms and goals are compatible with organizational objectives in some situations, but some of whose team norms and goals are not compatible with organizational objective in some situation. Norms mean rules or standards that regulate the team's behaviour and providing direction and are part of the team's mental model. When individual team members violate team norms, some type of punishment is usually applied. Although, norms allow teams be function smoothly, who can sometimes be harmful to team members. It is important that teams develop norms that both foster team productivity and performance and promote the welfare of individual members. This company goal was that it's factory team needed to finish identified wire assemblies of numbers to satisfy every business clients to meet whose identified schedules individually. Hence, Bill, the electronic factory team supervisor who needed to follow Dave, shop of supervisor's instruction to inform whose workers team to finish all wire assemblies of numbers to meet every business client's identified schedule on or before due date. Thus, Bill , factory team supervisor needed to give team norms to let whose team of workers to know whose factory's rules or standards that regulated whose workers teams individually behaviour and providing direction to let them to know when (what the client schedule date was) and what the wire assemblies of numbers the team which must need to finish to deliver to whose clients by shipping. Hence, this factory's rules and standards regulation could be one part to this factory team's mental models on this aspect to achieve this factory workers team norms were compatible with this organizational objective.

Although, the factory workers team norms allowed them to function smoothly, but Bill, factory supervisor could sometimes be harmful to the factory workers team to influence whether

the factory workers team productivity and performance standards level of those wire assemblies of products quality, such as Bill, factory supervisor informed to those factory workers team to increase to produce eight wire assemblies of numbers one hour for normal three wire assemblies of numbers one hour suddenly. It was caused these workers felt anxious whether who should be dismissed if who could not attempt to produce eight wire assemblies of numbers one hour from Bill, factory supervisor demand. It seemed that the factory workers team norms and goals were not compatible with this company organizational objectives because this company organizational objective was needed workers finished to produce three wire assemblies of numbers to deliver to every client before schedule due date. It was depended on the situation of the factory whether it had enough time and machine and skilful worker numbers to supply to finish the identified wire assemblies of numbers to every client identified schedule individually. Otherwise, currently, on this situation, it seemed that this factory lacked enough worker and machine numbers and enough time and training to those old(current workers), it caused who felt difficult that every worker needed to finish to produce eight wire eight assemblies of numbers minimum per hour to meet this Pacific electronic company client's identified schedule change suddenly. It also seemed that this company current organizational objective was not same to its prior (past) organizational objective, such as every team worker needed to finish to produce three wire assemblies of numbers minimum per hour before to meet this Pacific electronic company client's

identified schedule change suddenly. It was given more difficult to let this factory team every worker to attempt to finish to produce eight wire assemblies of numbers minimum per hour to meet this current Pacific electronic company client's sudden schedule change. Hence, in this situation, I should feel this factory team norms and goals were not compatible with their company's past organizational objective for this Pacific electronic company's earliest past three wire assemblies of numbers of every worker individual production demand in the identified schedule. In this situation, this Pacific electronic company client's wire assemblies of production numbers needed to be changed which caused this company factory team expectation schedule and wire assemblies of production numbers, such as every worker needed to produce eight wire assemblies minimum per hour of numbers of it's production goals and should be changed, but this factory team norms and production goals was still same to this Pacific electronic company client's earliest production numbers, such as every worker needed to produce three wire assemblies of numbers per hour. It meant that who needed have more time and worker and machine numbers to assist them to finish to produce if some workers had no enough effort to produce eight assemblies of numbers per hour to finish to meet this client's identified schedule change, otherwise, who needed to extend time to finish this client's production numbers schedule if none of them could produce eight wire assemblies of numbers at minimum one hour.

This, this factory team norms and goals seemed that who were not compatible with organizational client's current objective to every worker needed to increase to produce eight wire assemblies of numbers per hour to finish to meet this Pacific electronic company client prior (not changed) schedule possible. Otherwise, these current factory workers could increase to finish eight wire assemblies of numbers to meet this client's current schedule goals. If this factory team some workers could finish eight or even more wire assemblies of numbers of numbers per hour individually. Thus, this team productivity could still achieve this client's expectation goals to finish to meet on or before schedule. It implied that this team norms and goals was compatible with organizational current objective due to client's expectation wire assemblies of overall increasing numbers had been finished to meet schedule from this factory team overall productivity together. Thus, it caused why this factory team norms and goals would be compatible with organizational team objective of finishing enough wire assemblies of overall numbers to meet this client's schedule date goals possibly or this factory team norms and goals would not be compatible with organization team objective of not finishing enough wire assemblies of overall numbers to meet this client's schedule date goals possibly.

How does the team function to meet individual needs?

This company, Steve and Jack were electronic wire assemblies products factory manufactory workers (members) among of this factory team, who had worked in this factory team five years. Bill was this company factory supervisor, who needed to supervise this workers team to help every business client to finish every electronic wire assemblies of products order to meet whose identified schedule, then delivered to them by shipping channel. Hence, if Bill, factory supervisor

who could not lead whose workers team to co-operate to produce the identified electronic wire assemblies of products of numbers to finish to meet the individual business client's identified schedule before due date to deliver to them by shipping. It would cause that this company and the and the client would feel this company Mr Martin, office manager and Dave, shop of supervisor could not achieve their service agreement to finish electronic wire assemblies identifies numbers to deliver to them before schedule due date. The result would cause this company lost this client, even this company would accept guilty from this client's complaint. Hence, Bill, factory supervisor needed to lead whose workers team to work efficiently to achieve whose job responsibility to finish every individual business client identified good quality and non damaged of electronic wire assemblies of products of numbers to deliver to them by shipping before schedule due date.

In fact, this factory workers team was combined (co-operated) by every individual worker. Hence, if Bill, factory supervisor expected whose factory team could have good productivity and efficiency, who must individual needs. Otherwise, if some workers did not like to work hard, who would cause this team to delay to finish the identified electronic wire assemblies of numbers to deliver to the individual business client before the schedule due date. Hence, if ill, factory supervisor could

satisfy every individual worker needs, then Bill could lead this team to perform more effectively and efficiently. If this factory work could be done by individual without any need for teamwork was not necessary in this factory. I supposed that this factory needed different workers worked in different steps to cooperate to finish every electronic wire assembly product. The reason was possible that because the employer felt every worker could be more proficient to practise to finish the identified step to co-operate to work together in one team, thus every worker could be raised productivity and efficiency in team, it could get more benefits than individual worker did all steps to finish every electronic wire assembly product alone in this factory. However, as the number of this factory team workers increased, the need for cooperation also increased. As some point, the effort of Bill, factory supervisor who managed the factory team who would outweigh the benefit of having more workers and this factory team performance would began to decline. Hence, if this factory team of worker numbers increased suddenly.

Although, every business client's electronic wire assemblies of products individual order finishing time would be reduced possibly, but it seemed that Bill, factory supervisor would feel more difficult to spend more time to lead this team to manage every individual worker who how to co-operate to work more efficiency and who should also feel difficult to satisfy individual worker needs if this team increased many worker numbers sudden seriously. Hence, this factory team overall performance of efficiency and effectiveness would begin to decline for long term due to this factory team increased many worker numbers suddenly to cause every individual worker felt that who could not satisfy more needs than before. Team structure means of coordinating formal team efforts. Leaders are appointed and work rules and procedures are detailed and job descriptions specify individual task responsibilities. It is necessary to coordinate the efforts of individuals assigned to the different tasks. Otherwise, tasks may not be performed in the correct sequence and employees may duplicate their efforts or work against each other. It seemed that this factory workers team which electronic wire assembling steps could be similar to bank loan department and collection department steps. If one individual worker who had much effort to finish whose wire assembling job step more quick to compare another less effort worker individual wire assembling job step. It seemed that the much effort worker could have much time to attempt to help the another less effort worker to finish whose step. Hence, it was possible that this factory team function could compare every individual worker's effort whether who could had more effort and time to help other worker to finish whose wire assembly job step during the less effort worker could not finish whose wire assembling step quickly. Thus, this factory team function could evaluate whether who individual worker had more effort and much time to attempt to help another less effort individual worker to finish their wire assembling job step for every individual client. It implied that these much effort individual workers who had needs to pay to optimal compensation more than the less effort individual workers for whose better performance in the factory team. It was possible that the piece pay rate compensation was not suitable to these more effort individual worker to satisfy whose individual needs to accept in the team because who could increase return to multi tasking, in which the same workers did both easy to observe tasks, such as wire assembling production of every step and hard to observe tasks, such as process improvement of wire assembling production of every step and producing exact wire assembling quantities of output (no more and no less). I suggest this factory ought change piece rate compensation to time rate compensation and gain sharing payment method to the more effort individual worker productivity , the individual more effort worker who could receive time rate compensation plus a usually small amount bonus linked to the productivity of the establishment to this factory team during who could increase return to multi tasking to assist whom to finish the another job step of less effort worker's wire assembling job duty for any individual client's wire assembling products delivering order before schedule due date.

I supposed that this factory team function adopted transfer lines in which individual worker was transferred between stations either by machines or by a moving conveyor assembly line. In either case, time rates compensation were more advantages than piece rates compensation due to it was more fair to the every more effort individual worker if who could finish whose wire assembling individual step before schedule due date and who had more time to assist another less effort worker to help who to finish whose wire assembly step immediately. In result, these every individual workers could raise this team efficiency to help this factory team to finish the identified wire assembly numbers to deliver to any client by shipping before the schedule due date normally. Bill, factory supervisor and Dave shop of supervisor who both could obtain high effort from this factory workers on observable tasks by noticing where the wire assembly inventory piles up between stations, without incurring the costs of piece rates. I supposed that the wire assembling products required operations on different machines, performed in different orders setting up fixed paths for work to travel would have made low effort in production more observable, but would have made the wire assembling production process very inflexible. Therefore, Bill, factory supervisor needed put each individual worker in charge of a machine that could do several jobs. (each with a negotiated rat) and encouraged this team workers to do each job quickly via piece rates. Since there was recurring demand for each wire assembling product for a long time, management did not have to negotiate new piece rates very often. I suggested that Bill, factory supervisor should design the observable tasks , e.g. the step of wire assembling production to be done by one group of factory workers and the unobservable making improvement to the step of wire assembling production, fixing problems to be done by another group with a different compensation scheme and observable and unobservable tasks were separated in this factory team. Thus, wire assembly production workers focused on producing output and were paid to piece rate. Quality was the responsibility of other departments workers, such as inspectors, who identified defective parts and engineers , who attempted to design less defect wire assembly products and processes, these all individual workers who every was paid time rates. All else equal, the low rates compensation was paid to less effort individual worker per piece and the higher rates and bonus compensation was paid to high effort individual worker per time rate to finish every individual business client's order. Finally, this factory team function could give synergy to achieve an effect of the total output of this factory team is greater than the combined outputs of individual worker working alone. In conclusion, this factory team function could use time rates and bonus compensation method to pay to the individual more effort every worker to let who to feel this employer was more fair to every individual worker performance. The more effort workers ought have more reasonable compensation to compare the less effort workers in this factory team.

● If I was Dave, shop supervisor, what team concepts should I apply? why?

If I was Dave, shop supervisor, I should apply these team concepts to this electronic factory wire assembling team. When, managers assign associates to teams, who often make three common assumptions, which can lead to mistakes; such as, who assume that a large team size always better and who assume that everyone knows how or is suited to work in a team and who assume that people who are similar to each other will work better together and so they can co-operate happily. Group means two or more interdependent individuals who influence one another through social interaction. Thus, if I was Dave, shop supervisor, I and my shop staffs would be one group. Bill, factory supervisor and factory team workers who would be another group factory workers team ; Mr Martin, office manager and office staffs would be another group top managers team. Our company needed these three groups communicate and co-operate to work together to deliver message between about of us about every individual business client's wire assembly product numbers demand and schedule due date to ensure when every client's order could confirm to finish to deliver to the client by shipping factory supervisor and whose workers was a team because this team had two or more workers with work roles that required them to be interdependent who operated within a large social system, as our factory performing tasks, such as every individual worker needed to produce every part of wire assembling in different stage relevant to our organization's mission , such as finishing the indicated wire assembling numbers to meet individual client's schedule to deliver to whom by shipping with consequences that affected others inside, such as Bill, factory supervisor and others outside, such as Dave, shop supervisor and Mr Martin , office manager of our organization, such as company and Bill, factory supervisor had membership that was identified to these on factory team and those not on the team, such as Dave, shop supervisor and sellers teams as well as Mr Martin, office manager and office administration teams. Effective team performance can be more difficult to achieve when team members belong to difficult identify groups or when their identification with these groups conflicts with the goals and objectives of the team, such as these factory some workers who felt difficult to raise to produce eight wire assembling from these wire assemblies in this factory team, but Mr Martin, office manager needed Dave, shop supervisor to notify to Bill, factory supervisor to let whose factory workers every one to know whether who could raise productivity to this eight numbers and who could not, then who decided whether how to solve that Pacific electronic company client could not receive wire assemblies of identified number before schedule due date by shipping. In fact, Dan shop supervisor would had conflict, with Mr Martin, office manager who explained workers felt wages were less, so who would not worked hard to raise effort to produce more wire assemblies, but Mr Martin , office manager disagreed whose suggestion and who enforced Dan, factory supervisor to enquire whether these factory workers who could do eight wire assemblies possibly, it would cause some workers felt anxious to be dismiss if who could not finish this numbers. This, these group conflicts caused non effective team performance with the factory group goals and the shop group goals and management group goals which were more different. If I was Dave, shop supervisor of this electronic company, I would apply management team concept to my shop group because I believed we were both the senior level shop manager and office manager who needed to coordinate the activities of our respective units, e.g. shop top management teams and office top management teams as well as Mr Martin, office management group . Otherwise, Bill, factory supervisor would be production team because workers who needed to supervise whose factory workers group to produce tangible products, such as identified wire assemblies of numbers to meet every individual client's schedule due date.

A final consideration in Dave, shop supervising team effectiveness is whether a supervising team is needed to perform the work at all or whether the work is best performed by Dave, shop supervisor individually. I this case, it would have been better to have individual separately, Dave, shop supervising team effectiveness is measured

on knowledge criteria, affective criteria and outcome criteria. Knowledge criteria reflected the degree to which Dave, shop supervisor individually increased its performance capability . Affective criteria addressed the question of whether Dave, shop supervisor individually
had a fulfilling and satisfying to supervise shop experience, such as whether Dan could manage whose shop and factory effectively. Outcome criteria referred to Dan 's personal quality of the shop supervisor how to supervise whose shop and factory teams effectively. Hence, if I was Dan this electronic company shop supervisor, I shall apply these team concepts to apply to whose shop and factory teams management in this situation.

● Fair compensation solve baseball organization players cooperation challenge

Brooklyn Bluebirds baseball organization was the best professional team for ten years win competition. A new owner, Trudy Mills, who acquired it to rebuild the team by acquiring big name players intention. However, during the first month end, the team was in the first place with a record of 20 wins and 7 losses, but then conflicts problems began. Conflict is a process in which one party perceives that its interests are being opposed or negatively affected by another party. Firstly, Bluebirds organization encountered of conflict between players were reported in the sports columns. Russ Thompson, a five years veteran and starting first baseman team player, publicly stated that who wanted to renegotiate his contract. In fact, the reason to Russ, this baseball team player who caused this conflict, due to he was unhappy that whose baseball team current employer, Trudy had brought many baseball players at much higher salaries than him. Hence, it caused Trudy, baseball team player who felt dissatisfactory to whose current employer, he felt who had fire year baseball competitions experiences and who had fire year baseball competitions experiences and who had helped whose baseball team, such as Brooklyn Bluebirds to win much competitions. Hence, who felt Trudy, current Brooklyn Bluebirds baseball owner could not give him higher salaries than this team's other baseball team players. It was unfair to him. In the result, Russ, baseball team player met with Trudy, Brooklyn Bluebirds baseball team owner and Trudy's lawyer and Bluebird's general baseball team manager to discuss whose salary increasing issue, but the meeting ended in disagreement and both Russ, baseball team player and Trudy, Brooklyn Bluebirds baseball team owner were angry, it was caused by salary could not increased to Russ, baseball team player disagreement to achieve negotiation conflict within Bluebirds organization. It seemed that Russ, baseball team player and Trudy, Bluebirds baseball team employer (owner) whose interpersonal conflict which occurs between their both individuals in this organization. They are personal conflict, it means Trudy, Bluebirds baseball team employer and Russ, baseball team player both conflict that arises out of personal differences between people, such as differing goals, values or personalities, such as the baseball it was possible that Trudy, Bluebirds baseball team owner who would not give high salary to Russ, baseball team player due to who needed to evaluate whose baseball competitions performance with team members to judge whether who ought to increase whose salary, but Russ, baseball team player felt who was unfair to pay him less salary than other baseball players due to who had five years baseball competition experiences.

Thus, their differing values were very
different to cause this personal conflict in this Bluebirds baseball team organization. It also seemed that Trudy, baseball team owner existed substantive conflict that involved work content and goals to Russ, baseball player, such as Trudy needed time to evaluate Russ, baseball competitions performance (work content) whether who could help whose baseball team to win competitors (goals) to decide whether who could increase salary. I felt the main factor to cause their personal conflict was that Russ, baseball player felt Trudy, baseball team owner paid him less salary than other baseball players. Instead of this factor, it had also other factors, such as, baseball team organization needed interdependency co-operation specially. Interdependency means work must be coordinated between groups (such as baseball team) or individuals (baseball players). The more interdependent two
groups on individuals are the more the potential for conflict exists. Interdependency can result from limited resources or from required coordination in the timing and sequencing of activities. Due to Russ, baseball team player needed to co-operate with other baseball team players to attempt to carry on practising to learn how to achieve to win any baseball competitions intention. Hence, it was possible that Russ would listen of conflict between players who were reported in the baseball players in the baseball sports columns about their salary issue, even it was possible that

Russ and other baseball players who felt Russ and other baseball players who felt difficult to attempt to co-operate to carry on baseball team training within limited time and sequencing of activities before any baseball competitions.

It would cause this baseball team group conflict occurrence between baseball team individual players because this baseball team individual players and baseball team group had less control over own team cooperation in this situation. Russ, baseball team player felt who individual abilities were exceed to other baseball team players in this baseball team. In fact, Russ's individual abilities did not sum up to influence this baseball team performance. Russ, individual baseball player skill was only moderately good predictor when two or more team players interacted in a precise way. Due to baseball sport team needed more cooperation and interaction to team every players, so it was necessary the importance of individual ability decreases and groups processed increased.

Hence, the more closer the team players were in their abilities, the more likely who would fully put to use their combined abilities . Thus, it was possible that Russ would feel whose baseball skill and ability was exceed to this team other baseball players to cause who felt more difficult interdependent to co-operate with the other team baseball players in this baseball team to cause this team difficult co-operational conflict. Hence, the difficult baseball team cooperation also caused the group conflict due to Russ felt dissatisfactory reward and who felt the other baseball players performance would influence whose performance to be poor to win any further baseball competitions indirectly. Russ, baseball team player was discouraged to leave Trudy, Bluebirds baseball team organization by Marty, baseball team manager indirectly.

Next, Bluebird baseball team organization also encountered conflict between Marty, baseball team manager and Russ and Mickey baseball team players as well as conflict between Marty, baseball team manager and Trudy, baseball team employer (owner) about who planned leaving. Trudy, current baseball employer. This conflict was caused due to Marty, baseball team manager discouraged these two baseball team players both Russ and Mickey continued to serve this employer and encouraged who signed another baseball team employer who could give more salary to them. However, Trudy, this baseball team employer (owner) still felt Russ and Mickey both were the best baseball player and the clients paid to see them player. Hence, Trudy phoned to Marty, baseball team manager to require who to apologize to them and persuaded them did not plan to leave.Then, Marty baseball team manager made conflict with whose employer, Trudy to indicate himself had been a good baseball team manager to manage whose baseball team players effectively and who felt that who did not need to apologize to Russ and Mickey, these two baseball team players because who had not leave Trudy currently and who had already trained them to play further baseball competitions. This conflict was caused because Marty, baseball team manager who encouraged these two team players to leave due to whose salaries were paid less than other baseball team players. Then, Trudy baseball team employer needed Marty to persuade who did not leave his baseball organization, but Marty refused to tell them about whose employer instruction. Thus, it caused group substantive conflict due to Russ and Mickey both baseball team players felt dissatisfaction to work in this baseball team to achieve team cooperation goal with other team players to win any baseball competitions as well as it also caused individual procedural conflict between Trudy and Marty due to that Trudy, baseball team owner gave responsibilities to Marty, such as Marty, baseball team manager needed to apologize to these two team players and persuaded them did not plan to leave, Marty felt it was not whose responsibilities due to who had finished to manage this baseball team effectively and who ought not need to apologize to them due to who was their manager. However, Trudy felt it was also whose responsibilities. Thus, unreasonable responsibility was a factor to cause Marty felt dissatisfactory to Trudy, baseball team employer to require him to do this apologizing issue.

suggestion of solvable method:

● Describe the types of conflict that seem to exist within the Bluebirds organization.

What are the causes?

Is the conflict functional, dysfunctional or both? explain

Dysfunctional conflict is different to functional conflict as below:

Dysfunctional conflict is conflict that interferes with performance to organizational goals and objectives, such as doubting about the organization's future performance in the minds of shareholders; conflict can cause people to exercise their own individual power and engage in political behaviour directed toward achieving their own goals; conflict can have negative effects on interpersonal relationships, so it needs to take time and resources and emotional energy to deal with conflict, both on an interpersonal and an organizational level.

Functional conflict is beneficial to organizational goals and objectives . Any organizations without functional conflict frequency lack the energy and ideas to create effective innovation. Conflict can have a number of functional consequences for organizations, such as facilitation of change, improved problem solving or decision making, enhanced morale within a group, more ability in communication and productivity and creativity and stimulation. I felt this Bluebirds baseball team organization had only dysfunctional conflict, such as Trudy baseball team owner and Marty, baseball team manager who had negative effects on interpersonal relationship. Trudy needed to take time and resources and emotional energy to deal with Marty's individual conflict both on an interpersonal level. For example, in fact, Marty encouraged Russ and Mickey to leave Trudy's baseball team, but Marty refused to follow Trudy's requirement to apologize to them and persuaded them to stay. It would cause this baseball team other players turnover numbers to be increased due to these two the best baseball players leaving influence and Trudy would lose these two the best baseball performance players final.

On conclusion, all of conflicts are caused by unfair compensation to this baseball organizational every players, so this basball organization needs to spend time to decide every player whether whom ought pay the reasonable compensation for his performance. Then, these conflicts will be solved to reduce in possible.

● Fair compensation strategy solves compensation director poor working performance challenge

This is one case applies expectancy theory provides a useful framework for organizing those factors : people will be committed to goals that carrying a reasonable expectation of being attained and are more viewed as desirable to attain. It aims to solve the senior management working performance challenge.

When you are one entrepreneur to manage one compensation director behavior, how you manage him/her successfully. Frances Mead , compensation director for Puma corporation , who paid well to hire Don Coggin to fill position of benefits administrator for her company in corporate personnel department at Puma, headquartered in Salt Lake city, Utah and the job was located in Utah. Hence, Don could always enjoyed the outdoor and he liked to backpack, camp and did some mountain climbing sport entertainment conveniently. Hence, it ensured that this job location could give Dan to enjoy his likely mountain climbing ,camp, backpack sport entertainment conveniently was also an important reason to influence Don to choose this job.In fact, Dan's financial background aided him greatly in his new benefits administrator job, where he was responsible for development and administration of the pension plan, life and health insurance package, employee stock purchase plan and other employee benefit programs within one month. Dan has learned how to do duties. Frances Mead, she was satisfied with her selection for Dan to do this benefits administrator position. Hence, she expected Dan to move up to in the department rank rapidly, but Dan only concern was that who did not seem to have enough time to enjoy his outdoor activities after he had seem promoted to do further duties absolutely. It implied that Dan disliked to promote to spend more time to do more job duties.
Even, his salary would not be increased and his rank would be promoted in this moment. After six months, Dan had his job proficiently and who was quite talented and the job did not present a strong challenge to him. During to Frances, compensation director for Puma corporation recognized Dan's talent and wanted him to evaluate Puma corporation's complete benefits package for the purpose of making needed changes without the help of costly outside consultants and Frances believed that Puma's benefits package was outdated and needed to be revised. However, Frances felt Dan disliked to discuss with her to evaluate the total benefits package from her several encouraging because Dan seemed to be constantly thinking of and discussing his outdoor activities and he seemed lack of commitment to do his job. As ERG theory indicated that a person's existence needs don't necessarily have to be satisfied before who can became concerned about whose relationships with others or about using whose personal capabilities, whose desire to meet the existence needs may be stronger than whose desire to meet the two other types of needs, such as relationship with others or about using those personal capabilities, but the other needs may still be important. As this case, Dan , this company 's benefits administrator who chose to serve this company, instead of salary was paid well reason, the other reason was his job was located to let him to enjoy the outdoors sport activities

conveniently. Hence, it is Dan's existence needs in this company. Hence, even Frances , this company compensation director accepted to increase Dan's salary to promote him to do higher rank after six months, due to Dan's personal capabilities was very good. Dan whose behaviour performance disliked to discuss with Frances to evaluate and Dan seemed to be constantly thinking of and discussing his outdoor activities and he seemed lack of commitment to his job. As ERG theory indicated Dan could not motivated by Frances because Frances needed him to forgive to enjoy his outdoor sport entertainment when Frances needed him to spend much time to discuss with her to evaluate the total benefits package at this moment. However, Dan felt the reason of his existence was staying in this company was because his new job could located in Utah to always enjoyed the outdoor entertainment. If he could not spend extra time to enjoy this kind of entertainment. It would cause Dan lost commitment to serve this employer.

suggestion of solvable method:

Using ERG theory, explain the reasons for the situation described in the case.

ERG theory suggests people are motivated by three hierarchically ordered types of needs: existence needs (E), relatedness needs (R) and growth needs (G). A person may work at the same time, although satisfying lower order needs often takes place before a person is strongly motivated by higher level needs.Work motivation and job satisfaction means the relationship between the organization and its members is influenced by what motivates them to work and the rewards and fulfilment they derive from it. Motivation is typified as an individual phenomenon. Every person is unique and all the major theories of motivation allow for this uniqueness to be demonstrated in one way or another, it is as intentional to assume to be under the worker's control and behaviours that are influenced by motivation, such as effort expended. Motivation is through an understanding of internal cognitive processes, that is what people feel and how who think. This understanding should help the manager to predict likely behaviour of staff in given situations. The two factors of greatest importance are what gets people activated and the force of an individual to engage in desired behaviour (direction or choice of behaviour). The purpose of motivation theories is predict behaviour. Motivation isn't the behaviour itself and it is not performance. Motivation concerns action and the internal and external forces which influence a person's choice of action.

Maslow's hierarchy of needs theory suggests people are motivated by their desire to satisfy specific needs and that needs are arranged in a hierarchy with physiological needs at the bottom and self actualization needs at the top. People most satisfy needs at lower levels before being motivated by needs at higher levels. However, ERG theory differs from Maslow's theory. Firstly, a person's existence needs don't necessarily have to be satisfied before who can become concerned about whose relationships with others or about using whose personal capabilities, whose desire to meet the existence needs may be stronger than whose desire to meet the two other types of needs, such as relationship with others or about using those personal capabilities, but the other needs may still be important. Otherwise, the need hierarchy theory proposes that the hierarchy is fixed and that physiological needs must be largely satisfied before other needs become important. Hence, using ERG theory to apply to this case, it may explain why Don Coggin did these behaviour. Although, Frances Mead , compensation director for Puma corporation , who paid well to hire Don Coggin to fill position of benefits administrator for her company in corporate personnel department at Puma, headquartered in Salt Lake city, Utah and the job was located in Utah. Hence, Don could always enjoyed the outdoor and he liked to backpack, camp and did some mountain climbing sport entertainment conveniently. Hence, it ensured that this job location could give Dan to enjoy his likely mountain climbing ,camp, backpack sport entertainment conveniently was also an important reason to influence Don to choose this job.In fact, Dan's financial background aided him greatly in his new benefits administrator job, where he was responsible for development and administration of the pension plan, life and health insurance package, employee stock purchase plan and other employee benefit programs within one month. Dan has learned how to do duties. Frances Mead, she was satisfied with her selection for Dan to do this benefits administrator position. Hence, she expected Dan to move up to in the department rank rapidly, but Dan only concern was that who did not seem to have enough time to enjoy his outdoor activities after he had seem promoted to do further duties absolutely. It implied that Dan disliked to promote to spend more time to do more job duties.

Even, his salary would not be increased and his rank would be promoted in this moment. After six months, Dan had his job proficiently and who was quite talented and the job did not present a strong challenge to him. During to Frances, compensation director for Puma corporation recognized Dan's talent and wanted him to evaluate Puma corporation's complete benefits package for the purpose of making needed changes without the help of costly outside consultants and Frances believed that Puma's benefits package was outdated and needed to be revised. However, Frances felt Dan disliked to discuss with her to evaluate the total benefits package from her several encouraging because Dan seemed to be constantly thinking of and discussing his outdoor activities and he seemed lack of commitment to do his job. As ERG theory indicated that a person's existence needs don't necessarily have to be satisfied before who can became concerned about whose relationships with others or about using whose personal capabilities, whose desire to meet the existence needs may be stronger than whose desire to meet the two other types of needs, such as relationship with others or about using those personal capabilities, but the other needs may still be important. As this case, Dan , this company 's benefits administrator who chose to serve this company, instead of salary was paid well reason, the other reason was his job was located to let him to enjoy the outdoors sport activities conveniently. Hence, it is Dan's existence needs in this company. Hence, even Frances , this company compensation director accepted to increase Dan's salary to promote him to do higher rank after six months, due to Dan's personal capabilities was very good. Dan whose behaviour performance disliked to discuss with Frances to evaluate and Dan seemed to be constantly thinking of and discussing his outdoor activities and he seemed lack of commitment to his job. As ERG theory indicated Dan could not motivated by Frances because Frances needed him to forgive to enjoy his outdoor sport entertainment when Frances needed him to spend much time to discuss with her to evaluate the total benefits package at this moment.

However, Dan felt the reason of his existence was staying in this company was because his new job could located in Utah to always enjoyed the outdoor entertainment. If he could not spend extra time to enjoy this kind of entertainment. It would cause Dan lost commitment to serve this employer. Hence, as ERG theory indicated that Dan felt he and Frances relationship would become worse and he would feel this company was not to be valued for whom to grow further and Dan would plan to leave current employer possibly if Frances continue to force Dan to discuss with her to evaluate the total benefits package for her employer. Moreover, ERG theory also indicated that when a need is satisfied, it may remain the dominant motivator if the next need in the hierarchy can't be satisfied. As Dan , benefits administrator who had satisfied whose relatedness needs to Frances, as Frances had believed who was satisfied with her selection to do this benefits administrator position absolutely within this six months. Basically, Dan felt his existence needs was satisfied with Frances, compensation director relationship. Hence, during Dan was stilling doing this benefits administration position within these six months, it might remain Dan to be this company dominant motivator, even, he could not promote to do higher rank and he could earn higher salary from Frances after these six months. In result, Dan's performance began to be poor after six months, e.g. complaints from employees regard errors and time delays in insurance claims and stock purchases began to increase. Also, Dan was package and thus no progress in the design of new benefit programs and he began to call in sick occasionally. Interestingly, he seemed to be sick on Friday and Monday, allowing for a three day weekend. It was obvious that Dan had the ability to perform the job and even more challenging tasks. In conclusion, Dan changed his behaviour and performance poorly in this company because Dan felt not he had existence needs, as he needed to spend time to discuss with Frances to evaluate the total benefits package employees, she could not let him to have more extra time to enjoy his sport entertainment as well as Dan, benefits administrator and Frances, compensation director both co-operation relationship was broken because the reason of Frances needed Dan to spend much time to discuss with her to evaluate Puma corporation's completion benefits package for the purpose of making needed changes was that she did not without the help of costly outside consultants and Frances was still not ensuring to increase his salary, she was examining Dan's ability in this stage. Hence, Frances's decision would cause Dan lost existence needs and relatedness needs and growth needs in this company. Due to these needs had been found to decrease to Dan as they were not satisfied and the lesser needs were not satisfied and the lesser are desired . Hence, it would cause Dan's behaviour and performance to be poor because Frances could not motivate Dan to get these psychological needs absolutely in this company after six months.

Using expectancy theory, explain the reasons for the situation.

Expectancy theory suggests motivation is a function of an individuals expectancy that a given amount of effort will lead to particular level of performance and judgement that indicates performance will lead to certain outcomes. Expectancy is the subjective probability that a given amount of effort will lead to a particular level of performance. Hence, manager needs to consider the factor of probability that a given amount of effort will lead to a particular level of performance and the second factor individuals consider is the perceived connection between a particular level of performance and important outcomes and the third factor is the importance of each anticipated outcome.Hence, it means individual may have different goals or needs and individual may have different connections between actions and achievement of goals to consider alternatives, weigh cost and benefit and choose action of maximum utility. Different reward can be given to individual as a result of effort or performance. Hence, expectancy theory indicates that people are influences by the expected results of their actions.

Concept of motivation is some driving force within individuals by which they attempt to achieve some goal in order to fulfil some need or expectation. People's behaviours are determined by what motivates them.Their performance is a product of both ability level and motivation. Motivation is a function of the relationship between effort expended and perceived level of performance and the expectation that rewards (desired outcomes) will be related to performance and the expectation that rewards (desired outcomes) are available. Motivation includes extrinsic and intrinsic two kind of motivations. Extrinsic motivation is related to tangible rewards such as salary and benefits, security, promotion, contract of service, the work environment and conditions of work as well as intrinsic motivation is related to psychological rewards, such as the opportunity to use one's ability, a sense of challenge and achievement, receiving appreciation, positive recognition and being treated in a caring and considerate manner.People are capable and willing to perceive fairness in their immediate environment, compare input , ability, skill, age, education, effort and training to outcome like monetary reward, praise, status, improved promotion opportunities to compare reward to others. It implies needs and expectations of staffs at work, it includes economic rewards, social relationships, intrinsic satisfaction. Hence, motivation is as psychological forces that determine the direction of a person's behaviour in an organization and a person's level of effort and a person's level of persistence. It is important that managers attempt to reduce potential frustration, for example, through, effective recruitment, selection and socialisation, training and development, job design and work organization, equitable human resource management policies, recognition and reward, effective communications,participative styles of management, attempting to understand the individual's perception of the situation. Proper attention to motivation and to the needs and expectation of people at work will help overcome boredom and frustration induced behaviour.

To apply this expectancy theory to this case study. In fact, Dan who had lack effort and motivation to do this benefits administrator position from Frances after six months, so Dan should choose to perform whose normal job duties poorly. e.g. complaints from employees regarding errors and time delays in insurance claims and stock purchases began to increase. Even, Dan was making no progress in the evaluation of benefit package and thus no progress in the design of new benefit programs and he began to call in sick occasionally. Interestingly, he seemed to be sick on Friday and Monday, allowing for a three day weekend. It was obvious that Dan had the ability to perform the job and even more challenging tasks.The expectancy theory could explain reasons why Dan's behaviour and performance was became poor. Due to expectancy theory suggests motivation is a function of an individual's expectancy that a given amount of effort will lead a particular level of performance and judgement that indicates performance will lead to certain outcomes. Before the six months, Frances could give motivation to Dan, such as she could give good salary and good job location to satisfy Dan's life needs and outdoor sport entertainment needs and Dan and Frances both felt this job's working hours and Dan's ability and performance was very reasonable.

However, after six months, Frances needed Dan to spend much time to discuss with her to evaluate the total benefits package for her employees, but Frances could not tell Dan to ensure to increase Dan's salary and promotion after Dan should finish this extra evaluation job duties with Frances. Even, Dan felt who could not enjoy this outdoor sport entertainment due to he needed to spend much time to discuss with Frances about the total benefits package evaluation to whose employees issue. Hence,Dan would felt that who spent much effort to do this job, but he could not get fair salary and position . It would cause him to decide to change his job performance and personal behaviour to be poor , e.g. complaints from employees regarding, errors and time delays in insurance claims and stock purchases began to increase. Even, Dan was also making no progress in the evaluation of benefit package and this no progress in the design of new benefit programs and he began to call in sick occasionally. Interestingly, he seemed to be sick on Friday and Monday, allowing for a three day weekend. It was obvious that Dan had the ability (effort) to perform to job (benefit administrator position) in this Puma corporation company, but he chose to perform to do this position poorly. The reason was because Dan had judged that his expectancy was not reasonable from Frances demand because Dan needed to spend much time to discuss with Frances and who could not get higher salary and higher rank and who could not have extra time to enjoy his outdoor entertainment. Hence, Dan's decision to make poor performance and bad behaviour, his aim was to make Frances felt who had ability to change another new job possibly. Unless, Frances could change her decision not needed Dan to spend much time to discuss with her to deal this extra job duties. Otherwise, who would find another new job possibly. It implied Dan's job expectancy was not same to Frances's performance need expectancy to Dan to cause Dan's poor performance occurred after six month.

Using the integration framework found in the last major section of the chapter, describe what actions Frances should and should not take.

In fact, Dan Coggin, benefits administrator, whose behaviour performance indicated that who chose to do this job because he felt be well paid and this job was located in Utah to always enjoy the outdoors activities of backpack, camp and do some mountain climbing. Before six months, Dan's job performance was satisfied with Frances, compensation director, so it caused Dan expected Dan to move up in the department ranks rapidly . Due to Frances felt Puma's benefits package was outdated and needed to revised and who proposed to making needed changes, without the help of costly outside consultants. Thus, Frances decided to recognize Dan's talents and wanted him spent extra time to evaluate with her to discuss how Puma corporation's complete benefits package to make changed to satisfy Puma's employees benefits of needs. However, after six months, Dan's performance and behaviour began to be poor, e.g. complaints from employees regarding errors and time delays in insurance claims and stock purchase began to increase. Also, Dan was making no progress in the evaluation of benefit package and thus no progress in the design of new benefit programs and he began to call in sick occasionally. Interestingly, he seemed to be sick on Friday and Monday, allowing for a three day weekend. It was obvious that Dan had the ability to perform the job and even more challenging tasks.

However, why Dan became lazy and who disliked to spend extra time to discuss with Frances to evaluate how to change Puma corporation's complete benefits package to its employees. It was obvious that Frances forced Dan to spend extra time to discuss with her to do evaluation issue that who did not enquire Dan's desire(ideas) whether who liked or disliked to do this issue and Dan would feel who would not have time to enjoy his sport activities in this job Utah location and who also felt it was unfair to him why whose salary was not increased and position was not promoted when Dan needed to spend extra time to do extra job unreasonably.

I shall use integration framework to find whether what Frances Mead, compensation director should take actions and should not take actions. On the one hand, Frances should take these actions as below:

In common, formulating strategies that can deliver competitive advantage is not easy. Senior managers needed to work with other individuals engage in meetings, experiments, discussion and analyses in order to create or modify company strategies. Implementing strategies and engaging in the day-to-day behaviours that help to create competitive advantage also are not easy task. Hence, staffs must be motivated if who are to effectively engage in the behaviours and practices that bring advantage and success to a firm. Hence, Frances mead, compensation director should need to choose to use different strategies to require different types of people (staffs) and behaviours and therefore different approaches to motivation. To fully motivate such Dan, benefits administrator staff, resource for trying new ideas, must be available, including time and opportunities to develop new skills to change old pension plan, life and health insurance package, employee stock purchase plan and other employee benefit programs benefit package. I believe human resources and time was not enough to Frances and Dan two people to evaluate this issue. Frances ought to enquire Dan's idea whether Dan felt what cause whose performance began to be poor, e.g. complaints from employee regarding errors and time delays in insurance claims and stock purchase began to increase. To investigate whether Dan felt the issue of evaluation Puma corporation's complete benefits packageissue with her or other factors that was influenced to his normal job performance to be poor. The benefits were that Frances could let Dan to tell what the reasons were to cause his performance poor honestly and their conservation could let Dan felt France could spend extra time to consider to discuss whether what Dan felt needs and dissatisfaction to cause Dan's performance poorly. Hence, Frances could judge whether Dan's ability could deal to evaluate Puma corporation's complete benefits package and this issues could not influence Dan's daily normal job duties for this benefits administrator position or not. If Frances should prefer to spend extra time to discuss with Dan about what difficulty and needs and dissatisfaction who felt to cause whose job performance began to be poor. Frances should know whether it was job factors or other factors were influenced to Dan to feel dissatisfaction to cause whose performance poorly to let Frances to revise whose strategies. The factors could include such as, unreasonable market salary, poor working environment, increasing job responsibilities and feeling difficulties, lacking opportunity for advancement or promotion, challenging work and potential for personal growth, lacking personal commitment and recognition and achievement needs to this position,lacking work and life balance needs, unreasonable company policies and working conditions and administration procedures, poor interpersonal relationship with peer and poor status security issues.

As goal setting theory suggests challenging and specific goals increase human performance because whose effort and persistence attention can be committed to affect motivation. Due to Frances didn't indicate clear specific goals to let Dan to know whether how and what steps who should use to evaluate Dan's ability to judge whose job performance was achieved to goal to promote higher rank before Dan began to do this job. Hence, Dan should feel doubt why Frances needed him to spend extra time to evaluate with Frances about making changes to Puma corporation's complete benefits package issue after six months. Hence, Frances should need to explain why who needed Dan to spend extra time to evaluate with him and they also needed to discuss further issue for this evaluation report job of about how difficult Dan felt his performance goal should be achieved whether the goal should be easy, moderately difficult or very difficult to achieve to Dan's ability, how the expert outcome should be specific or goals could be more do best what Dan needed to make commitment to achieve this goal; to what extent of feedback needs Dan should be informed of their report in this evaluation progress toward his performance goal. Hence, if Frances could let Dan to know what Dan needed to perform to achieve. Frances goal to evaluate Dan's ability clearly. Then, Dan's could judge whether Frances was a right employer for his continue staying or leaving further decision. An understanding for the factors that motivate workers are critical not only to corporate executive who concentrate on the bottom line, but more importantly to the security of companies as it relates to compete in the global market. However, the internal process view that motivation needs that activate, guide, and motivate behaviour (especially goal directed behaviour) is one of the most important concerns of modern organizational managers , as Frances Mead, compensation director for Puma corporation. The traditional motivator for a worker is his salary, but in many cases that isn't enough. As Puma corporation, Frances Mead, compensation director, it implied to use only material rewards to motivate Dan, benefits administrator staff , it was not enough and it needed to use only motivators to satisfy Dan's needs. Supposing to Dan's tasks such as development and administration of pension plan, life and health insurance and employee stock purchase package etc duties whose solution was obvious extrinsic motivators, e.g. increasing salary reward were working as which should be increase performance, but for task whose solution were more complex, such as revision and evaluation of complete outdated benefits package for the purpose how to make needed changes, extrinsic motivation should have negative effects on performance to Dan. Hence, if the task was complex, the motivation users must be intrinsic e.g. achievement, chance, promotion to give to Dan employee. Due to revision and evaluation of complete outdated benefits package was one complex and if also needed to spend more resources and time discussion tasks for Puma corporation. Hence, Frances should ought to tell Dan who should use job with performance related pay to attract him of higher ability and induced who to provide greater effort. Frances should focuses on Dan's role as an incentive system. Hence, Frances should consider compensation as a return for Dan's services rendered and saw Dan's performance was as a reflection of whose personal worth in terms of skills and abilities as well as whose education and training also had acquired. However, Frances should view compensation from two perspectives: as a major expense and as a possible influence on Dan's attitudes and behaviours through compensation based motivational strategies. This potential to influence Dan's work attitudes and behaviours and subsequently the productivity and effectiveness of Puma corporation.

Attribute theory indicated that when an outcome, such as poor performance is attributed to a stable cause. such as low intelligence, it is logical to expect that the employee's performance isn't going to change in the future. If the same poor performance is attributed to a less stable factor, such as insufficient effort, a employer can expect that the employee could improve whose performance by working harder in the future. Thus, Frances should consider what attributions were to influence Dan's job performance began to be poor, then who should revise whose actions should be changed to solve this issue. The attribution should influence Dan's performance to be poor, internal and stable attribution, such as whether Dan's intelligence could deal his normal job duties and extra job duties of evaluation on Puma's benefits package both at the same time; external and unstable attribution, such as whether Dan had enough effort and time to attempt to discuss with Frances to finish this extra job duties of
evaluation on Puma's benefits package within limited time or external and unstable attribution, such as whether Frances' temporary strategy or decision was without the help of outside consultants to evaluate Puma's benefits package whether which should give pressure or effort to Dan to attempt to help him to finish this evaluation job, it meant that Dan would do this duties, even which should also influence whose normal duties to be poor if Dan felt pressure to attempt to do this extra duties. Frances should need to provide feedback to Dan about whose progress toward performance goals was well established . In fact, feedback on performance was likely to have a positive effect on motivation. Moreover, Dan's feedback was important when benefits package of evaluation of performance goals existed and when Dan was relatively difficult to achieve. Hence, Frances's feedback should encourage Dan to discover (find) errors to know what he should need to improve during evaluation was progressing and Frances should not have due date limitation to let Dan felt pressure to finish this benefit plan evaluation job ,even if influenced to whose normal job duties poorly .

Expectancy theory provides a useful framework for organizing those factors : people will be committed to goals that carrying a reasonable expectation of being attained and are more viewed as desirable to attain. Frances should judge whether human resource inputs were enough to do this benefit package evaluation job with Dan. It was possible that Dan felt human resource inputs were out enough to cause who felt pressure to attempt to dot this extra job duties with Frances and Dan should feel inequity and unfair treatment and unreasonable due to who should need to spend extra time to do this extra evaluation job with Frances. Hence, Frances should need to explain to let Dan to know why who needed Dan to attempt to do this extra evaluation job as well as what benefits were Dan should give reward if Dan's evaluation job performance could satisfy Frances' requirement. Then Dan would be committed to goals that carrying a reasonable expectation of being attained and was more viewed as desirable to attain. On the other hand, Frances should not take these actions as below: Although Dan performance began to become poor after six months due to Dan needed to spend extra time to discuss with Frances to evaluate how to change Puma corporation old benefits package issue. However, Frances should not angry to blame Dan immediately. The reason was that Dan's performance was still good before six months. It meant that who had ability to do this position.Hence, Dan ought have ability to assist Frances to evaluate the changed needs to current benefits package evaluation to Puma corporation's employees with Frances discussion together.
Otherwise, if Frances should blame to Dan. it would cause Dan felt Frances was not a good compensation director to manage and co-operate with him to work together and it was possible that would choose to leave Puma corporation to find any employer immediately. Then, Frances would feel difficult to spend more time to choose applicants to re-employ another new staff to do this benefit administrator position, instead of Dan and Frances should also need to spend more time to train this new staff. Hence, Frances should not blame Dan. Otherwise, Frances should need to enquire why Dan's performance to be poor whether Dan's poor performance behaviour was caused by extra evaluation job duties factor or other personal factors to revise Dan's errors to expect Dan to continue to assist Frances to finish this evaluation job effectively and efficiently.

In conclusion, I did not agree Frances, compensation director should blame Dan immediately because Dan believed himself had owned market competitive ability due to Dan had worked in Puma corporation six months .

It should give Dan had confidence to change another new employer if Dan felt Frances' personal attitude was not friendly to arrange any further new jobs to him to do. Hence, Frances should enquire Dan why who performed poorly in order to solve whose personal trouble issues and then Frances should also attempt to find some methods to satisfy Dan's personal needs to motivate and persuade Dan to continue to co-operate with Frances in this company together.

Crisis management and time management strategy solves nuclear factory team cooperation challenge

This case concerns how this nuclear factory repair teams often face difficulties to make any kinds of decisions in suddenly. So, management decision making is one important factor to assist how they can deal any problems in any time when they are working in this nuclear factory. In academic decision theory, one fundamental decision rule is that of maximizing expected utility. This is the idea that when company management needs to make a decision and there are different choices, each choice has a set of possible outcome with different probabilities.

Nuclear factory team making the most right decision challenge:

When you are one nuclear factory entrepreneur, how you manage you nuclear team work efficiently. Dan was the supervisor of technical maintenance in the nuclear power facility factory and who had noticed that several of his people were reluctant to follow maintenance procedures. He had been told that the specifications were too complex to understand, that the procedures were often unnecessary,and that the plant engineers did not really appreciate maintenance problems. On the one hand, Dan realized that most of their complaints were just excuses for doing things their own way. On the other hand, Dan did not really know which procedures were important and which were not. That's why Dan had asked Mary, design engineer to meet with him. Mary, design engineer knew nuclear power plants' procedures are complex and potentially risky and every specification and every procedures had a reason for being there. If Dan, supervisor of technical maintenance ignored one procedure, they might get by with it and nothing happens. But one of them just might do it at the wrong time and it caused serious wrong result in this nuclear power plant. So, Mary needs Dan to explain that they had safety and cost to consider. If they lost expensive equipment how they should lie to pay for it. Dan referred that if they lost a finger or got exposes to much radiation, they would not like that happened either.

However, Mary needed Dan to follow her specification and procedures to do, but Dan told Mary this really wasn't what his maintenance staffs wanted and they hoped for a little flexibility and who felt who would not like it, but they would have to do it. Lately that afternoon, Dan decided to met his unit and relayed the instructions and who reminded them of the rules and disciplinary actions for not following procedures. At the end of the meeting, who couldn't decide whether whose decision had done any better than Mary's decision. Harry, technical maintenance staff noticed that he had been assigned the routinely scheduled maintenance on the three feed water pumps. The pumps were normally used only for start up and shutdown and as emergency backup. When the main feed water system malfunctioned, these pumps would activate to keep the steam generator from drying out. The procedure also specified that the pumps should be serviced and test one at a time and that one pump should be out of service at a time. Harry thought that who needed to take three hours to service the pumps that way, but who could do it in two hours if who shut don together. Finally, who did not follow specification and procedures to do maintenance job from Mary demand and who decided to shorten the normal three time to two hours to finish this pump maintenance service job. This case indicated that the nuclear power plant maintenance job needed Mary, design engineer and Dan, supervisor of technical maintenance to co-operate to give their opinions to make any important decision to follow the specification and procedures to reduce the incident crisis occurrence to cause serious death to workers and damage to nuclear power plants. However, due to Dan who had noticed that several of his people were reluctant to follow maintenance procedures. He had been told that the specifications were too complex to understand, that the procedures were often unnecessary, and that the plant engineers did not really appreciate maintenance problems. In fact, I believe that the bad result would be caused seriously. Hence, Mary needed Dan to discuss this issue urgently. However, Mary needed Dan to follow her specification and procedures to do, but Dan told Mary this really wasn't what his maintenance staffs wanted and they hoped for a little flexibility and who felt who would not like it, but they would have to do it. It implied that Dan still agreed whose technician opinions and refused to accept

Mary's opinion to follow specifications and procedure in the maintenance procedure as well as Dan decided to meet whose technicians to notify them the rules and disciplinary actions either who might choose to follow procedures or who might choose not to follow during their maintenance. Hence, it implied Dan gave whose technicians to choose freely and Dan's attitude was not forced to need them to follow easily. I agreed that Dan handled this decision was not the best way.However, it was not right that Dan made decisions to choose of nuclear power plant maintenance job whether technicians ought follow specifications and procedure from Mary or technicians ought not follow specifications and procedure from maintenance units actions in the short time. Because it would increase Dan, supervising maintenance unit technicians death or hurt chance and nuclear power plant damaging change if whose decision was wrong. So, Dan ought need to spend time to discuss and gather information to evaluate whether Mary or technicians' suggestion was more safe and less cost to work in nuclear power plant for long term benefits in their meeting together.

In fact, Dan had not follow the correct steps to make final decision before he accepted whose maintenance units did not need to follow specifications and procedures during who needed to maintain nuclear power plant. The decision making steps include that as defining the maintenance problem, e.g. what maintenance problems were the most important to need technicians followed all specifications and procedures to carry on working; identifying criteria, gathering and evaluating information, e.g. other nuclear power plant maintenance procedure methods; listing and evaluating information; selecting best alternative; implementing and following up and giving feedback to let Mary to know the reason either why who disagreed Mary's suggestion or why who agreed whose maintenance units suggestion or none of final decision was made that Mary and Dan and technicians needed to carry on meeting to discuss clearly. An effective decision was as one that was timely, that was acceptable to those affected by it, and that satisfied the key decision criteria, and it was in the systematic and logical process. Mary and Dan and maintenance units had not ever sat down to discuss this issue in any once meeting together. Dan only met Mary and Dan only met maintenance units individual to discuss this issue separately.He did not give chance to let them to discuss with him in meeting room by face to face contact. Hence, they could not have complete knowledge about all possible alternatives to achieve their potential results effectively because who lacked enough time to make decision making and one good decision making needs a cognitive activity that relies on both perception and judgement. If two people used different approaches to solve problem in the processes of perception and judgement, they were likely to make quite different decision, even if the facts and objectives are identical. As Mary and Dan used different approaches to solve maintenance procedure problem in the process of perception and judgement to decide decision whether the maintenance units needed to follow specifications and procedure or they did not need to follow during technicians did maintenance job in nuclear power plant. Thus, Dan could not ensure technicians' decision whether which was better than Mary's decision because who lacked complete knowledge about all possible alternatives to make final decision before. In conclusion, Dan ought spend time to follow correct decision steps to make decision and who also needed to give them to discuss this issue by face to face contact in meeting and he ought not own objective judgement to agree any one suggestion, who ought give them to make subjective judgement to discuss to accept whose decision freely. Hence, Dan ought to be one participant role and ought not be one controller role in this decision making procedure.

suggestion of solvable method:

Analyze the critical problem in Part A of the case.

Did Dan handle it in the best way?

What decision styles did he use?

Decisions are reflected the person's preference for one of two perceptual styles and one of two judgement styles. Dan seemed to use intuition style decision, who disliked details and time required to sort and interpret them and whose decision made using this style was based on imagination and Dan believed that whose creativity could help Mary and technicians both to choose whose decision was more suitable. For example, Dan did not spend time to follow decision steps to make decision and Dan did not let Mary and maintenance units and him had chance to meet to discuss this issue by face to face contact to decide whether whose decision was less risky and logical to maintenance units work in nuclear power plant easily. Dan was also a feeling style person to make whose judgement.

A feeling style meant a decision style focused on subjective evaluation and the emotional reactions of others. Dan preferred to rely on whose emotions and personal subjective judgements to agree maintenance units‘ decision. At the earlier, Dan had noticed that several of his people were reluctant to follow maintenance procedures. He had been told that the specifications were too complex to understand, that the procedures were often unnecessary, and that the plant engineers did not really appreciate maintenance problems. So, Dan had accepted maintenance units' suggestion to make judge and Dan had not think and analysed their suggestion clearly. So, Dan chose maintenance units decision was based their feeling and emotion reactions. Before,Dan was met to enquire whose suggestion from Mary. Dan would not accept her suggestion easily, even Mary let Dan to know what the serious crisis would have more chance to occur if his maintenance units did not follow specifications and procedure during they were carrying on maintaining job. However, Dan had not change to accept maintenance units‘ suggestion easily due to they had influenced Dan's feeling and emotion to judge this issue early.

In what important ways is Harry's behaviour different from Marv's?

During the nuclear power facilities occurred problem, Mary and Harry's both behaviour performance could be seemed as these four aspects to evaluate, such as judgement effort and decision making effort and crisis management effort and time management effort aspects.The important ways is Harry's behaviour different from Marv's included as below: Marv Bradbury, technician was working shift time in nuclear power facility plant. In fact, most technicians did not like this shift, but Marv discovered that who enjoyed this job after few months and who also liked sleep in the mornings and many of this co-workers complained his behaviour to influence poor team work. Marv's job in the nuclear power plant was particular important. Marv's primary was to monitor a series of dialsand readouts in the control room. In fact, the system was so automatic, so who did not spend much time to do this duty of control and manage this system. However, if the readings indicated some variance in the system whose responsibilities were great, who would needed to do duty of interpret the readings, diagnose the problem as well as who would needed to do initiate corrective actions if the automatic correcting system failed. For two reasons, Marv never worried about his responsibilities because the system was fault free and self correcting and it was a good system with no weaknesses as well as Marv had confidence to understand about the system and he was trained always knew what he had to do in the event of a problem and was capable of doing it. In fact, the system occurred problem and who attempted to solve, but who felt difficult to deal. Hence, Marv felt the system was in serve trouble and decided to phone to get help. Although, who could not solve this system problem, but who knew the result if the systems dried out, the temperature was really going to go up and that the core was going to be damaged. Hence, the nuclear power facilities would cause to damaged. However, it took minutes to get someone to attempt to solve this system trouble, but it was too late and no one seemed to know what to do.

On judgement effort and decision making effort aspects, Marv's behaviour performance was seemed as team co-operation managed style person. On the one hand, who lacked decision making effort and who could not attempt to solve problem himself and who needed team co-operation to work together to increase confidence to solve problem. On the other hand, who lacked judgement effort to know whether what who ought need to attempt to solve any during crisis occurred. Moreover, Marv also lacked time management and crisis management efforts.

However, Marv needed to wait eight minutes to get someone to attempt to solve this system trouble, but it was late and no one seemed to know what to do. If the technicians took longer time to arrive, even Marv could not phone to contact them successfully. The result would be more poor seriously. It seemed that Marv could not have confidence to continue to maintain this system. Otherwise, if Marv could attempt to maintain, it was possible that the system could be maintained successfully.

Because Marv felt to make decision making have some degree of risk at this immediate accident occurrence, it would seem that risk taken by a group should be the same as the average risk that would have been taken by the individual group members acting alone (himself). Hence, who decided not to do action to attempt to solve this trouble, who decided to phone other technician team members to wait their arrival after eight minutes to attempt to solve this trouble, but it was too late and no one seemed to know what to do. However, if who could attempt to solve this trouble within eight minutes, it is possible that this trouble would solve from himself alone.

Harry, technical maintenance staff noticed that he had been assigned the routinely scheduled maintenance on the three feed water pumps. The pumps were normally used only for start up and shutdown and as emergency backup. When the main feed water system malfunctioned, these pumps would activate to

keep the steam generator from drying out. The procedure also specified that the pumps should be serviced and test one at a time and that one pump should be out of service at a time.

Harry thought that who needed to take three hours to service the pumps that way, but who could do it in two hours if who shut don together. Finally, who did not follow specification and procedures to do maintenance job from Mary demand and who decided to shorten the normal three time to two hours to

finish this pump maintenance service job. Two hours later he was done and he packed up his tools and hurried to get home.

On crisis management and time management effort aspects, Harry's behaviour performance was seemed as self managed style. He could attempt to accept risk to decide how to solve problem from himself effort and who had effort to judge how to deal in any crisis occurrence and time management. Hence, it could prove who could deal any crisis occurrence alone and who did not spend time to wait any team members (technician group) assistance, although who could not ensure whose decision whether it was right or wrong. Hence, it implied who was one confident person.Harry, technical maintenance staff noticed that he had been assigned the routinely scheduled maintenance on the three feed water pumps. The pumps were normally used only for start up and shutdown and as emergency backup. When the main feed water system malfunctioned, these pumps would activate to keep the steam generator from drying out. The procedure also specified that the pumps should be serviced and test one at a time and that one pump should be out of service at a time. Harry thought that who needed to take three hours to service the pumps that way, but who could do it in two hours if who shut don together. Finally, who did not follow specification and procedures to do maintenance job from Mary demand and who decided to shorten the normal three time to two hours to finish this pump maintenance service job. Two hours later he was done and he packed up his tools and hurried to get home. On judgement and decision making effort aspects, Harry's behaviour performed who can attempt to judge what action was possible more right to solve this trouble, although who could not ensure whose action is right or wrong, who could make decision to attempt to finish whose job and who felt who would not need to spend time to wait other team members (technicians) to make any decision to work together. Hence, who performed that who was one confident person. In conclusion, risk exist when the outcome of a chosen course of action is not certain. Most decisions in business carry some degree of risk. In choosing between less and more risky options, an individual's risk taking propensity, or willingness to take chances, often plays a role. Two persons with different propensities to take risks may make different decisions when confronted with identical decision situations and information. One who is willing to face the possibility if loss, for example, may select a riskier alternative, whereas another person will choose for taking risks. As Harry and Marv who were working in this same nuclear power facility plant, when the crisis occurred, whose performance would have different to decide to cause different result. Due to Harry performed behaviour was more confident and more judgement effort and self managed person who could accept risk to attempt to make decision alone and disregarded whether the result was right or wrong . Otherwise, Marv performed behaviour was lacked confidence and less judgement effort and team managed person who could not accept risk to attempt to make decision alone and regarded whether the result was right absolutely. Hence, their performance caused the result was also different, as Harry decided to spend two hours to solve the system trouble alone. Although Marv was not sure that Harry's action whether was correct or incorrect and it needed time to wait whether the system would occur trouble again or not. However, Harry had attempted to finish whose duties. Otherwise, Marv decided to phone to ask technicians to assist whom and they arrived after eight minutes and who attempted to co-operate to work together. But it was too late and no anyone seemed to know what to do and the system trouble would not still be solve. Hence, it was ensure that the system must be existed trouble and Marv decided not to continue to solve this problem individually and it seemed that Marv could not finish whose duties definitely. Otherwise, Harry could attempt to solve this system trouble alone although it needed time to wait.

It seemed that Harry, technician had more strategic decision ability and performed better to compare Marv to deal any crisis occurrence in the nuclear power plant and it seemed that who could assist Dan, supervisor technical maintenance in whose team effectively, although the system needed time to wait to confirm whether it was needed to maintain or needed not maintain again after Macv spent two hours to attempt to maintain. However, it seemed that Harry had more judgement and decision making and crisis management and time management efforts to compare Marv to do this technician position in this nuclear power plant.

How might group decision making be applied at the end of Part B?

The group decision making might be applied to Marv, technician shift team as below:

In general ,in high involvement organizations, associates participate in many decisions with lower level and middle level managers and where low level and middle level managers participate in decisions with senior level managers as well as teams of associates can also make some decisions without managerial input. In this way, human capital throughout the organization is utilized effectively. However, group decision making is similar in some ways to individual decision making because the purpose of group decision makes to arrive a preferred solution to a problem, the group must use the same
basic decision making steps: such as defining problem, identifying criteria, gathering and evaluating information, listing and evaluating alternative, choosing the best alternatives and implementing it finally. Groups are made up of multiple individual, however, resulting in dynamic and interpersonal processes that make group decision making different from decision making by individual. For instance, some members of the decision group will arrive with their own expectation, problem definition and predetermined solutions. These characteristics are likely to cause some interpersonal problems among group members. Also some members will have given more thought to the decision situation than other members' expectation about what is to be accomplished may differ. Thus, a group leader may be more concerned with a collection of individuals into a collaborative decision making team than with the development of individual decision making skills.

In fact, group processes that occur during decision making often prevent full decision of facts and alternatives. Group norms, member roles, dysfunctional communication pattern, and too much cohesiveness may deter the group to produce ineffective decisions. Marv Bradbury, technician was working shift time in nuclear power facility plant. In fact, most technicians did not like this shift, but Marv discovered that who enjoyed this job after few months and who also liked sleep in the mornings and many of this co-workers complained his behaviour to influence poor team work. Marv's job in the nuclear power plant was particular important. His primary was to monitor a series of dials and readouts in the control room. In fact, the system was so automatic, so who did not spend much time to do this duty of control and manage this system. However, if the readings indicated some variance in the system whose responsibilities were great, who would needed to do duty of interpret the readings, diagnose the problem as well as who would need to do initiate corrective actions if the automatic correcting system failed. For two reasons, Marv never worried about his responsibilities because the system was fault free and self correcting and it was s good system with no weaknesses as well as Marv had confidence to understand about the system and he was trained always knew what he had to do in the event of a problem and was capable of doing it. One day, the system occurred problem and who attempted to solve, but who felt difficult to deal. Hence, Marv felt the system was in serve trouble and decided to phone to get help. Although, who could not solve this system problem, but who knew the result if the systems dried out, the temperature was really going to go up and that the core was going to be damaged. Hence, the nuclear power facilities would cause to damaged. However, I felt that it was wrong decision that Marv decided to phone to technicians to wait eight minutes to attempt to find them to solve this system trouble, but it was too late and no one seemed to know what to do. In the beginning, Marv could attempt to solve this system trouble by individual decision, but then who decided to phone to technician team members to assist who because who wanted to reduce whose action risk alone. After eight minutes, these technician team members arrived the nuclear power plant. Marv did not anticipate any actions finally and Marv did not tell technicians how to attempt to act, so who did not anticipate any group decision among their actions finally. In the result, these technicians group decided to auxiliary pump room and discovered that the three valves were still closed and they decided to open the valves, but it was too late and no one seemed to know what to do. During these technicians group decided to do any actions immediately, their group leader would think to build a positive image (believing this system trouble could solve immediately) under threat (nuclear power facilities would occur damage possibly). Hence, this technician group leader had already failed possibly and who would decide to attempt to maintain this system together and who decided not to enquire Dan, supervisor of technician to assist them immediately. It was possible that who felt time was not enough to wait supervisor assistance or who could attempt to solve by themselves. Because Marv believed that group think decision making was more successful than individual decision making.

Although, group think did not guarantee a better decision but simply increased that likelihood of such a result. When good judgement and discussion were suppressed, the group decision could be more effective to compare to individual decision, Hence, it was possible that , the group decision making could give some benefits to Marv's individual decision making, which included that group decision making could reduce more errors to than Marv's individual decision alone; group decision making could reduce pressure when technicians gave their opinions to solve this system trouble at the same time; members who could been quiet were assumed to be in complete this job together; they could build complex rationales that effectively discount warnings or information that conflict with their thinking; they could reduce chance to cause them to ignore any dangers when they worked at the time and they could discussed any facts, criticisms or evaluations to solve this trouble together at the short time possibly. Hence, it implied that group making decision still had these benefits to compare to Marv's individual making decision.

What alternatives do you use for reducing the possibility of a similar problem in the future?

In academic decision theory, one fundamental decision rule is that of maximizing expected utility. This is the idea that when company management needs to make a decision and there are different choices, each choice has a set of possible outcome with different probabilities. The problem with this procedures

is that in real life the probabilities and utilities are often different to determine. Of course, if the outcomes are more or less certain. There might be more than one item you like and you might have a hard time to choose just one, but choose any one of choice will be a rational choice. More generally, what we should be when we make decisions is to list the pros and cons of each option available to use (the reasons supporting the option and the reasons against it). Management then choose the option that on balance has the most reasons in its favour. A good decision process requires all time parts being implemented correctly. For example, Is it clear what we have to decide? What is the most important or urgent decision? Are all the options realistic? Are there other options we should consider? Are we overlooked any good or bad consequences of an option? Is there any special criteria for the decision, we should be aware of?

Have the criteria been applied wrongly?

Main reasons why people are failure in their creative idea because failure due to lack of part knowledge and relevant skills and failure of concept and wrong with the initial idea or theory and failure of judgement due to management can have the right idea, but make the wrong decision in executing and developing it and due to failure of attitude and forging a new path where others have not gone before requires courage and the right balance of attitude and due to fear to failure to cause management to abandon an idea before it comes to success.

I recommend that Harry, engineer and Dan, supervisor and Dan's group of normal shift and part time technicians who needed have group discussion to decide what were the serious or common problems as well as whether these system problems which needed to follow specification and procedures

or which needed not to follow specification and procedures during who needed to carry on working daily in this nuclear power plant. Because who should not have enough time to predict or evaluate to judge whether which system troubles issues were serious and which system troubles issues were common to decide whether which needed to follow specification and procedures to carry on maintaining job.

Thus, this decision ought be more fair between Harry and technicians to reduce their conflicts. However, in this situation, group decision making (Harry, engineer and Dan, supervisor of maintenance groups and technicians discussion together) must be better than individual decision making (Harry, engineer and

Dan, supervisor of maintenance group discussion together).

The group decision making advantage is better quality, or least a significant chance of better quality, particularly when complex decisions are being made. The advantage is based on the fact that groups bring more knowledge and facts to make decision and engage in a richer assessment of alternatives. Other advantages include making better of decisions and greater satisfaction in the organization and personal growth for group members. However, time is one several disadvantages associated with using a group to make a decision. Thus, if they had already discussed this issue to make group decision making before any system troubles existed trouble . Then, these technicians would know whether which system troubles were more serious and which system troubles were common to judge whether either which system troubles needed to follow specification and procedures or which system troubles did not need to follow specification. For example, as the shift time technician, Marv and another full time technician who could not judge whether system troubles were serious or not, so who should felt doubt and difficult whether who ought follow all instruction to finish system maintained work or who ought not follow al instruction to finish system maintained work. Even, Marv decided to phone to technicians to ask their help. Marv would cause these technicians felt difficult to make group think to make decision in the short time. Group think is a more extreme problem where the pressure to conform hinders critical analysis and creativity, resulting in poor decision making, it might include outsiders who disagree and morality superior. These members are likely to feel more comfortable with each other, but who might also mistakenly perceive themselves as creative. In conclusion, group decision making ought be needed between Harry, engineer and Dan, supervisor of maintenance and technicians before other new system troubles occurred. Hence, if this nuclear factory management can have crisis management and time management strategy to know how to assist these different repair teams to work together, then their cooperation challenge must be solved more easily.

● Time management hotel staff workplace stress emotion challenge

When you are one hotel entrepreneur, how you manage chef have high moral performance. Walt and Tony were working in the Frontier hotel, Walt was head waiter and Tony was head chef. Then, Tony encouraged Walt to start a restaurant and who promoted himself to be Walt's restaurant's head chef. Finally, after several meetings and a lot of planning, Walt and Bill decided to open a Italian restaurant and employ Tony to be head chef. After then, Walt and Bill both partners tried to encourage Tony to join them in partnership, but Tony had refused and his personal reason was to lose his freedom. However, Walt dissatisfied Tony's performance because Tony had begun waking up late for work and who had missed several shifts altogether and who also often liked to drink alcohol. Hence, Tony performed bad behaviour to cause this conflict with Walt. Although their age were late thirties years old and before they were head positions in the Frontier hotel, but Tony had personal problem, such as marriage was broken and who liked to spend much time to meet girlfriend and who often drank alcohol in his private life. Tony's private life was seemed to influence whose head chef cooking job in Walt's Italian restaurant. Although, the Italian restaurant could expand to a large location. Walt and Bill two partners could earn profit and Tony head chef could earn Frontier hotel and Italian restaurant both employers' salaries in the same time within one year. However, Tony's performance was became poor, e.g. who didn't come to work and who had called in sick to Walt. In fact, who told lie to Walt, Tony spent sick time to meet whose girlfriend. Sometime, Tony arrived Walt's restaurant to work , but sometimes who was absent. Tony had also often drunk alcohol for two years during who had worked in Frontier hotel and Italian restaurant in the period.

suggestion of solvable method:

Could Tony's problem with alcohol be stress related?

Explain why or why not?

Walt and Tony were working in the Frontier hotel, Walt was head waiter and Tony was head chef. Then, Tony encouraged Walt to start a restaurant and who promoted himself to be Walt's restaurant's head chef. Finally, after several meetings and a lot of planning, Walt and Bill decided to open a Italian restaurant and employ Tony to be head chef. After then, Walt and Bill both partners tried to encourage Tony to join them in partnership, but Tony had refused and his personal reason was to lose his freedom. However, Walt dissatisfied Tony's performance because Tony had begun waking up late for work and who had missed several shifts altogether and who also often liked to drink alcohol. Hence, Tony performed bad behaviour to cause this conflict with Walt. Although their age were late thirties years old and before they were head positions in the Frontier hotel, but Tony had personal problem, such as marriage was broken and who liked to spend much time to meet girlfriend and who often drank alcohol in his private life. Tony's private life was seemed to influence whose head chef cooking job in Walt's Italian restaurant.

Although, the Italian restaurant could expand to a large location. Walt and Bill two partners could earn profit and Tony head chef could earn Frontier hotel and Italian restaurant both employers' salaries in the same time within one year. However, Tony's performance was became poor, e.g. who didn't come to work and who had called in sick to Walt. In fact, who told lie to Walt, Tony spent sick time to meet whose girlfriend. Sometime, Tony arrived Walt's restaurant to work , but sometimes who was absent. Tony had also often drunk alcohol for two years during who had worked in Frontier hotel and Italian restaurant in the period.

I believe Tony's problem could be with alcohol stress related. I shall give these reasons as below:

Stress means a feeling of tension that occurs when a person perceives that a situation is about to exceed whose ability to cope whose ability to cope and consequently can endanger whose well being and who feels whose capabilities or resources or needs don't match the demands or requirements of the job. In fact, it was possible that Tony would feel stress because Tony was working two head chef positions in Frontier hotel and Italian restaurant at the same time. He should feel very busy to work and who could not use enough time to meet his girlfriend. Although Tony could earn double salaries from these two employers, but he felt stress after one year. Hence, after one year, Tony did poor performance (behaviour) to let Walt to know, e.g. Tony had begun waking up late for work, who had missed several shifts although. Thus, Tony's stress had poor consequences to Walt's Italian restaurant and to Tony's himself. These poor consequences followed from the effects on Tony's individual's performance that include lower motivation, dissatisfaction, low job performance, increased absenteeism and lower quality of relationships at work, increased safety risks in kitchen and increased health care and increased costs to Tony's alcohol drinking problem. Thus, stress would cause Tony's bad behavioural consequences, e.g. abusing alcohol, late work, absenteeism and Tony's individual's frequently missed work due to stress related illness personal problems. In fact, Tony needed to do two head chef cooking jobs for two employers at the same time. It would cause psychological stress to Tony, e.g. anxiety, depression, low self esteem, sleeplessness, frustration or family problems(marriage was broken). Tony's drinking alcohol problem would increase stress to influence whose job performance to be poor. It caused Tony could not wake up early to work lately, Tony would absent to work to follow shift time often and Tony could not cooperate with kitchen cookers team and waiter team easier and became increasing isolated with them. Thus, Tony's problem with alcohol influenced whose work and private times could not adopt to cause a serious source of stress related. Due to Walt's restaurant work demands had increased to Tony to need spend longer working hours, fast and short time cooking speed needs to satisfy client increasing numbers needs. The most important, Tony needed to work for head chef two jobs for Frontier hotel and Italian restaurant both employers at the sane time. Hence, Tony's work overload could be quantitative increasing too much cooking work. In conclusion, Tony's bad behavioural habit, such as abusing alcohol drinking problem could be caused to stress related due, to influence his sickness, woke up late for work and lacked enough nervous and energy to do cooking job and felt not enough sleeping time. Thus abusing alcohol drinking problem was cause nervous stress to Tony's cooking job performance absolutely.

What should Walt do in this circumstance to help Tony cope?

In fact, it implied Tony would feel stress to perform those behaviours, such as who had begun waking up late for work, who had missed several shifts altogether to work to Walt and Bill two partners' Italian restaurant. Due to Tony was working Frontier hotel and Italian restaurant as two head chef positions as the same time. It was possible that Tony felt who needed to spend too much nervous and energy to do cooking job in these two employers and who needed to do shifts job duties for Walt's Italian restaurant and Frontier hotel both as well as Tony had also bad drinking alcohol habit two years, it would influence who could not have nervous to concentrate on cooking job in Walt's Italian restaurant's Kitchen. Because cooking head chef job was needed to spend too much energy (effort) and nervous and time if Tony hoped to cook good tactic foods to Walt's Italian restaurant's clients to eat and who hoped to lead his cooking team work efficiently with waiters team to provide good service to Walt restaurant clients. However, Tony had missed several shifts, it was possible that Tony preferred to spend his private time to meet whose girlfriend, who felt who spend shift time to work in Walt's Italian restaurant which would reduce he could enjoy his private life time with her as well as Tony had begun waking up late for work, it was possible that Tony had alcohol drinking abused problem long time , it would caused Tony has serious psychological stress responses, e.g. depression, low self esteem, sleeplessness, frustration or family problems(marriage broken). The most important, although Tony could earn double salaries due to who had been working Frontier hotel and Italian restaurant both employers at the same time, but Tony would enough lack nervous and energy and who would feel difficult to adopt to arrange time to do cooking jobs with whose team efficiently. So, Tony would feel very hard to earn double salaries after Tony had begun to choose to do Walt's Italian restaurant and Frontier hotel cooking jobs at the same time after one year. However, I shall recommend that Walt should attempt to use these methods to help Tony cope in this circumstance.

Workplace stress can occur when individual (Tony) perceive the demands of the workplace to outweigh whose resources for coping with those demands as well as workplace demands are aspects of the work environment that job holder (Tony head chef) must handle. Hence, Tony was current stressor but who had little control over this situation from Walt's fear authority to him. The most important, Walt should not let Tony to feel who gave more stress to Tony's cooking duties because Tony should choose to leave Walt's cooking job to serve only Frontier hotel employer or who should perform to lead whose cooking team to influence waiter team co-operation poorly and who could not cook better taste to foods to satisfy clients needs if Walt's behaviour should let Tony to feel more stress and unhappy to work. Hence, Walt needed to use organizational stress management method to help Tony to reduce stress or helped Tony to deal more efficiently with Tony's stress. Walt could attempt to let Tony to increase his individual's autonomy and control to his working time, e.g. Tony could choose to arrange what shift working times were the most suitable to him to work every day in order to make Tony could arrange what shift times to work in Frontier hotel or Italian restaurant every day.Walt should ensure that Tony was compensated properly and maintained job demands / requirements at healthy levels to ensure that Tony had enough nervous and energy and time to prepare to cook and lead whose cooking team to co-operate with waiter team efficiently. Demand control model that suggests experienced stress is a function when demands are high , but individuals have little control over situation. The two factors can create situations of job strain and the experience of stress include the workplace demands faced by employer and the control that an individual has in meeting those demands. In fact, Tony felt pressure due to who needed to do both shift time jobs at the same time. If Walt could employ more cookers to assist Tony to do cooking job and Walt could change Tony to do part time shift job. It would reduced Tony nervous workload to do both cooking jobs and it could let Tony had more relax time to sleep. Effort reward imbalance model that suggests experienced stress is a function of both required effort and rewards obtained. Stress is highest when required effort is high but rewards are low. It focused two factors include the effort required by employer and the rewards an individual receives as a result of the effort. Hence, it was possible that Tony felt who required effort and nervous and time were high but rewards were low to work in Walt's Italian restaurant to compare to Frontier hotel employer. It implied that Walt needed to increase Tony's salary if who hoped Tony could serve whose Italian restaurant long time. Otherwise, Tony would choose to leave Walt's cooking job.

Is Tony saveable?

Do the benefits outweigh the costs of trying to save him?

Tony can be attempt to saveable to work in Walt's Italian restaurant in the one to three months probationary period to evaluate whether the benefits outweigh the cost of trying to save Tony or not save.

Effort required relates to performance demands and obligations of the jobs. It is more narrowly focused on the job itself rather than on broader aspects of the overall work environment. It indicates a combination of strong required efforts and low rewards to any employees in organization to cause whose have strong negative emotions and harmful changes. Although a individual facing such a situation could simply exist, many stay because of limited opportunities in the labour market, hope for changes in the situation and excessive work related over commitment. (it is driven by achievement , motivation and approval motivation). In fact, Tony had enough effort and cooking skill and experience to choose which hotel or restaurant employer who liked to work in this labour market. Hence, Tony felt no worry his poor behaviour to cause Walt should dismiss him. Moreover, Tony was also working head chef shift job in another hotel at the same time. So, it was possible that Tony performed absent and woke up late to work and told lie to sickness and drunk alcohol of bad behaviour that who wanted Walt knew that they ought to discuss salary rising issue. Otherwise Tony should leave Walt's employment.The reason was because Tony felt spend much effort and time and nervous to do head chef job in Walt's Italian restaurant, but Walt could not give reasonable rewards to Tony to compare Frontier hotel employer at the same time. Hence, Tony begun waking up late for work and who begun to miss several shifts after he worked one year in Walt's Italian restaurant. Hence, Tony did action to complaint Walt to imply whose dissatisfaction to Walt's employment. However, Walt could attempt to increase Tony's salary and let Tony to choose to change to do part time shift.

Even who could let Tony to choose what shift time who preferred to work and who could suggested Tony who would not spend much time to meet girlfriend and drunk alcohol , who would spend time to sleep to prepare to do cooking job every day. Walt could enquire Tony whether who needed extra cookers and assistant head chefs staffs to assist him when the restaurant was busy time. If Tony felt who lack enough cookers and assistant head chef to assist him to do cooking job in kitchen when the restaurant was busy time. Walt ought need to spend extra salaries to employ extra staffs to assist Tony. Hence, Walt needed to discuss with Tony about how to change his shift job time and whether Tony accepted full time or accepted part time shift job and whether how many extra cookers and assistance head chefs who needed . After they had negotiated successfully, Walt could begin to give one to three months probationary period to evaluate whether Tony was suitable to do whose staff or not.

In conclusion, Walt could give one to three months probationary period to evaluate(measure) whether Tony could have enough effort and nervous to continue to do this cooking job. However, if Walt felt Tony's performance was still dissatisfactory. Walt needed give final chance to Tony to chose either who didn't work full time shift head chef job in Frontier hotel or leave Walt's job immediately.

Marketing mix strategy solves supermarket store organizational cooperation challenge

● This case concerns chain involved in the supply of fresh
fruit and vegetables to Tesco stores cooperation challenge

The place(P) of the traditional marketing mix decides about channel intermediaries or middlemen to use an outdated, yet user friendly, term and the management of physical distribution. Placing products involves managing the process supporting the flow of goods or services from producers to consumers.

The process has sometimes been described as developing the best routes to market for a firm's products. Products must be made available in the right quantity, in the right location, and at the times when customers wish to purchase them. Marketing channels can perform an important role in the later stages of a value chain, in particular outbound logistic (e.g. order processing, storage and transportation); marketing and sales (e.g. market research, personal selling, sales promotion) and after sales service. However, it depends on which kinds of business to need outbound logistic, such as Tesco supermarket only needs ordering fresh fruit and vegetables from local farmers, then these foods need to be stored in refrigerate in warehouse and transport these foods to different supermarkets by vans. So, Tesco value chain only needs outbound logistic activity, but it does not need marketing and sales and after sale service to sell its fresh fruit and vegetables to its clients from its supermarkets (stores). In fact, Tesco stores is such UK farmer's intermediaries which can add value by breaking bulk. This might involve purchasing in large quantities of fruits and vegetables from UK local farmers and then selling smaller, more manageable, to keep volumes of fresh food stock in warehouses, then its vans will deliver these fresh fruits and vegetables to different stores daily. Discrepancies of fruit foods quantity are reduced by Tesco (intermediary) who provides every store clients with individual preferable fresh foods items that suit their needs daily. Tesco stores can offer superior knowledge of a target market compared with farmers, for example by ensuring which kinds of vegetables or fruits foods numbers are stocked in every store to match the economic and lifestyle needs of Tesco store shoppers who live in the area. Probably the most important gaps between Tesco store shoppers and UK local farmers in channel management are indicated at those of location and time. A location gap occurs owing to the geographic separation of farmers and the store shoppers of their fresh fruit and vegetables foods. UK farmers generally want to grow their fruits and vegetable food in one central location (farming), but farmers' food buyers typically want to buy their growing foods locally. A time gap arises when the UK local farmers' fresh foods buyers want to buy whose fresh growing foods at a time when a UK local farmer may considerate it inconvenient to make the available. UK local farmers may like to grow fresh fruits and vegetable foods at night from 8:00 PM to 12:00PM, then who will collect these fresh foods from 5:00 AM to 7:00 in the morning, but their buyers may want to buy in the evenings or at weekends afternoon. Tesco stores (intermediary) need to facilitate vans to transport these fresh fruits and vegetables foods from farmers' farming to its one central warehouse to deliver to different stores to sell the budget numbers of different kinds of foods to every local store consumers more exactly (Adrian, P. 2012).

Tesco stores is one of the world's largest retailers, it has social responsibility to protect fresh fruit and vegetable to sell to clients. It had attempted to predict customer behavior about hope much fresh fruit and vegetable and what kinds of fresh fruit and vegetable whose consumers will buy from data statistic in warehouse. It aims to reduce excess fruit and vegetable stocks in warehouse to cause perishable. In the winter might have seen choice reduced to basic items such as potatoes, cabbage, apples, supplemented by canned fruit and vegetables. Look in a Tesco supermarket today, and clients may find difficult to tell the season of the year or the distance from the countryside, simple based on the fruit and vegetables with are on display. In UK supermarket sector is intensely competitive, and has seen continuous innovation in the way it seeks to satisfy customers' needs. As consumers have become wealthier, the supermarkets realized that buyers would no longer be content with the staple foods such as cabbage and potatoes in the depths of winter-significant numbers of them now wanted excitement on a plate, and all year round. Furthermore, if they were planning a menu, they wanted to be sure that when they went to their local supermarket.

By and large, supermarkets have been key drivers of the value for the groceries that they sell. They have been close to their customers and identified their changing needs. They have built confidence with their customers, who can trust freshness and provenance of food they sell and the reliability of supply. It is therefore the supermarkets who have gone seeking sources of supply, rather than growers aggressively seeking to sell the produce that they have available. Before, the development of very large supermarket chains, retailers were more fragmented. They did not have the power or resources to innovate with new product lines which they could then commission a grower to produce. Today, supermarket such as Tesco invest heavily in their food technology laboratories, and can then go to suppliers and place large orders with exacting standards with regard to price, quality, and delivery. Above all else, supermarkets have put themselves at the center of a slick distribution system which connects an international networks of growers through transport networks of trucks, ships and planes to put fresh produce in their network of stores, every day, all year around. The efficiency of the logistics, and the bargaining power of the supermarkets has often led to the price being charged at a British supermarket being lower than the price changed in supermarkets thousands of miles away where fruit and vegetables were grown. Tomatoes grown in Bulgaria and sold in Britain can be cheaper in Britain in local Bulgarian shops. The bizarre situation has occurred where the supermarkets import apples from France to be sold in Kent, the traditional home of British apple growing, plums from Poland to be sold in the grown product in Lincolnshire. Supermarkets argue that sourcing from overseas is not just an issue of cost saving more importantly, the supermarkets seek a continuity of supplies from large growers who can guarantee to deliver a specified quantity at a specified quantity at a specified time and place. The supermarkets capable of achieving this. British supermarkets are among the most efficient in the world, and their desire to ensure that customers can always get what they want may explain the mass transport of food. Local farmers' market may could environmentally friendly, but they rarely guarantee a continuity of supplies. As part of their drive for efficiency, supermarkets have a tendency to move food , such potatoes could being transported several hundred miles between distribution centers before they end up on a supermarket shelf just a few miles from where potatoes were grown. The environmental campaigning group Sustain has estimated that the average children travels 2,000 between the farm where it was grown and the supermarket shelf and furthermore the distance products travel from farm to end customer increased by an estimated 25 per cent between 1980 year and 2007 year (Priesnitz 2007).

Global warming had become an important issue with many clients and there was growing concern that supermarkets' practice of transporting fresh produce long distances around the world was irresponsibly adding to greenhouse gas emissions. Hence, distance travelled was one of value chain factor Terso supermarket needs to consider their fruit and vegetables food to keep fresh in refrigerate to transport to retailers to sell in UK. The most contentious food miles are clocked up by fresh fruit and vegetables flow in by plane from overseas. Although, air freighted produce accounted for less than 1 per cent of total UK food miles, it was the fastest growing way of moving foods around. One response By Tesco was to introduce a greatest proportion of local produce. To achieve this, it placed buyers and marketing teams in the regions in order to get a clear picture of local markets and to develop relationships with suppliers. By 2007 year, Tesco claimed to have 7,000 regional lines from throughout the UK, which were promoted as local produce, supporting local growers and reducing greenhouse gas emissions. Throughout its history, Tesco has demonstrated its ability to listen to what customers want, and this has been true in respect of its distribution system. The weaknesses of commodity systems are particularly for major customers, such as Mc Donalds, commodity systems do not lead to reliability in supply, quality, quantity or price nor high rates of innovation on which they can differentiate their offer from their competitors. The opportunity and challenge of fresh food product differentiation, so Tesco stores need to innovation to give rise to a number of strategic options to keep vegetables and fruits to be fresh in the short time to sell full numbers. If a firm, such as Tesco is the lowest cost producer than commodity market strategy can be an attractive strategic option. As Tesco stores fresh food sale that it's larger competitors shall find difficult to copy. Otherwise, Smaller size stores can sometimes be a competitive advantage.

Tesco stores (fresh food retailer) need to co-operate with suppliers and fresh food growers to align the whole chain to the changing needs of consumers. The food chain strategy aims to deliver superior value to specific groups of customers.

Tesco stores work closely with its fresh food suppliers to develop specific products for each range. Both the supplier and growers understand the Tesco marketing strategy and their role in the innovation process. Tesco is actively seeking new

chain ideas and is prepared to pay for such efforts. From a primary producer and supplier perspective the range of brands enables Tesco to work with suppliers to market the total crop .

2. Critically discuss the factors influencing Tesco's sourcing of fresh fruit and vegetables.

At a time when the media enjoyed the big supermarkets, such as Tesco, being seen to source fresh fruit and vegetables food locally and being good to the environment helped to restore. One observe from Friends of the Earth noted the local produce sold at a branch of Tesco in Excess had in fact travelled served hundred miles as it was moved from the grower to a regional processing center, then to a regional distribution center, and finally back to the supermarket where it was sold. There has also been debate about where sourcing fruit and vegetables locally actually reduces greenhouse gas emissions. There is an argument that Tesco supermarket would be better for environment to grow them in countries where fresh fruit and vegetables need less heating and fertilizers than if they were grown in British. The greenhouse gas emissions resulting from growing them locally in Britain may be more than the emissions associated with transporting them from warmer countries.

The first factor influences Tesco's sourcing of fresh fruit and vegetables is the main stages of horticultural value chain are as follows: The first stage is inputs elements needed for production, such as seed, fertilizers, agrochemicals fungicides and pesticides, farm equipment and irrigation equipment, production for export includes the production of fruit and vegetables and all processes related to the growth and harvesting of the produce, such as planting, weeding, spraying and picking, packaging and cold storage means grading, washing, trimming, chopping, mixing, packing and label are all processes that may occur in this packing stage of the value chain . Once the produce is ready for transport, it is chilled produce is ready for transport, it is chilled and placed in cold storage units ready for export, processes fruit and vegetables include dried, frozen, preserved, juices and pulps. May of these processed add value to the new foods by increasing the shelf life of the fruit and vegetables and the final stage is distribution and marketing means the produce is distributed to different channels, including supermarkets and small scale retailers and wholesalers and food services.

The second factor indicates several basic conditions must be for a country to enter the fresh fruit and vegetables value chain. These include climate allowing for year found supply, adequate road and transport infrastructure, such as ports and airports, essential for moving fragile foods to market efficiently, establishment of sanitary and to prevent disease spreading. The value chain needs to upgrading into the packing segment and processing segment. Upgrading into parking is dependent on understanding the market needs investment in capital goods and availability of supporting activities within the country, such as United Kingdom. Maintaining open lines of communication regarding demand preferences in fresh foods, quality, packing and fostering buyer involvement is critical in all stages of the value chain. For example, organize trips to key markets and they observe interactions at the point of fresh food purchase, a wide variety of equipment to attain very high standards of hygiene within the pack house operations as well as on site laboratories for fresh fruit and vegetables research and staff health tests, horticultural sector has been greatly inhibited in its upgrading along the value chain by the lack of fresh food quality packing materials. Much of produce destined for the Europe is shipped to neigh countries where it is repackaged, resulting in a significant of value. However, upgrading into the processing segment of the value chain has been difficult to achieve for low income developing countries since the processing of fruit and vegetables is cost prohibitive at low levels of crop production. Therefore, countries must gain a level of expertise during the production stage to increase output to a level that will enable the country to upgrade to the fruit and vegetable processing stage. For example, given the importance of ability to read pesticide labels and understand barcodes amongst others, standards have led to additional training initiatives to improve adult literacy. Skills training must be carried our in all job categories of value chain to maximize growth and upgrading opportunities. Investments in training are required for all job categories, from farm workers to managers, such as farming activities and the workforce within the agriculture sector, packing and storage positions and the processing stage in which workers are classified under the industrial workforce. Hence, fresh fruit and vegetables packing and processing services, such as washing, chopping, mixing as well as bagging, branding and applying bar codes are often carried out at the fresh foods source rather than at the end market destination. These processes which were previously based in the developed country, such as UK have created considerable new employment opportunities in developing countries.

The third factor influences Tesco's sourcing of fresh fruit and vegetables, which indicates today, the fruit and vegetables sector operators as a buyer driven value chain and large supermarket chains are the leading actors both in key export markets with controlling market and shares across the Europe and United States as well as increasing in emerging markets. These buyers including Sainsbry's Marks and Spencer and Walmart seek enhanced cost competitiveness, consistency and product differentiation, such as convenient, ready to eat fresh foods from their global supply chains. It causes considerable value chain method how fruit and vegetables are produced, harvested, transported, processed and stored to achieve how fresh fruit and vegetables characteristics of quality, size, pesticide use and the social and environment conditions of cultivation and post-harvest handling will influence buyer behavior decision. This ensures that the perishable food reaches its destination in good condition cold storage units are used throughout the chain to keep the produce fresh and both air and sea freighting supported by the cold chain are key elements to ensure timely delivery. Export is divided between production for fresh and vegetables and fruit consumption and production for processed fruit and vegetables that are not accepted for sale as fresh produce are as well as inputs for the processing stage, but in order cases, such as orange juice or preserved peaches a specific variety and grade quality is required and production occurs separately. The next segment is packaging and cold storage unacceptable low grade produce will be redirected to processing plants or the domestic market. Washing, trimming, chopping, mixing, packaging and labelling are other processes that may occur in this stage of the value chain. Once the produce is ready for transport it is chilled and placed in cold storage units ready for export. Packaging usually requires economies of scale due to the high costs of cold storage and other capital investment necessary at this stage .Processed fruit and vegetables include dried, frozen and preserved produce as well as juices. Processing plants purchase fruit and vegetables inputs from the producers. These firms may export their products under their own brands as well as under the buyer's brand. The last stage of the value chain before consumption is distribution and marketing. In this final stage, the produce is distributed to different channels including supermarkets, small scale retailers, wholesales and food services. Air freighting for horticultural foods and more cold storage segment of value chain in order to increase their access to key markets and avoid competition form new countries entering cold storage technologies allow suppliers to adapt to geographic constraints, such as size and distance to market.

3. Assess the level of power that Tesco exercises in the supply chain for fruit and vegetables.

The themes identified were the perceptions of freshness, having good relationships with growers and suppliers , good quality of fresh fruits and vegetables, competitive and pleasant environment for shoppers. Globalization of the fresh fruits and vegetables, retailer system has impacted on the distribution and marketing of fresh modern supply chain outlets now dominate the fresh food retail market. The increasing population and rising personal income is resulting in significant shifts in fresh food demand. Supermarkets are perceived to be the place where more wealthy consumers choose to shop. Consumers purchase almost everything there including fresh fruit and vegetable, meat, children and fish and other household supplier like dry food, bread, detergents, stationary and toys in supermarkets, such as Tesco stores, not choose to buy from fruit and vegetable markets or food retailers. The traditional markets and grocery stores comprise wet markets, fresh markets, farmer's markets are popular among consumers when purchasing fresh food are the oldest food distribution channel.

The traditional market has been defined as a market with little central control or organization that lacks refrigeration and doesn't process fresh foods into brands foods for sale where each vendor specialized in one fresh food line (meat, fish, fruit or vegetable) or in a sub line (fruit and vegetable). A fresh market and/or wet market generally occupies one or two floors of a building that is located adjacent to a housing area where there is a high population density and high traffic flow. The ground floor is normally rented to retailers who sell fresh food or ready to eat items.

The upper live level is occupied by retailers who sell ready to items or non food products/ These stores are family owned retailers that sell a limited variety of foods ,such as fish, fruit and vegetable, bread and milk, stationary , toys and household supplies. However, consumers may limit their purchase from these stores due to the high prices and limited product lines. Another distribution power level to Tesco supply its fruits and vegetable to deliver to its clients in the short time. Tesco faces its customers occurred with respect to its home delivery service. With the launch of its Tesco online service, it effectively extended the supply chain right through to customers' own homes, adding value to its product offer by avoiding the need for customers to even visit a supermarket. Was it good for the environment to have fleets of delivery vans around town and countryside? Simple evaluations were difficult to make supermarket buyers again, Tesco was keen to be seen as a good citizen in this final leg of its chain, for example by launching electric delivery vehicles which Tesco decided to reduce global warmth when its vans do not need to deliver fresh foods and vegetables to different supermarkets from its warehouse in the long distance. Tesco stores is a retailer to UK local farmers that buys their fresh fruits and vegetable for the purpose of reselling them to end consumers in its different local stores daily. The Tesco stores are large, self service stores carrying a very wide range of different kinds fresh fruits and vegetable foods to sell in its different local value chains from UK local farmers supply daily. For example, Tesco stores are often the first with new store shoppers initiatives such as loyalty cards and low fresh food prices are based on large scale efficiency to sell in Tesco smaller independent stores to match. Hence, the factors can influence Tesco stores channel selection power include that the expectations of store shoppers who expect to buy local stores or who prepared to travel to a retailer that the farmers' fresh fruit and vegetables keep to save more than one day or more days to buy. This might mean taking into consideration factors such as a geographical preference to buy locally, or a tendency to feel more comfortable visiting a particular type of store; Tesco fresh foods attributes can be important, fresh produce that is highly perishable requires fairly short channels. Bypassing channels, a UK local farmer may seek to cut out intermediaries , such as Tesco stores by dealing directly with the public and Tesco may feel difficult to open up any new local stores for the farmers. Over saturation, a farmer may be accused of using too many fresh fruits and vegetable food distributors within a given geographical area, making it difficult for any individual distributor to achieve a satisfactory level of fresh foods sale , such as Terco stores. Too many links, in the supply fresh foods chain, Tesco stores may be required to buy excessive fresh fruits and vegetable foods from any farmers daily, who may be perceived as a fresh food farming competitor, rather than a cooperative channel member. New channels, these can have a similar effect to bypassing an intermediary, for example, many UK local farmers have opened up internet sales channels, thereby taking fresh food sales away from established intermediaries, such as Terso stores. Cost cutting, in order to increase volume fresh fruit and vegetables food sales, a UK local farmer may seek to distribute through higher volume, low cost intermediaries, which may make it more difficult for a smaller, full service intermediary , such as Terso stores sell the farmers' any fresh foods and UK local farmers can give incentives and rewards to other intermediaries to help them to sell in UK any stores to raise Terso's competition in UK foods supply market.

A national chain of restaurant mobile advertising promotion strategy

1. Critically assess the likely opportunities and problems of mobile advertising for a national chain of restaurants.

A global crisis in the advertising industry largely linked to the impact of the internet is transforming the business models of media industries, the content they create and distribute, and the audiences who consume that contents. Such as consumers can use whose mobiles to find where the chain of restaurants are located and meal and drink prices and meal and drink types and restaurant opening and closing time etc. information for the national chain of restaurants from internet advertising when who leave at home conveniently. The opportunity to mobile advertising for a national chain of restaurants, it can expand its national chain of restaurants brand to different countries visitors and instead of its self country visitors to let them to know whether where its chain of restaurants can provide what kinds of food or drink to serve to them to eat before they prepare to go to any one of the national chain of restaurants immediately. Hence, when visitors travel to its country, it will be more easy to let them to remember where any one of the national chain restaurants are located in the nation when who enter the national chain restaurants website or enter yahoo website to type" national chain restaurants" word, then who can seek any one of the national chain restaurants from whose mobiles easily.

In fact, if a national chain of restaurants chose to use television advertising, due to the national chain of restaurants which locate at itself country locally. It is only concentrate on promoting it's country's domestic eating consumers target to know it's existence when its country's domestic eating consumers are watching television at homes. Usually, working people need to work and students need to go to school to study from morning 9:00AM to 6:00 PM at night. Hence, the national chain of restaurants can only advertise at night time. Furthermore, the overseas travelers watch the nation's television when who are staying in the nation's hotels at night time. Hence, the national chain of restaurants can only use television to advertise to attract the largest numbers of local and foreign visitors to watch its advertisement at night time possibly.

Due to mobile advertising exists, television advertising is more difficult to attract the durability of audience segmentation models to build upon demographic and it also lacks new opportunities to implement psychographic and behavioral models for understanding audiences. Such as, many young people who accept to use mobile to communicate, so it implies every family usually has a mobile to use and mobile advertising also have much opportunity to help any businesses to promote whose services or products to let many families to know whose advertising. In fact, mobile users can use mobile to watch movies or news, so who ought to link internet to watch during who are sitting on any transportations or walking, so when the nation's people who feel hungry, who can use their mobiles to link to internet to seek any restaurants to decide which restaurants are the most close to their locations to choose. As a national chain of restaurants, it is more effective to advertise it's different chain of restaurants' locations to let any it's different locations of national mobile users to seek its any one of chain restaurant conveniently when who are walking on the street if who feel hungry who can turn on mobile to find map to seek the national chain of restaurants immediately. In fact, the global households who the average viewing audience composition, the number of global households using the television set and the various times it is in use, the average audience (home viewing during an average minute of a program) and the total audiences (homes viewing the program in excess of minutes) which are decreasing. Otherwise, the mobile phone users view mobile advertising numbers are increasing. Broadcast channels as well as whatever is available on their various devices, including computer, mobile devices, gaming devices, time-shifting devices or internet enables devices. As such, it is providing more and more difficult to track the audience and known who they are and the best way to target them. Additionally, the rise of social media adds another dimension to audience research. Social media provides new ways of segmenting audiences that currently can not be done on television. Hence, a national chain of restaurants can get better ways of segmenting its viewers from mobile advertising over a variety of platforms.

So mobile networks can be better package to the nation chain of restaurants advertising programming and the national chain of restaurants advertiser can make a more effective to attract foreign visitors or domestic visitors to make them to enter its website to view its advertising from their mobiles. For example, car owners, such as those who own a BMW or Audi famous brands cars, which have very homogeneous demographic characteristics, but each car brand has a specific type of owner with a unique personality. A similar look as television audiences could allow advertising of those car brands (who attend the upfront presentations every year) to match their car buyers to specific television shows. Demographics have not caught up with these changes and presume that viewers are still watching in only the conventional way. For instance, there is not yet a way for the networks to get credit for online viewers and it is as more viewers more to online platforms, like a network in landing site.

Instead, a psychographic profile of the audience, one based on psychological segmentations , such as behaviors, attitudes, interests, values, opinions feelings which is a valid and valuable way of narrowing down the audience into segments for an advertiser. So, psychographic data can measure, such as peoples' activities how who spend whose time, their interests what they place importance on in their immediate surroundings, their opinions how their view of themselves and the world around them and some basic characteristics, such as their stage life cycle and income and education and residence location. The result of the research then provides a detailed profile that allows the marketer to be better visualize the target audience.

Psychographics start with people and reveal how the people feel client specific subjects, which can lead to be more effective marketing. When psychographic segmentations are used, the consumers are divided into group based on lifestyle and personality, often with all of this in mind, the research questions proposed here as follows: What psychographic measurements are being used right now to determine the television audience or mobile advertising ?

How are the various branches of the industry , such as restaurant industry adaptive to the new television landscape ,such as mobile advertising and what actions are they taking?

What are some challenges and resistances to psychographic measures between television advertising and mobile advertising?

What incentives or lack are there to change between television and mobile advertising?

What would be helpful for advertisers , such as a national chain of restaurants or networks , such as internet advertising to know or do in order to more towards wider use of psychographics?

A reason behind dividing audiences based on engagement can be illustrated with the Pod mobile phone, such as the national chain of restaurants organization has shown that audiences‘ attachment to specific the restaurants' brand corresponds directly to how much the audience will pay attention to the national restaurant brand's advertisements from mobile and how likely who are the actually to choose to go to the national chain of restaurants to eat lunch or dinner or breakfast more than its other restaurants.The problem is how the national chain of restaurants to advertise it's foods taste, price and service and locations uniquely to win its other restaurant competitors from mobile specific program, providing the network to be best convenient that it's restaurant brand to advertise on that specific program. Another key problem is trend segments viewers based on domestic and foreign consumers‘ behavior are more specifically their viewing behavior mixed with their restaurants choosing eating behavior in whose countries, watching the national chain of restaurants television advertising from whose mobile , what who are watching to know its existence and on how to let them to know what their actual eating taste to the national chain of restaurants can provide. Hence, I suggest the national chain of restaurants can attempt to use surveys to carry on researching the different countries foreign visitors and domestic visitors whether what whose tastes are preferable to choose what kinds of foods and drinks who hope to eat in this national chain of restaurants from mobile advertising website. The problem is who may choose not to fill its surveys from its mobile website advertising. If they use computer to fill its surveys at home, it will have more opportunities to gather data from survey due to who can sit down to fill surveys in quiet environment. Hence, I suggest it ought use computer internet to do market research about what whose tastes are preferable to eat in its restaurants. When it estimates whether the foreign visitors and domestic visitors numbers, how many people choose to eat different kinds of foods and drinks to its identifications. After it can achieve mobile advertising to promote its restaurant brand more confidently in this mobile marketing advertising strategy.

2. Discuss methods that could be used to assess the effectiveness of mobile advertising.

Measuring social media marketing , such as mobile advertisement, effectiveness and identifying the target market. The use of social media sites as part of company's marketing strategy has increased significantly. Regardless its popularity, there is still very limited information to answer some of the key issues concerning the effectiveness of social media marketing , ways to measure its return on investment and its target market. The social media was started around ten years ago. It began with linked in, which was launched in 2003 year, followed by both My space and face book in 2004 year. You tube in 2005 year and Twitter in 2006 in year. The popularity of social media sites has also spread to companies as part of their strategies. Executives are concerned with their budget justification for a social media plan in computer or media online advertising, when there is lack of supporting materials to confirm the effectiveness of the social media platform , i.e. conversion rate, the relation between buyer-seller relationship and increase in sales and the rate of return investment that they can earn from this plan. Others also believe that their companies' performance are not affected by their lack of involvement in the social media sites.

Clearly, the fact that social media marketing is still relatively new among business practitioners has raised some major concerns , such as its effectiveness, the main purpose of including social media mobile advertising in a company's media platforms, it's relation to the existing platforms and the target audience of this strategy. The methods to assess effectiveness of mobile advertisement include that marketing research method is about target client segment of respondents' social media activities and buying decisions relationship survey. Survey questions can include whether how long time and how often who turn on mobile phone to use internet, such as a week is less than 20 hours average or a week is between 20 hours and 30 hours average or a week is between 30 hours and 50 hours or a week is more than 50 hours, why who like to use mobile to use internet and not use home computer to use internet, e.g. reducing to use home electricity, interesting, convenience, no computer at home, what who will seek to see from mobile advertisement, e.g. advertisement , news ,email , message, movie, whether who decide to buy products or consume services choice is from which kinds of channel advertisement influence mostly, such as television, radios, newspapers, magazines, computer internet, mobile internet. It aims to gather target client segment of respondents' social media activities and buying decision relationship to estimate whether there are how many numbers of target client will decide to buy the company's product or use it's service from mobile advertisement channel.

Hence, the survey result can indicate these five respondent groups, such as highly affected, somewhat affected, neutral somewhat not affected and not affected at all groups. Mobile phone advertisement is needed to any organizations to use internet to operate. Hence, to access the effectiveness of mobile advertising which may begin by using measures that were very easy to capture and understand, such as the number of website hits or percentage of users who clicked on an advertisement. These measures were very useful fro examining trends in traffic patterns, but the impact of this traffic on sale and other marketing objective was sales and other marketing objectives were little understand. Standardized approaches for capturing and summarizing websites behavior were eventually developed to help make sense of web traffic and patterns. Metrics, such as number of unique visitors and the amount of time who spent viewing web pages provided marketers with new insights into who was assessing the site and how who were using it. But even with a high level of detail about how customers were interacting with the company via the web, marketing manager often lacked the information how user behavior data translates into increased profits and business value. For example, organizations using websites primarily for after sales support have used exactly the same kinds of metrics as these selling directly from the site. This is not due to a lack of available data. Many organizations using web analytics gather and store vast amounts of information and develop large, complex databases to house it. But much of that information is never used. Because organizations who first began to market over the internet often lacked a clearly formulated strategy. In addition, the rapidly changing internet environment made it difficult for marketers to formulate clear expectation about the impact of activities. Both the amount of returns and amount of investments are difficult to measure. I suggest organizations may estimate the value of a visit to a particular web page by estimating the number of visitors who will become customers and then multiplying that number by the average value of all clients to estimate returns. What the 'clicks and hits' and 'measurement driven' approached have in common organization's strategic objectives and provide quantified models that plan and track internet marketing investments from intermediate outcomes to financial results. Hence, it can indicate how marketing expenditures in mobile internet advertising method to lead to increase shareholder value aim. I think investment in internet marketing , organizations will need follow these stages. In the beginning is inputs stage:

Organization and business unit strategy includes structures, systems, resources as well as marketing strategy includes structures, systems as well as information strategy includes structures, systems and market strategy transfers to websites, search marketing , advertisement and public relations, mobile marketing and marketing research. Next, it is outputs stage: It includes intermediate outputs, such as awareness and perceptions, attitudes and intentions, value provisions, channel optimization and market information as well as it includes final outputs, such as marketing assets: customer value, brand equity, knowledge as well as financial flows: increased revenue, cash flows, reduced revenue, lower cost, lower working capital, lower fixed capital and reduced risk. Finally, it is outcomes stage includes shareholder value, return on investment and corporate profitability. For example, Donald restaurant uses its website to promote lower calorie food and fruit options as well as its global campaign tied to the Olympics, nutrition (Business week 8-7-06). Each organization should carefully identify the outputs it seeks to achieve. How can process produce these outputs? Organization can attempt to enhance of website functional or initiation of an email campaign. The final question to organizations which will ask : How outputs contribute to the long term financial performance of the organization from mobile advertising ? Is critical for organizations seeking to enhance return on investment from mobile advertising? In addition, whether mobile advertising can give these benefits to any companies, such as market capitalization and shareholder value can be enhanced by increases in marketing assets (customer value, brand equity and knowledge base) that produce future corporate financial flows from mobile internet advertising method. Hence, marketing assets include customer value, such as using dynamic pricing to manage demand, supporting sales through online information sites, shipping directly to reduce need for inventory possession, shifting in store sales to online sales, eliminating clients with prior post sales problems from promotion lists; brand equity, such as additional revenue through brand premiums, using customer relationship to speed adoption of next generation products target marketing to loyal clients during predicted slow periods, reducing customer turnover and support costs, shifting responsibility and risk for inventory management to major suppliers, pool inventories with suppliers and clients to reduce warehouse space across the supply chain, using trust in brand to reduce unwarranted lawsuits, knowledge base, such as developing mass customization capability, reducing time to market through online concept trials, time promotions to smooth demand, eliminating product features that are not valuable to clients. Watching production timing to demand, direct in store sales to products that generate high contribution margin per square foot of fixed space and anticipating and respond to stakeholder concerns. Finally, customer value and brand equity and knowledge base shall transfer to financial flows aim, such as increased revenue, accelerated cash flow, reduced revenue volatility, lower cost, lower working capital requirement, lower fixed capital requirement and reduced risk.

However, Metrics can be used to access effectiveness of mobile advertising, both financial and non financial metrics are needed to effectively measure performance. Some non financial items , such as market research activities are difficult to measure and companies often avoid measuring those items. However, if the item plays a critical role in delivering organizational value. Measuring it, preferably in quantifiable terms, such as monetary changes or percentages. Even when such measures are difficult to obtain or depend a rough estimates, they provide a basis for examining trends over time and can provide useful information to managers. For example, two metrics for the output awareness are: The number of emails opened recipients and the number of clients that clicked on a promotional mobile advertising. Those two metrics can provide different perspectives on the meaning of awareness, thus the choice of metrics helps clarify the objectives, just as clear objectives can help in identifying specific and to be relevant must be specific and to be relevant they must be customized to meet the unique dynamics of the organization . It aims to achieve the best to capture and reflect the organization's unique sets of activities and results some may be relevant to all organizations and many can be readily adopted to be useful for decision making.

3. Discuss the relationship between mobile advertising and other elements of the promotion in campaign planning.

Mobile advertisement defines as the use of the mobile medium, it is as a communications and entertainment channel between a brand and an end user. In basic terms, it is the process of planning and execution conception, pricing, promotion and distribution of products and services through the mobile channel. Advertising is a form of communication intended to convince an audience (viewers, readers or listeners) to purchase or take some action upon products, information or services etc. The relationship between independent variables elements and mobile advertising which are environmental response and emotional response with behavioral aspect of consumer buying behavior with mobile advertising. It is time that people purchase those brands with which who are emotionally attached elements. Almost every one grows up in the world which is flooded with the mass media, e.g. television, films, videos, magazines, movies advertising and internet channel is either mobile advertising or computer advertising. Advertising is a subset of promotion mix which is one of the 4'p in the marketing mix, i.e. product, price, place and promotion. As a promotional strategy, advertising serve as a major tool in creating product awareness in the mind of a potential consumer to take eventual purchase decision. Advertising, sales promotion and public relations are mass communication tools available to marketers.

Telecommunication technology, such as mobile advertising enables business and industry to grow at a faster pace when contributing to the economic development and at the same time telecommunication infrastructure can be reliable. Cellular phone industry has been one of the profitable businesses in Asian. The country's growing population and huge demand potential have always been an attraction for many high-technological multinational companies. Societies used symbols and pictorial signs to attract their produce users. There elements were used for promotion of products. A company can't make dream to be a well known brand until which invests in their promotional activities for which consumer market have been dominating through advertisements. As the primary mission of advertiser is to reach prospective customers and influence their awareness, attitudes and buying behavior.

The major aim of advertising is to impact on buying behavior, however this impact about brand is changes or strengthened frequently in peoples' memories. Memories about the brand consist of their associations that are related to brand name in consumer mind. These brand cognition influence consideration, evaluation and finally purchases. The promotion in campaign planning to mobile advertising focuses on young people because who choose advertising information and characters as whose role models, who may not only identify with them but also intend to copy them in terms of how who dress and what who are going to buy. As the market is surplus with several products or services, so many companies make similar functional claim, so it has became extremely difficult for companies to differentiate their products or services based on functional attributes alone. Differentiations based on functional attributed, which are shown in advertisement, are never long lasting as the competitors could copy the same. Mobile advertising may differentiate companies' products or services promotion channel to attract client's attention, e.g. the company can use movable product images on internet video to show on mobile. However, mobile advertising time ought depend on the business nature, e.g. facial health products target segment is female, so it's mobile advertising time ought choose form 9:00 AM to 6:00 PM working time between Monday to Sunday, due to housewives or working women shall go back home to cook, who shall not turn on mobile phones at home. Hence, if the company had differentiated which brand and it had chose what time is the more popular to accept to let mobile users to turn on their mobile from mobile advertising. The company mobile advertising will have more promotion effort. For example, if the company sold toys, it's target segment would be 3 ages to 10 ages old. It's mobile advertising ought let every family to find its company website easily. If the family didn't know it's brand, but is was difficult to let the family to find what its toys sale from whose mobile phone because there are many toy companies were using internet advertising to promote which toys. So, it might let every family types " toy" word on yahoo, Google websites, then this toy company name would appear on their websites, the family only clicked its name on their mobile phone, it could show it' toys images, prices, which country manufacturing and which year manufacturing different kind of toys, sale payment and delivery method, e.g. visa card payment, air or land or shipping transportation flight delivery, toys manufacturing ingredients indication from website advertising and it's toys advertising time ought to choose family working time, such as between 9:00 and 6:00 PM , due to who shall bring their mobile to work usually. Hence, the toy company needs to consider family will choose what time to use mobile phone. It ought not choose night time to advertise its toy products from mobile due to family would not turn on whose mobile at home at night time usually. Economic theory has sought to establish relationships between selling prices, sales achieved and consumer's income, similarly before the company chooses to spend mobile advertising expenditure, it ought frequently compared it with sales actual income each month.

Social media marketing, such as mobile advertising effectiveness is highly influenced by three aspects: content quality, involvement and integration with the other media platforms methods to assess whether effectiveness of mobile advertising.

On the first aspect, content quality isn't quantity. It shows that managers should not totally reply on the monitoring software to measure and analyze their social media campaign. For example, the twitter website analysis show that some brands/companies, e.g. Microsoft used their Twitter account to connect and to

communicate with customers . Their Tweets were about communicating and connecting with their follows, through some personal conversations in subjects. That were relevant to their customers . As a results, Microsoft clients were able to

beat their main competitors in financial performances and Twitter activities. So, Microsoft can use twitter website to assess whether how many numbers of people use internet service to enter phone, then who decide to buy its software products . If Microsoft found the result of the number of buyers who decide to buy its software from mobile phone Twitter website advertisement channel which is more than mobile phone Yahoo or Google websites advertisement channel after who turn on mobile to see advertising. On the another aspect, building trust and long term relationship to mobile advertising to indicate to how to persuade to increase many shippers to decide to buy any products or seek service, e.g. travel tickets booking service after who use mobile to seek advertising habitually. Today, media marketing is about building relationship and trust through effective two way communications , e.g. talk about something that customers are interested in and creating products or service that will help to solve customers' problems from mobile advertising. Some of today's social media marketing campaigns are still driven by the old fashioned marketing and focus on short-term effect sales, which is also known as incentive induced behavior. To assess trust and genuine buyer/seller relationships achieved through consistent and engaging conversation will increase the messages (SMM) level of influence. Trust is the key factor to get the followers to actually to something , i.e. change in buying decisions influence their peers and turn it into revenue for the companies. It is crucial to build a strong relationship with customers and enhance brand loyalty. Hence, it implies mobile phone companies need to build trust relationship to let them to pay extract internet charges to aim to read email, news, watch movie habitually. Then, it will increase chance to let potential buyers to prefer to seek advertisement to choose to buy and products or consume service from mobile websites habitually. Hence, assessment of mobile internet habitual users who use mobile internet time per week from survey is one effective method. Also, firms should start their involvement by inviting their customers or prospects to join their social media community. For example, firms can post the icons of the social media main websites or giving some special deals to customers who become their fans or followers . In the online community, firms should start writing more effective posts. An effective post should reflect honesty and conciseness, it is as key elements of an effective post. It should also be informative to satisfy clients' need for information and experts; opinions. Effective contents should be able to actions from the audience (conversion) so that by the end of this process. Followers will place on order, subscribe newsletter or participate on online surveys. In the offline community, managers should share expertise with their speaker in the local community, which will help to attract more followers or fans and to strength connection with the community. A debate has been going on whether or not consumers are willing to receive mobile advertising. America consumers seem to willing to accept mobile advertising to subsidize the cost of other mobile services , such as email and news services.

A study conducted by HRI Research on behalf of Nokia brand found that the core mobile phone subscriber market (16 to 45 year old) is not only receptive to experiencing mobile advertising, but also actively welcoming mobile advertising in the form of electronic coupons promotion. The relationship between mobile advertising and the four key elements contributing to mobile advertising's acceptance of the promotion in campaign planning. There were mobile advertising should allow users to decide whether or not to receive messages, users could bypass sales messages easily, users should be filter the message received and users want to get mutual benefits of something back. The SMA advertising campaigns of mobile advertising industry plays and consumers have been made afraid of the spam phenomenon deriving from negative email spamming experiences. The personal nature of the website phone markets spamming especially invasive compared to spam received via other channels and devices. Mobile advertising has the potential to be one of the most powerful one to one digital advertising mediums of utilized in the right manner. SMS trials across the would have show the power of mobile advertising in building direct one to one relationship. The online companies like AT&T, AOC wireless, Microsoft and Nokia to mention few companies that are focused on the potential of mobile marketing via mobile handsets. Factors contributing to the success of mobile advertising include that ability, setting up research. measurement, tracking systems, availability of specialist expertise in agency, service provide and establishing consistent rate mobile cards. Other factors impact of drivers on the development of mobile advertising include that personalized medium, users able to opt in , call to action , i.e. immediate response possible , location specific, interactive profiling, appeals to younger customers , one to many communication.

In conclusion, the relatively between mobile advertising and other elements of the promotion in campaign planning include as below: The first element is by utilizing mobile advertising, companies can run marketing campaigns targeted to tens of thousands of people with a fragment of the costs compared to other direct marketing mediums, such as direct mail or telephone and this in just few seconds of line. The advertising industry uses two types of cost calculation cost per thousand impressions (CPM) and cost per rating point (CPP). CPM is used for both print and electronic media when CPP is more popular for electronic media. For instance, if an advertising campaign costs US$5,000 and has an audience of 300,000 consumers, the CPM will be approximately to the initial CPM measure in media selection , such as quality of the audience, audience attention probability and believability of media selection when the CPM for direct mail is between UA$500 to US$700. For email the CPM ranges from US$5 to US$7. However when email marketing is losing its efficiency, mobile advertising offers new ways to promote products and services. A significant factor contributing to consumers‘ willingness to accept mobile advertisement is the capability of mobile handsets to service certain type of messages , such as multimedia messages. Evidently, most consumers in the future will carry on smart phone with them. The smart phones allow advertisers to reach consumers in different locations with personalize messages at a given time. Another element is the industry of SG or 4G network service is faster connection speed is a obvious enables users to receive digital photographs, moving wide images, high quality sound for their mobile handsets. From advertisers; perspective this opens various opportunities to plan and implement more advance m-advertising campaigns and integrate those with existing marketing channels. However, to develop and provide applications, for example, interfaces to the carrier's wireless network need to be provided in multiple areas: location, presence, billing, personalization, provisioning, packet network, transport and messaging systems. Next element is location awareness cab be seen as the driving force of many wireless applications and suits also well types of mobile advertising. When mobile phones are almost always carried with and intelligent location awareness technical solution are available. The final element is personalization means building customer loyalty by building a meaningful one to one relatively by understanding the needs to each individual and helping to satisfy a goal that efficiently and knowledgeably addresses each.

Personalization is about mapping and satisfying of client's goal in specific contest with a business's goal in its respective context. Personalization means understanding different kinds of individual preferences , needs, mindsets and lifestyles and cultural as well as geographical differences. Mobile are already equipment with a profiting options, e.g. silent, meeting, outdoors. For example, the utilization of time and location awareness as personalization variables has the benefit that mobile advertising is a marketing medium has features that other marketing channels lack. Hence, email advertising needs to keep every mobile users' personal information to be confidential, solicited message, relevance to users need and the right frequency.

A global crisis in the advertising industry largely linked to the impact of the internet is transforming the business models of media industries, the content they create and distribute, and the audiences who consume that contents. Such as consumers can use whose mobiles to find where the chain of restaurants are located and meal and drink prices and meal and drink types and

restaurant opening and closing time etc. information for the national chain of restaurants from internet advertising when who leave at home conveniently. The opportunity to mobile advertising for a national chain of restaurants, it can expand its national chain of restaurants brand to different countries visitors and instead of its self country visitors to let them to know whether where its chain of restaurants can provide what kinds of food or drink to serve to them to eat before they prepare to go to any one of the national chain of restaurants immediately. Hence, when visitors travel to its country, it will be more easy to let them to remember where any one of the national chain restaurants are located in the nation when who enter the national chain restaurants website or enter yahoo website to type" national chain restaurants" word, then who can seek any one of the national chain restaurants from whose mobiles easily.

In fact, if a national chain of restaurants chose to use television advertising, due to the national chain of restaurants which locate at itself country locally. It is only concentrate on promoting it's country's domestic eating consumers target to know it's existence when its country's domestic eating consumers are watching television at homes. Usually, working people need to work and students need to go to school to study from morning 9:00AM to 6:00 PM at night. Hence, the national chain of restaurants can only advertise at night time. Furthermore, the overseas travelers watch the nation's television when who are staying in the nation's hotels at night time. Hence, the national chain of restaurants can only use television to advertise to attract the largest numbers of local and foreign visitors to watch its advertisement at night time possibly.

Due to mobile advertising exists, television advertising is more difficult to attract the durability of audience segmentation models to build upon demographic and it also lacks new opportunities to implement psychographic and behavioral models for understanding audiences. Such as, many young people who accept to use mobile to communicate, so it implies every family usually has a mobile to use and mobile advertising also have much opportunity to help any businesses to promote whose services or products to let many families to know whose advertising. In fact, mobile users can use mobile to watch movies or news, so who ought to link internet to watch during who are sitting on any transportations or walking, so when the nation's people who feel hungry, who can use their mobiles to link to internet to seek any restaurants to decide which restaurants are the most close to their locations to choose. As a national chain of restaurants, it is more effective to advertise it's different chain of restaurants' locations to let any it's different locations of national mobile users to seek its any one of chain restaurant conveniently when who are walking on the street if who feel hungry who can turn on mobile to find map to seek the national chain of restaurants immediately. In fact, the global households who the average viewing audience composition, the number of global households using the television set and the various times it is in use, the average audience (home viewing during an average minute of a program) and the total audiences (homes viewing the program in excess of minutes) which are decreasing. Otherwise, the mobile phone users view mobile advertising numbers are increasing. Broadcast channels as well as whatever is available on their various devices, including computer, mobile devices, gaming devices, time-shifting devices or internet enables devices. As such, it is providing more and more difficult to track the audience and known who they are and the best way to target them. Additionally, the rise of social media adds another dimension to audience research. Social media provides new ways of segmenting audiences that currently can not be done on television. Hence, a national chain of restaurants can get better ways of segmenting its viewers from mobile advertising over a variety of platforms.

So mobile networks can be better package to the nation chain of restaurants advertising programming and the national chain of restaurants advertiser can make a more effective to attract foreign visitors or domestic visitors to make them to enter its website to view its advertising from their mobiles. For example, car owners, such as those who own a BMW or Audi famous brands cars, which have very homogeneous demographic characteristics, but each car brand has a specific type of owner with a unique personality. A similar look as television audiences could allow advertising of those car brands (who attend the upfront presentations every year) to match their car buyers to specific television shows. Demographics have not caught up with these changes and presume that viewers are still watching in only the conventional way. For instance, there is not yet a way for the networks to get credit for online viewers and it is as more viewers more to online platforms, like a network in landing site.

Instead, a psychographic profile of the audience, one based on psychological segmentations , such as behaviors, attitudes, interests, values, opinions feelings which is a valid and valuable way of narrowing down the audience into segments for an advertiser. So, psychographic data can measure, such as peoples' activities how who spend whose time, their interests what they place importance on in their immediate surroundings, their opinions how their view of themselves and the world around them and some basic characteristics, such as their stage life cycle and income and education and residence location. The result of the research then provides a detailed profile that allows the marketer to be better visualize the target audience.

Psychographics start with people and reveal how the people feel client specific subjects, which can lead to be more effective marketing. When psychographic segmentations are used, the consumers are divided into group based on lifestyle and personality, often with all of this in mind, the research questions proposed here as follows: What psychographic measurements are being used right now to determine the television audience or mobile advertising ?

How are the various branches of the industry , such as restaurant industry adaptive to the new television landscape ,such as mobile advertising and what actions are they taking?

What are some challenges and resistances to psychographic measures between television advertising and mobile advertising?

What incentives or lack are there to change between television and mobile advertising?

What would be helpful for advertisers , such as a national chain of restaurants or networks , such as internet advertising to know or do in order to more towards wider use of psychographics?

A reason behind dividing audiences based on engagement can be illustrated with the Pod mobile phone, such as the national chain of restaurants organization has shown that audiences' attachment to specific the restaurants' brand corresponds directly to how much the audience will pay attention to the national restaurant brand's advertisements from mobile and how likely who are the actually to choose to go to the national chain of restaurants to eat lunch or dinner or breakfast more than its other restaurants.

The problem is how the national chain of restaurants to advertise it's foods taste, price and service and locations uniquely to win its other restaurant competitors from mobile specific program, providing the network to be best convenient that it's restaurant brand to advertise on that specific program. Another key problem is trend segments viewers based on domestic and foreign consumers' behavior are more specifically their viewing behavior mixed with their restaurants choosing eating behavior in whose countries, watching the national chain of restaurants television advertising from whose mobile , what who are watching to know its existence and on how to let them to know what their actual eating taste to the national chain of restaurants can provide. Hence, I suggest the national chain of restaurants can attempt to use surveys to carry on researching the different countries foreign visitors and domestic visitors whether what whose tastes are preferable to choose what kinds of foods and drinks who hope to eat in this national chain of restaurants from mobile advertising website. The problem is who may choose not to fill its surveys from its mobile website advertising. If they use computer to fill its surveys at home, it will have more opportunities to gather data from survey due to who can sit down to fill surveys in quiet environment. Hence, I suggest it ought use computer internet to do market research about what whose tastes are preferable to eat in its restaurants. When it estimates whether the foreign visitors and domestic visitors numbers, how many people choose to eat different kinds of foods and drinks to its identifications. After it can achieve mobile advertising to promote its restaurant brand more confidently in this mobile marketing advertising strategy.

2. Discuss methods that could be used to assess the effectiveness of mobile advertising.

Measuring social media marketing , such as mobile advertisement, effectiveness and identifying the target market. The use of social media sites as part of company's marketing strategy has increased significantly. Regardless its popularity, there is still very limited information to answer some of the key issues concerning the effectiveness of social media marketing , ways to measure its return on investment and its target market. The social media was started around ten years ago. It began with linked in, which was launched in 2003 year, followed by both My space and face book in 2004 year. You tube in 2005 year and Twitter in 2006 in year. The popularity of social media sites has also spread to companies as part of their strategies. Executives are concerned with their budget justification for a social media plan in computer or media online advertising, when there is lack of supporting materials to confirm the effectiveness of the social media platform , i.e. conversion rate, the relation between buyer-seller relationship and increase in sales and the rate of return investment that they can earn from this plan. Others also believe that their companies' performance are not affected by their lack of involvement in the social media sites.

Clearly, the fact that social media marketing is still relatively new among business practitioners has raised some major concerns , such as its effectiveness, the main purpose of including social media mobile advertising in a company's media platforms, it's relation to the existing platforms and the target audience of this strategy. The methods to assess effectiveness of mobile advertisement include that marketing research method is about target client segment of respondents' social media activities and buying decisions relationship survey. Survey questions can include whether how long time and how often who turn on mobile phone to use internet, such as a week is less than 20 hours average or a week is between 20 hours and 30 hours average or a week is between 30 hours and 50 hours or a week is more than 50 hours, why who like to use mobile to use internet and not use home computer to use internet, e.g. reducing to use home electricity, interesting, convenience, no computer at home, what who will seek to see from mobile advertisement, e.g. advertisement , news ,email , message, movie, whether who decide to buy products or consume services choice is from which kinds of channel advertisement influence mostly, such as television, radios, newspapers, magazines, computer internet, mobile internet. It aims to gather target client segment of respondents' social media activities and buying decision relationship to estimate whether there are how many numbers of target client will decide to buy the company's product or use it's service from mobile advertisement channel.

Hence, the survey result can indicate these five respondent groups, such as highly affected, somewhat affected, neutral somewhat not affected and not affected at all groups. Mobile phone advertisement is needed to any organizations to use internet to operate. Hence, to access the effectiveness of mobile advertising which may begin by using measures that were very easy to capture and understand, such as the number of website hits or percentage of users who clicked on an advertisement. These measures were very useful fro examining trends in traffic patterns, but the impact of this traffic on sale and other marketing objective was sales and other marketing objectives were little understand. Standardized approaches for capturing and summarizing websites behavior were eventually developed to help make sense of web traffic and patterns. Metrics, such as number of unique visitors and the amount of time who spent viewing web pages provided marketers with new insights into who was assessing the site and how who were using it. But even with a high level of detail about how customers were interacting with the company via the web, marketing manager often lacked the information how user behavior data translates into increased profits and business value. For example, organizations using websites primarily for after sales support have used exactly the same kinds of metrics as these selling directly from the site. This is not due to a lack of available data. Many organizations using web analytics gather and store vast amounts of information and develop large, complex databases to house it. But much of that information is never used. Because organizations who first began to market over the internet often lacked a clearly formulated strategy. In addition, the rapidly changing internet environment made it difficult for marketers to formulate clear expectation about the impact of activities. Both the amount of returns and amount of investments are difficult to measure. I suggest organizations may estimate the value of a visit to a particular web page by estimating the number of visitors who will become customers and then multiplying that number by the average value of all clients to estimate returns. What the 'clicks and hits' and 'measurement driven' approached have in common organization's strategic objectives and provide quantified models that plan and track internet marketing investments from intermediate outcomes to financial results. Hence, it can indicate how marketing expenditures in mobile internet advertising method to lead to increase shareholder value aim. I think investment in internet marketing , organizations will need follow these stages. In the beginning is inputs stage:

Organization and business unit strategy includes structures, systems, resources as well as marketing strategy includes structures, systems as well as information strategy includes structures, systems and market strategy transfers to websites, search marketing , advertisement and public relations, mobile marketing and marketing research. Next, it is outputs stage: It includes intermediate outputs, such as awareness and perceptions, attitudes and intentions, value provisions, channel optimization and market information as well as it includes final outputs, such as marketing assets: customer value, brand equity, knowledge as well as financial flows: increased revenue, cash flows, reduced revenue, lower cost, lower working capital, lower fixed capital and reduced risk. Finally, it is outcomes stage includes shareholder value, return on investment and corporate profitability. For example, Donald restaurant uses its website to promote lower calorie food and fruit options as well as its global campaign tied to the Olympics, nutrition (Business week 8-7-06). Each organization should carefully identify the outputs it seeks to achieve. How can process produce these outputs? Organization can attempt to enhance of website functional or initiation of an email campaign. The final question to organizations which will ask : How outputs contribute to the long term financial performance of the organization from mobile advertising ? Is critical for organizations seeking to enhance return on investment from mobile advertising? In addition, whether mobile advertising can give these benefits to any companies, such as market capitalization and shareholder value can be enhanced by increases in marketing assets (customer value, brand equity and knowledge base) that produce future corporate financial flows from mobile internet advertising method. Hence, marketing assets include customer value, such as using dynamic pricing to manage demand, supporting sales through online information sites, shipping directly to reduce need for inventory possession, shifting in store sales to online sales, eliminating clients with prior post sales problems from promotion lists; brand equity, such as additional revenue through brand premiums, using customer relationship to speed adoption of next generation products target marketing to loyal clients during predicted slow periods, reducing customer turnover and support costs, shifting responsibility and risk for inventory management to major suppliers, pool inventories with suppliers and clients to reduce warehouse space across the supply chain, using trust in brand to reduce unwarranted lawsuits, knowledge base, such as developing mass customization capability, reducing time to market through online concept trials, time promotions to smooth demand, eliminating product features that are not valuable to clients. Watching production timing to demand, direct in store sales to products that generate high contribution margin per square foot of fixed space and anticipating and respond to stakeholder concerns. Finally, customer value and brand equity and knowledge base shall transfer to financial flows aim, such as increased revenue, accelerated cash flow, reduced revenue volatility, lower cost, lower working capital requirement, lower fixed capital requirement and reduced risk.

However, Metrics can be used to access effectiveness of mobile advertising, both financial and non financial metrics are needed to effectively measure performance. Some non financial items , such as market research activities are difficult to measure and companies often avoid measuring those items. However, if the item plays a critical role in delivering organizational value. Measuring it, preferably in quantifiable terms, such as monetary changes or percentages. Even when such measures are difficult to obtain or depend a rough estimates, they provide a basis for examining trends over time and can provide useful information to managers. For example, two metrics for the output awareness are: The number of emails opened recipients and the number of clients that clicked on a promotional mobile advertising. Those two metrics can provide different perspectives on the meaning of awareness, thus the choice of metrics helps clarify the objectives, just as clear objectives can help in identifying specific and to be relevant must be specific and to be relevant they must be customized to meet the unique dynamics of the organization . It aims to achieve the best to capture and reflect the organization's unique sets of activities and results some may be relevant to all organizations and many can be readily adopted to be useful for decision making.

3. Discuss the relationship between mobile advertising and other elements of the promotion in campaign planning.

Mobile advertisement defines as the use of the mobile medium, it is as a communications and entertainment channel between a brand and an end user. In basic terms, it is the process of planning and execution conception, pricing, promotion and distribution of products and services through the mobile channel. Advertising is a form of communication intended to convince an audience (viewers, readers or listeners) to purchase or take some action upon products, information or services etc. The relationship between independent variables elements and mobile advertising which are environmental response and emotional response with behavioral aspect of consumer buying behavior with mobile advertising. It is time that people purchase those brands with which who are emotionally attached elements. Almost every one grows up in the world which is flooded with the mass media, e.g. television, films, videos, magazines, movies advertising and internet channel is either mobile advertising or computer advertising. Advertising is a subset of promotion mix which is one of the 4'p in the marketing mix, i.e. product, price, place and promotion. As a promotional strategy, advertising serve as a major tool in creating product awareness in the mind of a potential consumer to take eventual purchase decision. Advertising, sales promotion and public relations are mass communication tools available to marketers.

Telecommunication technology, such as mobile advertising enables business and industry to grow at a faster pace when contributing to the economic development and at the same time telecommunication infrastructure can be reliable. Cellular phone industry has been one of the profitable businesses in Asian. The country's growing population and huge demand potential have always been an attraction for many high-technological multinational companies. Societies used symbols and pictorial signs to attract their produce users. There elements were used for promotion of products. A company can't make dream to be a well known brand until which invests in their promotional activities for which consumer market have been dominating through advertisements. As the primary mission of advertiser is to reach prospective customers and influence their awareness, attitudes and buying behavior.

The major aim of advertising is to impact on buying behavior, however this impact about brand is changes or strengthened frequently in peoples' memories. Memories about the brand consist of their associations that are related to brand name in consumer mind. These brand cognition influence consideration, evaluation and finally purchases. The promotion in campaign planning to mobile advertising focuses on young people because who choose advertising information and characters as whose role models, who may not only identify with them but also intend to copy them in terms of how who dress and what who are going to buy. As the market is surplus with several products or services, so many companies make similar functional claim, so it has became extremely difficult for companies to differentiate their products or services based on functional attributes alone. Differentiations based on functional attributed, which are shown in advertisement, are never long lasting as the competitors could copy the same. Mobile advertising may differentiate companies‘ products or services promotion channel to attract client's attention, e.g. the company can use movable product images on internet video to show on mobile. However, mobile advertising time ought depend on the business nature, e.g. facial health products target segment is female, so it's mobile advertising time ought choose form 9:00 AM to 6:00 PM working time between Monday to Sunday, due to housewives or working women shall go back home to cook, who shall not turn on mobile phones at home. Hence, if the company had differentiated which brand and it had chose what time is the more popular to accept to let mobile users to turn on their mobile from mobile advertising. The company mobile advertising will have more promotion effort. For example, if the company sold toys, it's target segment would be 3 ages to 10 ages old. It's mobile advertising ought let every family to find its company website easily. If the family didn't know it's brand, but is was difficult to let the family to find what its toys sale from whose mobile phone because there are many toy companies were using internet advertising to promote which toys. So, it might let every family types " toy" word on yahoo, Google websites, then this toy company name would appear on their websites, the family only clicked its name on their mobile phone, it could show it' toys images, prices, which country manufacturing and which year manufacturing different kind of toys, sale payment and delivery method, e.g. visa card payment, air or land or shipping transportation flight delivery, toys manufacturing ingredients indication from website advertising and it's toys advertising time ought to choose family working time, such as between 9:00 and 6:00 PM , due to who shall bring their mobile to work usually. Hence, the toy company needs to consider family will choose what time to use mobile phone. It ought not choose night time to advertise its toy products from mobile due to family would not turn on whose mobile at home at night time usually. Economic theory has sought to establish relationships between selling prices, sales achieved and consumer's income, similarly before the company chooses to spend mobile advertising expenditure, it ought frequently compared it with sales actual income each month.

Social media marketing, such as mobile advertising effectiveness is highly influenced by three aspects: content quality, involvement and integration with the other media platforms methods to assess whether effectiveness of mobile advertising.

On the first aspect, content quality isn't quantity. It shows that managers should not totally reply on the monitoring software to measure and analyze their social media campaign. For example, the twitter website analysis show that some brands/companies, e.g. Microsoft used their Twitter account to connect and to

communicate with customers . Their Tweets were about communicating and connecting with their follows, through some personal conversations in subjects. That were relevant to their customers . As a results, Microsoft clients were able to

beat their main competitors in financial performances and Twitter activities. So, Microsoft can use twitter website to assess whether how many numbers of people use internet service to enter phone, then who decide to buy its software products . If Microsoft found the result of the number of buyers who decide to buy its software from mobile phone Twitter website advertisement channel which is more than mobile phone Yahoo or Google websites advertisement channel after who turn on mobile to see advertising. On the another aspect, building trust and long term relationship to mobile advertising to indicate to how to persuade to increase many shippers to decide to buy any products or seek service, e.g. travel tickets booking service after who use mobile to seek advertising habitually. Today, media marketing is about building relationship and trust through effective two way communications , e.g. talk about something that customers are interested in and creating products or service that will help to solve customers' problems from mobile advertising. Some of today's social media marketing campaigns are still driven by the old fashioned marketing and focus on short-term effect sales, which is also known as incentive induced behavior. To assess trust and genuine buyer/seller relationships achieved through consistent and engaging conversation will increase the messages (SMM) level of influence. Trust is the key factor to get the followers to actually to something , i.e. change in buying decisions influence their peers and turn it into revenue for the companies. It is crucial to build a strong relationship with customers and enhance brand loyalty. Hence, it implies mobile phone companies need to build trust relationship to let them to pay extract internet charges to aim to read email, news, watch movie habitually. Then, it will increase chance to let potential buyers to prefer to seek advertisement to choose to buy and products or consume service from mobile websites habitually. Hence, assessment of mobile internet habitual users who use mobile internet time per week from survey is one effective method. Also, firms should start their involvement by inviting their customers or prospects to join their social media community. For example, firms can post the icons of the social media main websites or giving some special deals to customers who become their fans or followers . In the online community, firms should start writing more effective posts. An effective post should reflect honesty and conciseness, it is as key elements of an effective post. It should also be informative to satisfy clients' need for information and experts; opinions. Effective contents should be able to actions from the audience (conversion) so that by the end of this process. Followers will place on order, subscribe newsletter or participate on online surveys. In the offline community, managers should share expertise with their speaker in the local community, which will help to attract more followers or fans and to strength connection with the community. A debate has been going on whether or not consumers are willing to receive mobile advertising. America consumers seem to willing to accept mobile advertising to subsidize the cost of other mobile services , such as email and news services.

A study conducted by HRI Research on behalf of Nokia brand found that the core mobile phone subscriber market (16 to 45 year old) is not only receptive to experiencing mobile advertising, but also actively welcoming mobile advertising in the form of electronic coupons promotion. The relationship between mobile advertising and the four key elements contributing to mobile advertising's acceptance of the promotion in campaign planning. There were mobile advertising should allow users to decide whether or not to receive messages, users could bypass sales messages easily, users should be filter the message received and users want to get mutual benefits of something back. The SMA advertising campaigns of mobile advertising industry plays and consumers have been made afraid of the spam phenomenon deriving from negative email spamming experiences. The personal nature of the website phone markets spamming especially invasive compared to spam received via other channels and devices. Mobile advertising has the potential to be one of the most powerful one to one digital advertising mediums of utilized in the right manner. SMS trials across the would have show the power of mobile advertising in building direct one to one relationship. The online companies like AT&T, AOC wireless, Microsoft and Nokia to mention few companies that are focused on the potential of mobile marketing via mobile handsets. Factors contributing to the success of mobile advertising include that ability, setting up research. measurement, tracking systems, availability of specialist expertise in agency, service provide and establishing consistent rate mobile cards. Other factors impact of drivers on the development of mobile advertising include that personalized medium, users able to opt in , call to action , i.e. immediate response possible , location specific, interactive profiling, appeals to younger customers , one to many communication.

On conclusion, the relatively between mobile advertising and other elements of the promotion in campaign planning include as below: The first element is by utilizing mobile advertising, companies can run marketing campaigns targeted to tens of thousands of people with a fragment of the costs compared to other direct marketing mediums, such as direct mail or telephone and this in just few seconds of line. The advertising industry uses two types of cost calculation cost per thousand impressions (CPM) and cost per rating point (CPP). CPM is used for both print and electronic media when CPP is more popular for electronic media. For instance, if an advertising campaign costs US$5,000 and has an audience of 300,000 consumers, the CPM will be approximately to the initial CPM measure in media selection , such as quality of the audience, audience attention probability and believability of media selection when the CPM for direct mail is between UA$500 to US$700. For email the CPM ranges from US$5 to US$7. However when email marketing is losing its efficiency, mobile advertising offers new ways to promote products and services. A significant factor contributing to consumers' willingness to accept mobile advertisement is the capability of mobile handsets to service certain type of messages , such as multimedia messages. Evidently, most consumers in the future will carry on smart phone with them. The smart phones allow advertisers to reach consumers in different locations with personalize messages at a given time. Another element is the industry of SG or 4G network service is faster connection speed is a obvious enables users to receive digital photographs, moving wide images, high quality sound for their mobile handsets. From advertisers; perspective this opens various opportunities to plan and implement more advance m-advertising campaigns and integrate those with existing marketing channels. However, to develop and provide applications, for example, interfaces to the carrier's wireless network need to be provided in multiple areas: location, presence, billing, personalization, provisioning, packet network, transport and messaging systems. Next element is location awareness cab be seen as the driving force of many wireless applications and suits also well types of mobile advertising. When mobile phones are almost always carried with and intelligent location awareness technical solution are available. The final element is personalization means building customer loyalty by building a meaningful one to one relatively by understanding the needs to each individual and helping to satisfy a goal that efficiently and knowledgeably addresses each.

Personalization is about mapping and satisfying of client's goal in specific contest with a business's goal in its respective context. Personalization means understanding different kinds of individual preferences , needs, mindsets and lifestyles and cultural as well as geographical differences. Mobile are already equipment with a profiting options, e.g. silent, meeting, outdoors. For example, the utilization of time and location awareness as personalization variables has the benefit that mobile advertising is a marketing medium has features that other marketing channels lack. Hence, email advertising needs to keep every mobile users' personal information to be confidential, solicited message, relevance to users need and the right frequency.

Reference

Stredwick. J, (2005). An Introduction to human resource management. Elsevier Ltd, UK.

CHAPTER FOUR

Investing in office technology can bring efficient improvement

Why ought any kinds of businesses need to invest in technology to offices when businessmen began to do businesses? The reason is simple, such as
any offices need email to communicate to let different departments staffs can contact to do any tasks in short time. So, email can replace telephone calling communication channel between departments in offices. Moreover, for paper files, electronic files may replace to keep to save any office confident documents or general memos, letters, reports etc. documents. So, paper printing number may reduce. Even some businesses began to sell their products from online webstores to let customers to pat visa to buy their products from their webstores conveniently. Hence, computer technology is essential to nowadays any kinds of businesses offices.

The best are developed with the entire project-focused organization in mind. For example, a question on resourcing could involve looking a cariety of systems and files with no way to automatically generate the rught combination of data. Hence, any business offices ought need a single, centralised database which keeps accounting, project and even HR information and can integrate data when required.

ON the office investing in technology web-based system with mobile access benefit, due to investing globalization and pressure on fee rates means staff are in the office less
frequently than ever. A web-based system means data can be accessed from PCs and networked laptops with no other software needed. So, instead of offices can apply laptops and intra-internet communication technological tool, which can also offer the option of a mobile applications suite which means personnel working on -site can enter timesheet and expense reports from laptops, even when not connected to the central data base. This helps minimise time delays, streamlining the billing process and improving cash flow. So, office mobile onlinesite technology may help thme to bring real- time , easy access benefits. For exmaple, if a staff is
still making decisions based on information that is seven or eight weeks old, the staff will be surprised by the power of having real-time information at the
staff's fingertips. At any time this will give the staff an accurate "snapshot" of the health of the staff's
project, enabling the staff to take preventive action if the problems arise before it is too late.

This visualisation ensures that all key stakeholders can identify project problems immediately they happen . It's also an ideal way for directors or other managers to
grab headline information before a short notice meeting, for example, all of office laptop, mobile intra-internet, onsite technology may help to ensure more targeted decisions and better project control. Hence, office technology may help any business offices to save more time deal urgent tasks daiuly. It means that office technology may help any offices to save much time in long term.

For some businesses office technology may help their businesses to manage on projects to achieve rapid finishing in short time, such as all projects of harbour construction business aspect, some projects may face complex to prolong time to finish. SO, defining a discipline as " complex project management assumes that one can find projects cause of complexity". Also, any the harbour business projects do not really exist. The term project is a contract used to describe a particular human activity. Hence, if the harbour construction company managers can let its all harbour construction managers to apply mobile onsite technology, intra-internet communication channel to do daily

communication tasks in short time between their different construction teams. Then, these new harbour onsite mobile intra-internet communication technology ought help all
onsite harbour construction managers can supervise all harbour onsite workers to construct all harbour construction projects in short time efficiently and effectively.

Sp, on-site mobile intra-internet communication technology may be future construction industry which a kind of essential onsite mobile intra-internet communication
technoogy.Moreover, on-site mobile intra-internet communication technology can bring future construction industry on time to save cost and construction quality
improvement benefits. Due to increasingly construction industry and clients demand more for less and this is in a traditionalty high risk industry. The problem of
construction and its relatively slow pace of change seem to stem from its competive building living demand role in providing building buyer value. With its attendant
professions, it is often too remote from the customers' experience of their buildings.

When if the construction company really knew how to add value for building clients? What if the construction firm could improve productivity among those using the building?
How much is that worth? What if the school could improve performance of students in shcools and the recovery of patients in hospitals? Such improvements represent much cost
benefits that could mean that the building pays for itself. However, nowadays building technology can bring these key benefical features to any construction companies, such as
value success are committed leadership providing the vision, suitable values and effective shared processes.

How office technology brings intelligent thinking to office staffs? Finally, I beleive that if the company can invest technology in office. It will bring intelligent
thinking to office staffs in order to improve efficient and performance, because investing in office technology , which is a way to reduce risk without
going over the top through effective use of the company networks. Why can office technology working environment can help staffs to bring intelligent thinking in order to
improve performance and raise efficiency?

The reason of office technology working environment can excite staffs their intelligent thining to be raise. What's lacking is a way of mitigating against these risks and doing so cost- effectively. Because more recently, a new stage has been reached where office staffs rely not only on their technical and business knowledge, but now have methodologies and tools so sophisticated that they can forward predict and control any office projects to finish before due date more easily.Hence, with good technical knowledge, sound business underatanding, a good way of methodologies, and training in the very latest software technology to hand, these are the not investing in office technology staffs, those who still find it impossible to deliver projects successfully more easily before any their office projects finishing due date. What needs to be addressed to change this situation?
The main factors critical to improve office staffs performance and improve efficiency, the non-investing in office technology working environment ought to
changed to invest technology to office working environment in order to excite staff individual working emotion to bring raising efficiency, even improve performance effectiveness.

ON conclusion, any offices need to invest technology to offices in order to bring " improving technical skill to staffs their working environment", because
they need to know that skill does not equate to competence , and there fore, a competence and therefore a competency based assessment is essential so that a
prospective office employee knowledge and understanding, attitude and skills can be evaluated. So, technological office can help managers to evaluate office employee
individual job skill more easily in order to make decision whether skill is high or low to let high skillful staffs can continue to be trained to work
in offices as well as fire the low skillful staffs. So, when the office can attempt to spend more money to invest to its

office working environment, it means that the organization should be investing in training for permanent staffs in the scarce skills working markets. A small
investment in office technology can reap significant benefits further down the live, such as planning for skills scarcity on investing nowadays office technological working environment.

CHAPTER FIVE

9 798889 752271

Printed by Libri Plureos GmbH in Hamburg,
Germany